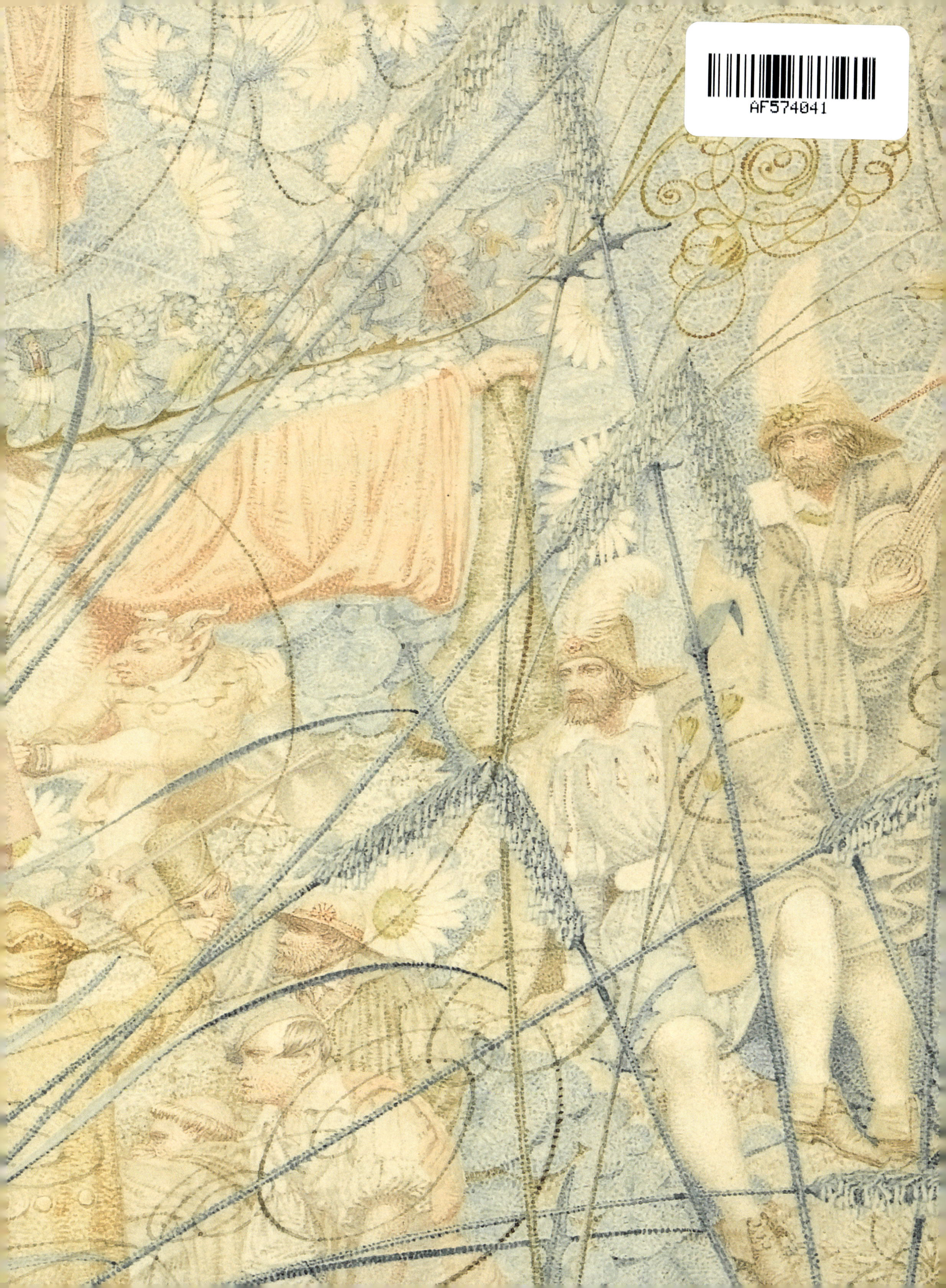
AF574041

This catalogue is dedicated to the memory of Sir Ivor Batchelor, a bibliophile, benefactor and friend, who enjoyed the subtleties – and piquancy – of word and image, and who always knew where to find the joke.

Literary Circles

Artist, author, word and image in Britain 1800-1920

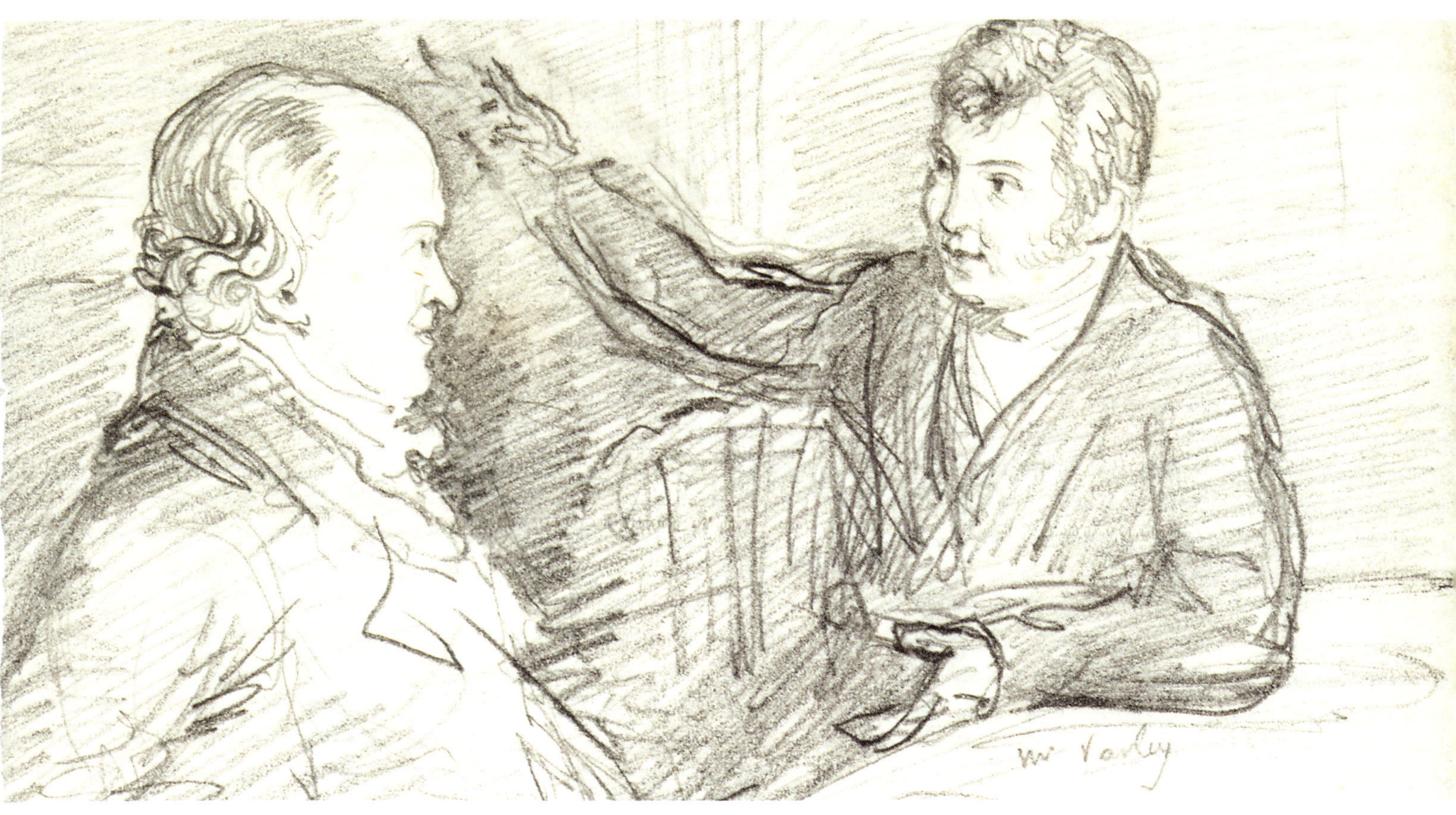

The
Fitzwilliam
Museum

This catalogue is published in conjunction with the exhibition

Literary Circles
Artist, author, word and image in Britain 1800-1920

held at The Fitzwilliam Museum, Mellon Gallery
17 October – 30 December 2006

Catalogue first published in October 2006 by
The Fitzwilliam Museum
Trumpington Street
Cambridge
CB2 1RB
Telephone 01223 332 900
Fax 01223 332 923
Email fitzmuseum-enquiries@lists.cam.ac.uk
www.fitzmuseum.cam.ac.uk

Editors: Jane Munro and Linda Goddard
Photography: Andrew Morris
Design: cantellday www.cantellday.co.uk
Produced by Fitzwilliam Museum Enterprises Ltd
Printed by Graphicom srl, Vicenza, Italy
The author of each chapter is acknowledged on the individual title page. Additional authors are acknowledged within the text as follows: GB: Grace Brockington, LG: Linda Goddard, EL: Elenor Ling, JM: Jane Munro.

For copyright permission, the publishers wish to thank Sue Denney, Anna Philps of the Sidney Sime Gallery, Diana Willis, The Bridgeman Art Copyright Library (nos. 24, 30 and 82), and the Society of Authors for permission to reproduce Laurence Binyon's *Dream-Come-True* (no. 74). Autograph manuscripts by Swinburne and his letter to Thomas Hardy (nos. 12, 13 and 25) are reprinted by permission of William Heinemann, an imprint of The Random House Group Ltd. The watercolour by Arthur Rackham (no. 82) is reproduced with the kind permission of his family. Every effort has been made to clear all images with their respective copyright holders. If there are any errors or omissions, please contact the publishers who will be pleased to make corrections.

ISBN (10) 0-904454-74-6
ISBN (13) 978-0-904454-74-1

© The Fitzwilliam Museum, University of Cambridge, 2006

All rights reserved. No part of this publication may be reproduced, stored in a retrieval system, or transmitted in any form or by any means, electronic, mechanical, photocopying, recording or otherwise, without the prior permission in writing from the publisher.

A catalogue record for this book is available from the British Library.

Front cover: no. 1. Joseph Severn, *John Keats*
Endpapers: no. 95. Richard Dadd, *Songe de la Fantasie (detail)*
Title page: no. 93. John Linnell, *Blake in conversation with John Varley*

Contents

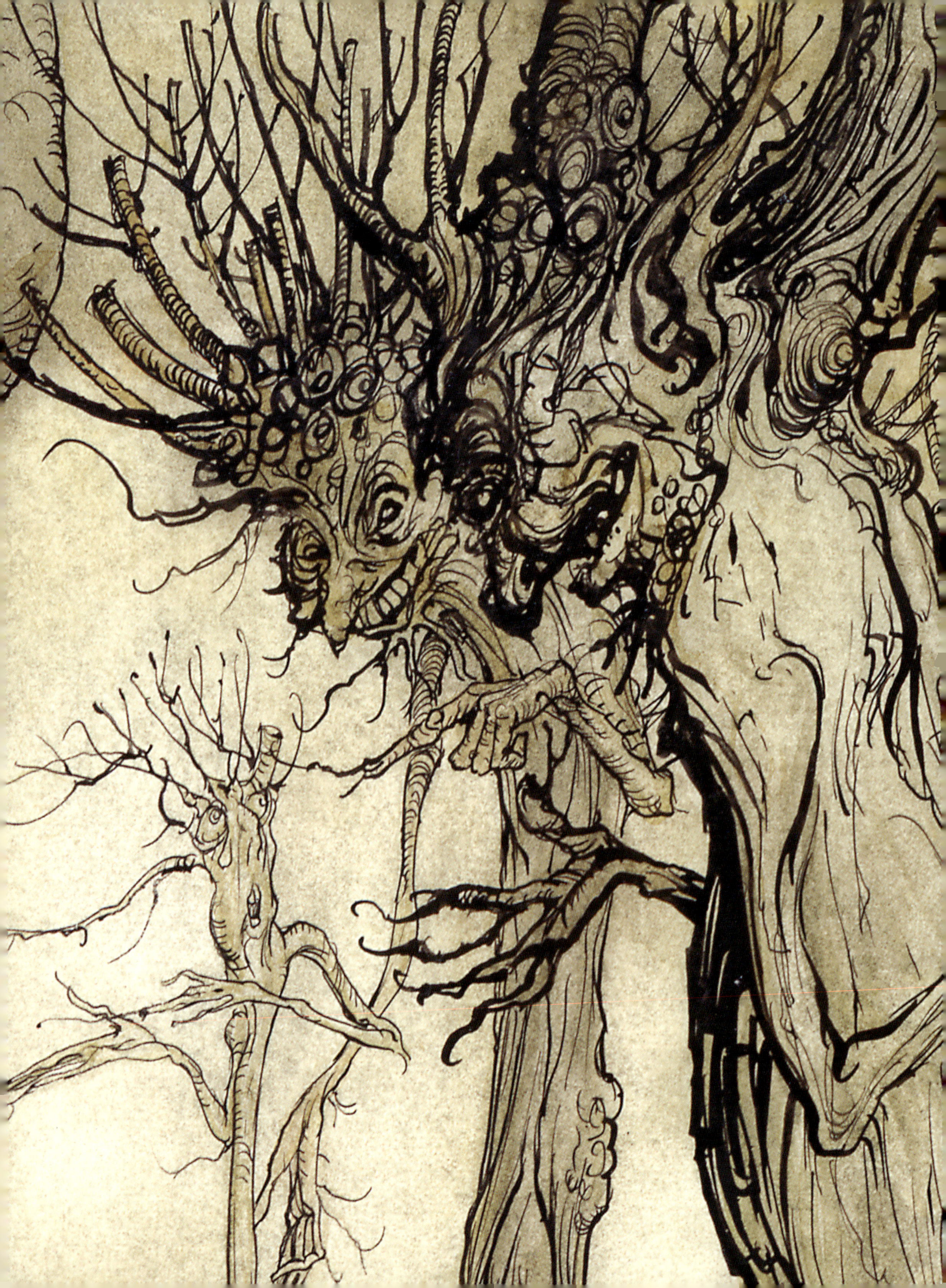

Preface

Literary Circles illuminates the networks of personal connections that fostered exchanges between artists and authors in 19th- and early 20th-century Britain. It also investigates the multiple ways in which text and image inform, or set up dialogues with, each other. In the context of the Fitzwilliam it shows how personal and professional relationships within circles of bibliophiles, critics, writers and book designers contributed in spectacular ways to the development and enrichment of its collections.

Whether artists and writers shared sources of inspiration or, like Dante Gabriel Rossetti, practiced both painting and poetry, the bonds between the 'sister' or 'double' arts were undeniably strong. They were not, however, consistently harmonious. As case studies of collaborative projects demonstrate, the degree of affinity between word and image, and the nature of the collaboration between artist and author, varied considerably. Similarly, while illustrations in the periodical press helped to encourage a wider readership for serialised fiction, they did not always relate explicitly to the text in question, and could function as independent 'visual narratives'. In contrast, the private press movement, spearheaded by William Morris's Kelmscott Press, aimed to restore coherence to all aspects of the printing process. However, even the complete unity of text, image and typography attained in the limited edition 'Book Beautiful' was compromised by the need to balance craftsmanship with economic viability.

Similar tensions structure the relationship between word and image in caricature and fantasy illustration. In the cartoons and caricatures published in *Punch* and other journals, pen and pencil complemented and vied with each other, using a combination of visual narrative and textual captions to deliver the joke. Painters of imaginary visions and dreams, meanwhile, progressed from creative interpretations of textual precedents, notably Shakespeare, to fantasy scenes of their own invention, often supplemented – though rarely explained – by their own verbal commentary.

Within and beyond these categories, the creative relationships between artist and author, word and image, were – and remain – subject to an infinite number of variables. While no exhibition or book could aim to explore these in any exhaustive way, the richness and depth of the Fitzwilliam's collections provide a stimulating point of departure.

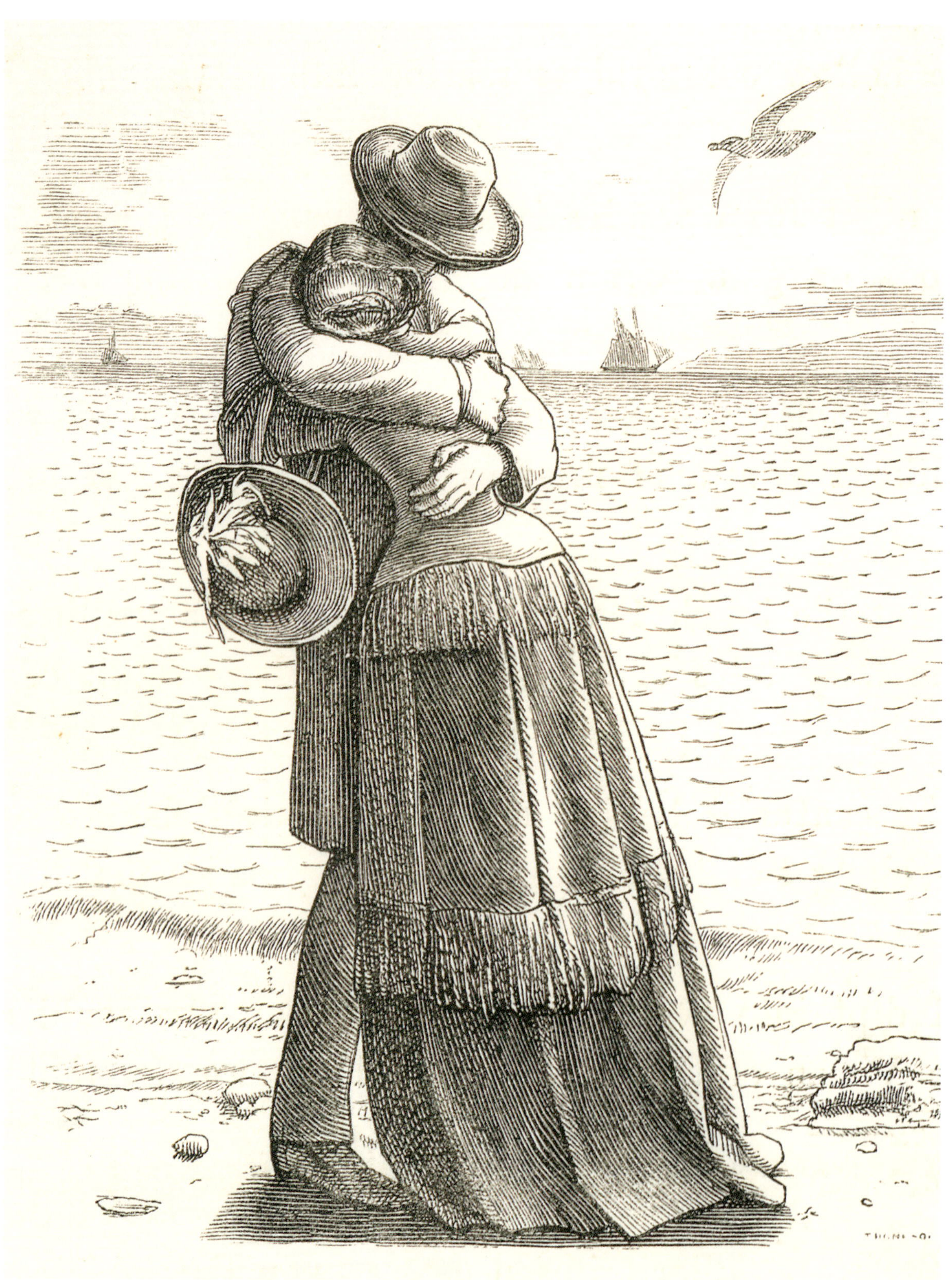

Acknowledgments

This exhibition has been selected from the Fitzwilliam's outstanding collections of paintings, drawings, prints, rare books and manuscripts and is complemented by a small number of loans from private collections. We extend our warmest thanks to the owners of these works for allowing them to enrich the exchanges between word and image within the exhibition.

The extent and quality of the Museum's collections makes the selection of a relatively small group of works a challenging, but highly enjoyable and rewarding, task. In making the selection the authors have benefited from the time, patience and expertise of colleagues at the museum. We should like to thank in particular Martin Allen, Mark Blackburn, Bryan Clarke, Craig Hartley, John Harvard, Kate Heawood, Elenor Ling, Stella Panayotova, Nicholas Robinson, Lewis Tiffany and Helen Strudwick. Bénédicte Ducastel gave invaluable organisational assistance in the early stages of the project. Anna Lloyd-Griffiths deserves special thanks for her support and most particularly for her boundless enthusiasm and good humour.

Translating words and ideas into the very specific form of an exhibition relies on those colleagues in the museum responsible for its installation; we are grateful to Andrew Bowker, Sean Fall, John Lancaster, Andrew Maloney, Jane Sargent and Nik Zolman for their consistently inventive technical responses.

Lady Honor Batchelor, Professor Mary Jacobus, Dr Brigid Lowe, Dr. Cathy Philips and Dr Mark Wormald have offered help, advice and ideas.

Thibault Catrice has overseen the book production with characteristic verve and imagination.

The exceptionally high quality of the images is due to Andrew Morris. He has been both meticulous and exceedingly generous of his time. We should like to thank him for his valued advice, and for more than once pulling rabbits out of hats.

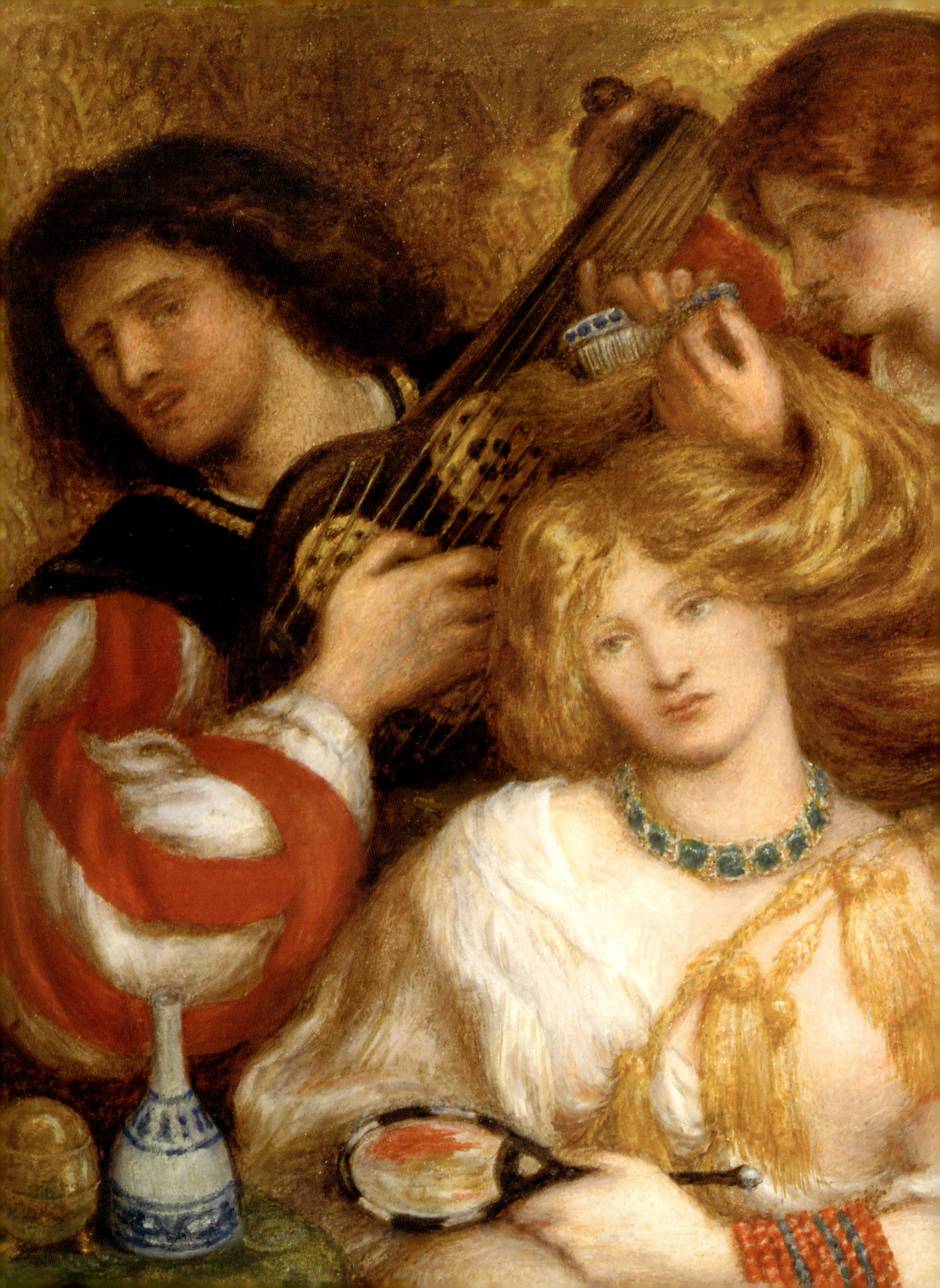

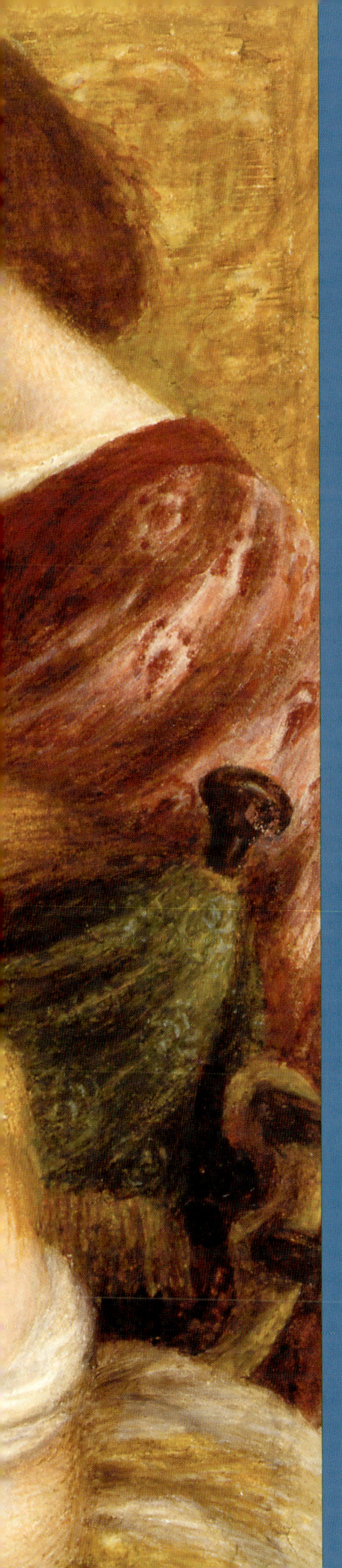

Creative Relationships, Creating Collections

Jane Munro

Creative Relationships, Creating Collections

Jane Munro

If the dialogue between word and image requires a mechanism to foster creative exchange, few function more naturally, more intensely – and, at times, more effectively – than personal acquaintance. At the same time, the operative mode can vary enormously, from the casual interaction of like-minded friends, united in the conscious pursuit of deeply-held ideals, to the satellite-orbiting of literary glitterati and formal societies intent on promoting, reviving or preserving particular literary forms. In each of its manifestations, the literary circle extends beyond the author, to embrace the advisors, listeners and critical commentators who form the necessary ballast in the creative enterprise. In some cases – and the Fitzwilliam is a notable one – these have embraced museum curators and directors possessed of both the critical acumen to recognise literary and artistic worth, and the determination to secure and preserve it for future generations.

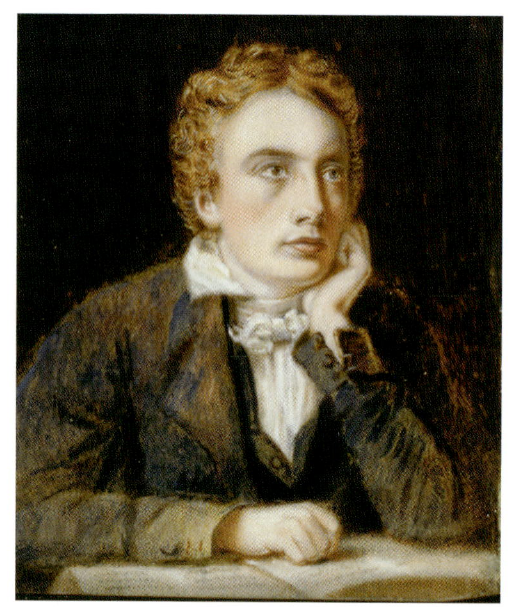

ABOVE LEFT
1. Joseph Severn
1793-1879
John Keats

One of the most significant spirals of influence to emerge in Victorian England did so through the formation, in 1848, of the Pre-Raphaelite Brotherhood, a group of seven artistically-committed young men with, at its core, William Holman Hunt, Dante Gabriel Rossetti, and John Everett Millais. Their self-appellation as a 'brotherhood' (Rossetti's chosen term) at once signalled the serious, and almost sacred, nature of their union, formed by and for art. And not just one art, or art form; for Pre-Raphaelite painting is an essentially literary art, one in which the bond between text and image is especially strong. Even before the creation of the 'Brotherhood', the Rossetti brothers, Dante Gabriel and William Michael, together with Hunt, Walter Deverell and other friends, corresponded regularly and excitedly about their latest literary finds, transcribed passages from poems which they hung on their walls,[1] created a league of 'Immortals', many literary (nos. 6 and 41), and formed a 'literary society' which met regularly on Saturday evenings. An unparalleled range of literary sources, past and present, from Dante, Chaucer, Malory and

Ode to the Nightingale
My Heart aches and a ~~painful~~ drowsy numbness ~~falls~~ pains
My sense as though of hemlock I had drunk
Or emptied some dull opiate to the drains

John Keats, *Ode to a Nightingale*

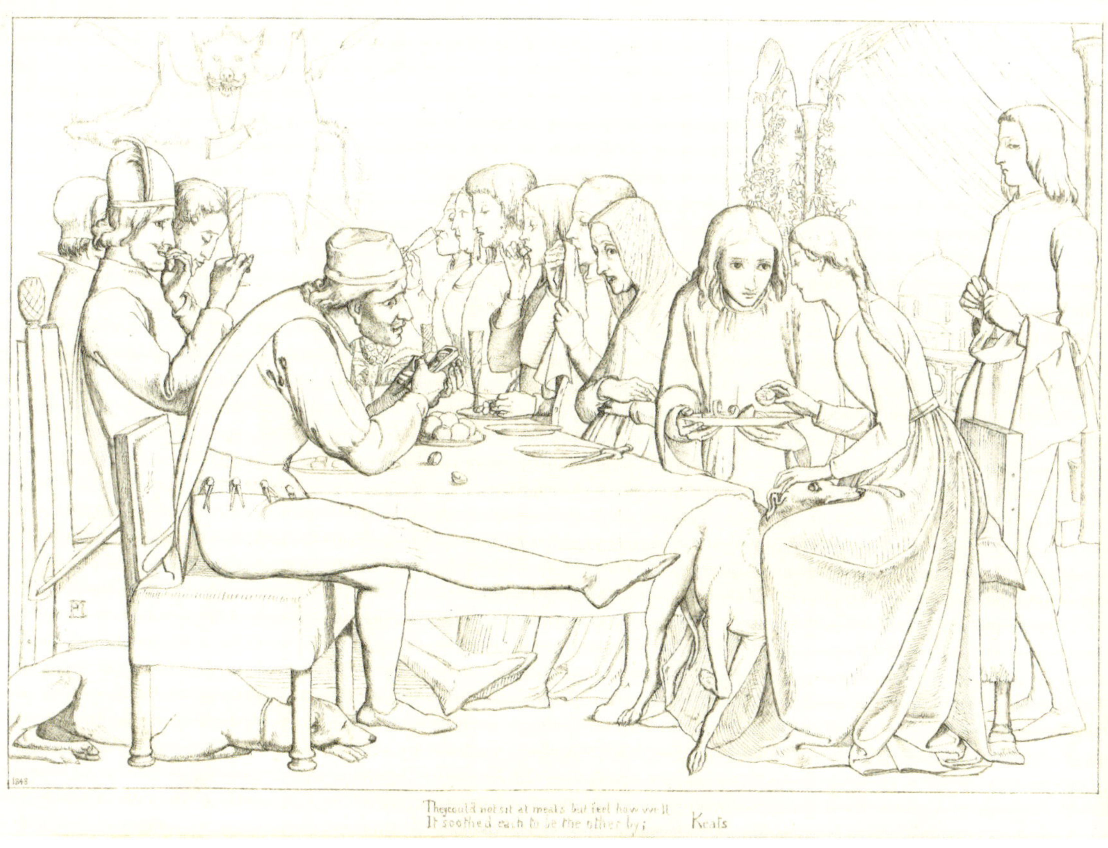

Shakespeare to Keats, Tennyson and Browning, inspired the themes of their paintings, reflecting the true catholicity of their taste. In responding to these sources, they sought an alternative to the subjects generally sanctioned as suitable material for painting by the artistic establishment. Their paintings themselves were often constructed so as to be 'read', using a series of well-placed symbols which elucidate meaning by directing the viewer back to the text (see no. 23); often, too, they extended the textual reference in quotes that accompanied the titles of their works at exhibition (no. 5, for example), and even in inscriptions on the frame (no. 21).

Rossetti was himself both a poet and a painter, but the Brotherhood counted among its wider circle of intimates, and sometimes their immediate family, poets and authors such as Algernon Swinburne, William Morris, William Michael Rossetti and Christina Rossetti, whose work and ideas nurtured their own. If the commonality of interest that originally brought them together was – to paraphrase and condense their own words – the wish to express passionately- and sincerely-held ideas through an attentive study of nature, it could be argued that one particular literary idol, John Keats, did more than any other to cement their union. It was mutual enthusiasm for Keats's poetry that first brought Rossetti and Hunt together in May 1848, after Rossetti had admired Hunt's painting *The Eve of St Agnes* (1848, Guildhall Art Gallery), on display at the Royal Academy. Knowledge of Keats's admiration of early Italian painters also went some way towards confirming them in their own aesthetic leanings: 'Seems to have been a glorious fellow,' Rossetti wrote to his brother in August 1848, 'says in one place (to my great delight) that, having just looked over a folio of the first and second schools of Italian painting, he has come to the conclusion that the early men surpassed even Raphael himself !';[2] indirectly, too, Keats's 'sanctioning' of the Italian Primitives may well have deepened their interest in consulting the same folio of Carlo Lasinio's 'grotesque'[3] and archaising engravings depicting the frescoes by Orcagna, Benozzo Gozzoli and others at the Campo Santo in Pisa. More generally, Keats's belief in the poet's ability – duty – to create through his art a separate world of beauty that transcended the inevitable inadequacies and contingencies of reality, could only have convinced the Pre-Raphaelites of the importance of their self-imposed artistic mission.

One of the undoubted stimuli to their interest was the publication in 1848 of Richard Monckton Milnes's biography, *The Life, Letters and Literary Remains of John Keats*, which re-evaluated the work of the then all-but-forgotten poet. Prompted by its successful reception, Hunt and Millais in 1849 were considering making etchings as illustrations to one of his poems, *Isabella*, although the project fell through due to copyright squabbles.

In the case of both Rossetti and Morris, Keats's influence extended as much, or more, to their poetry as to their painting. Morris, whose own poems, such as *The Defence of Guinevere*, are steeped in a Keatsian medievalism – his *Earthly Paradise* in particular contains echoes of Keats's *Ode to a Nightingale* –

ABOVE
John Everett Millais
1829-1896
Study for Lorenzo and Isabella

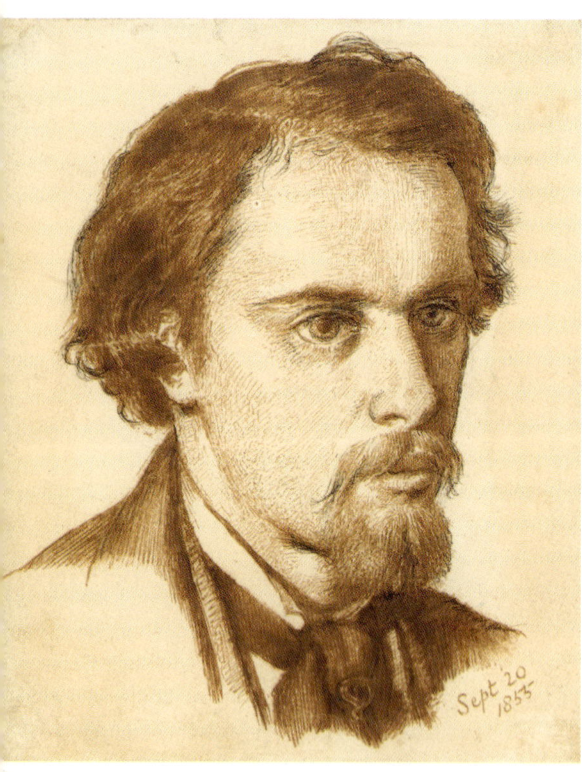

perhaps best summed up Keats's essential appeal to his 'clique' as being the visual resonance of his verse: he was, Morris wrote, 'a poet who respected semblances' in contrast to his contemporary, Shelley, who (for them) 'had no eyes.'[4] Later, while correcting the proofs for the Kelmscott Press edition of *The Poetry of John Keats* (no. 4), Morris was more specific, describing *La Belle Dame sans Merci*, as 'the germ from which all the poetry of [his] group had sprung.'[5]

Over a decade later, Rossetti could claim that, apart from his late wife's finest watercolour, the 'sole ornament' of his studio was a cast after a life mask of Keats;[6] and when he finally came to read *Endymion* in full, not long before his death, he marvelled at it: 'it is a brilliant labyrinth – a sort of magic toy.'[7] So pervasive was Keats's influence on the Pre-Raphaelite pictorial imagination, that by 1855, Burne-Jones – a relative late-comer to their 'clique' – could note with characteristic pithiness in his diary, 'Art – the chief subject going out, Keats coming back.'[8]

Personal curiosity and acquisitiveness sparked off another key 'rediscovery' among the Pre-Raphaelites, and one that would not only highlight the crucial role of the imagination in art, but help to define the role of art itself: the painting and poetry of William Blake. In 1847, the same year that Hunt stumbled across an old volume of Keats's poems at the bargain price of fourpence, Rossetti bought from Samuel Palmer's brother, William, an attendant at the British Museum, for a more extravagant ten shillings, a notebook by William Blake, containing emblems and diagrammatic drawings, drafts of prose essays and epigrams.[9] Over a decade later, having acquired at least two additional works by Blake,[10] and with ideas of a critical account of his work simmering in his mind, he took up a project for a biography initiated by the barrister, Alexander Gilchrist, and left incomplete on his death. The two-volume book on *The Life of William Blake* was eventually published in 1863, with contributions by himself, and his brother, William Michael. Rossetti's hefty editorial intervention in rewriting much of Blake's text for the second volume has been rightly disparaged by later generations of Blake scholars, but it nevertheless gives a measure of how directly he engaged with the older poet-painter on a creative level; indeed Blake's example as a practitioner of the 'double art' of painting and poetry would remain central to Rossetti's own artistic development.

It fell to Rossetti's close friend, Algernon Swinburne, to fulfil his ambitions to write an independent study of Blake's works, which he did in a brilliant essay published in 1868. In it, Swinburne uses the example of Blake and his art in order to articulate an argument for the independence and self-sufficiency of art. 'Handmaid of religion, exponent of duty, servant of fact, pioneer, she cannot become,' he insisted, 'She would be none of these things though you would bray her with bricks and mortar … Her business is not to do good on other grounds, but to do good on her own.'[11] The moral outrage that Swinburne had himself provoked two years earlier through the publication of his *Poems and Ballads* (see no. 12), can only have intensified his perception of Blake as an artistic liberator, and increased his determination to release art from enslavement to the mores of mortal man: 'Art for art's sake, first of all.'[12]

ABOVE LEFT
7. Dante Gabriel Rossetti
1828–1882
Self-portrait

RIGHT
21. Dante Gabriel Rossetti
1828–1882
Dante and Beatrice, meeting in Purgatory

For then the voice said in his heart,
"Even I, even I am Beatrice"

Dante Gabriel Rossetti, *Dante at Verona*

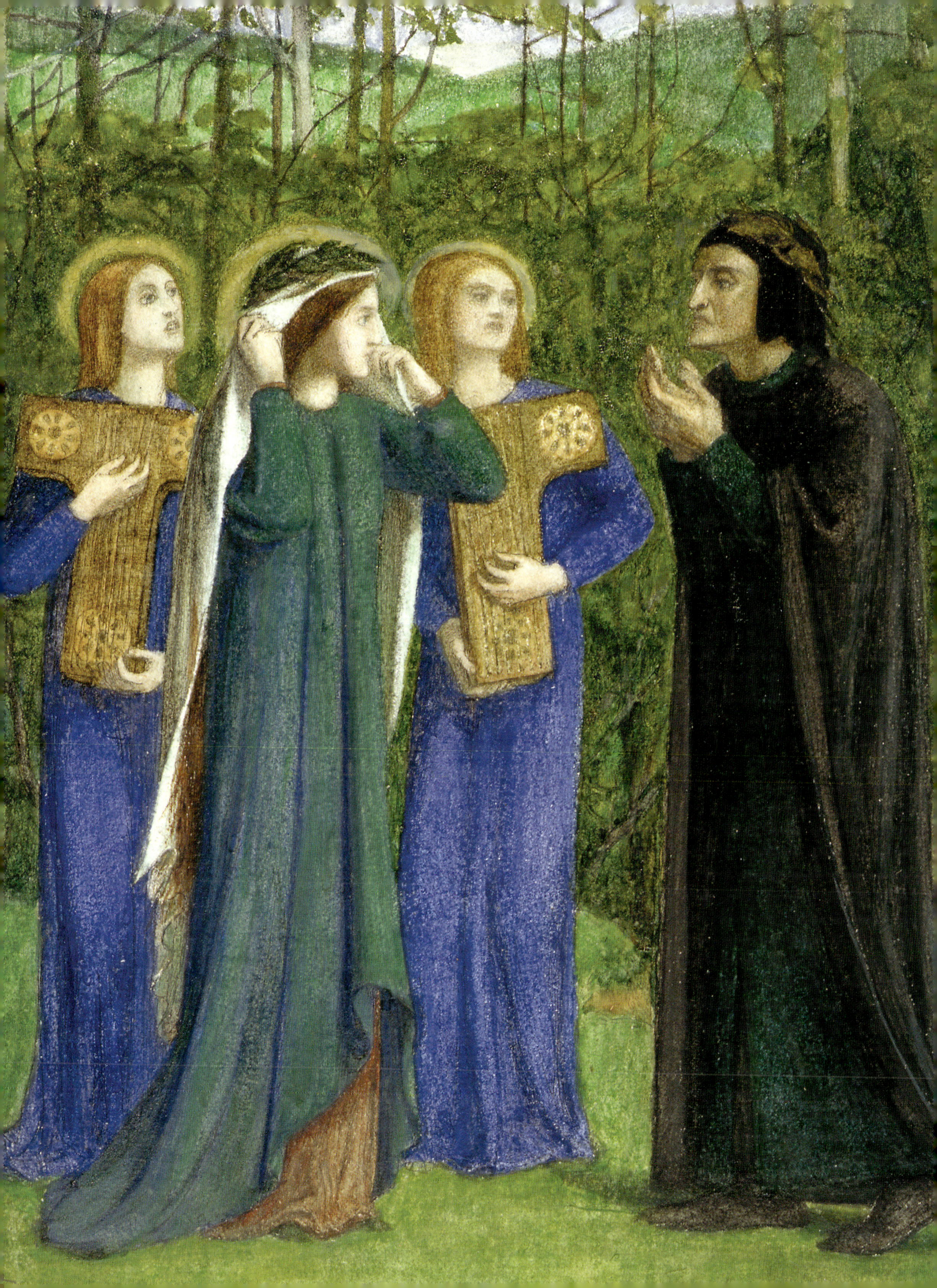

The copying of texts can double as an act of preservation and as a tribute to a given author, and it was perhaps in this dual spirit that, around 1864, Swinburne made a full, free-hand transcription of Blake's *The Marriage of Heaven and Hell* (no. 98), a book lent to him by Rossetti, and which he believed represented the 'high watermark of [Blake's] intellect.'[13] Unlike Keats's, however, Blake's poetry did not inspire the creation of imagery or direct visual responses, possibly because his own pictorial imagination set too powerful and personal a precedent. Rather, he remained an artistic beacon, an unshackled visionary genius who sought the truths of human existence not in the deceptive thralls of the material world, but in the unfeckled realms of the imagination.

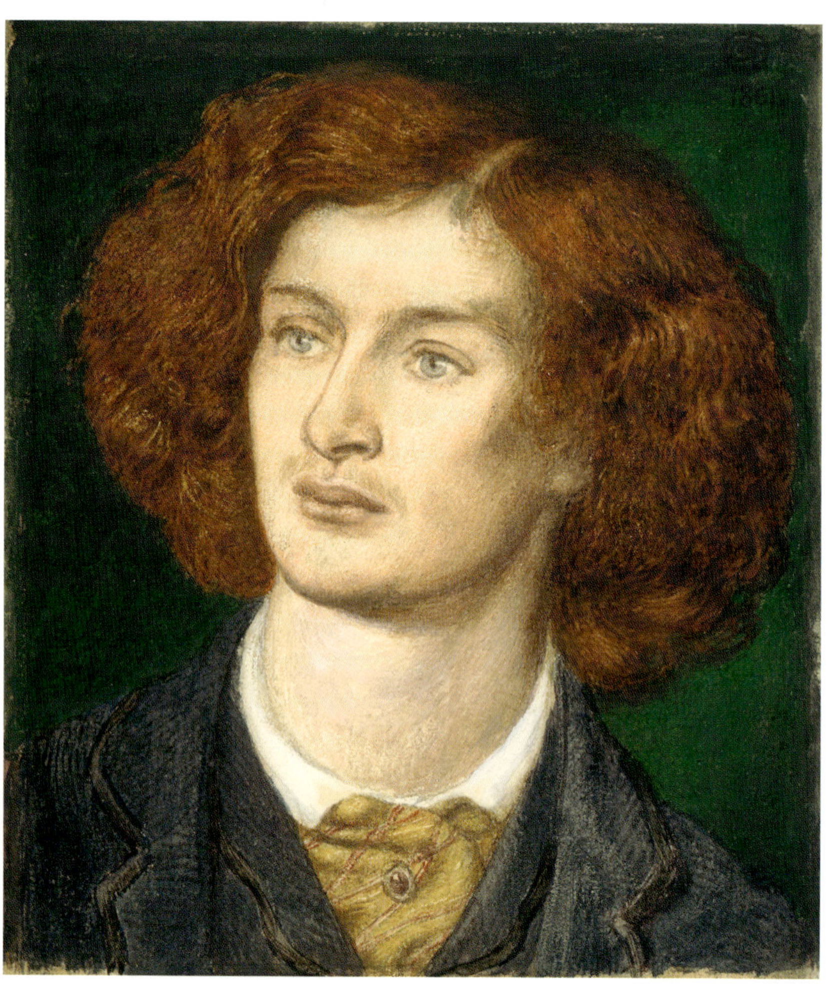

Of the Pre-Raphaelites, Swinburne found his closest visual equivalent in the paintings of his friend, Burne-Jones, to whom he dedicated his *Poems and Ballads.* Like him, Burne-Jones sought to create in and through his paintings a world apart, that spoke of 'a reflection of a reflection of something purely imaginary,'[14] 'a beautiful romantic dream of something that never was, never will be – in light better than any that ever shone – in a land no-one can define, or remember, only desire ...'[15] In this particular case, the closeness of their relationship means that discussion of precedence of text or image is often irrelevant; rather, as Swinburne recognised in an appropriately visual/musical analogy, it had more to do with expressing themselves in a common 'tone.'[16] Even when Burne-Jones's paintings clearly bear the title of one of Swinburne's poems – notably in the case of *Laus Veneris* (1873, Laing Art Gallery, Newcastle-upon-Tyne) – his visualisation is not so much a response to Swinburne's text as a product of a shared gestation of ideas. For his part, Swinburne not infrequently composed poems in direct response to a specific painter or painting, as, notably, *A Flower-Piece by Fantin, A Landscape by Courbet,* and *A Night-Piece by Millet,* all published in his 1883 anthology *A Century of Roundels.* However, to do so in the encapsulated literary form of a title represented for him a challenge of an entirely different order; as he told Georgiana Burne-Jones in 1886, 'hardly anything is so difficult as to find a name for another man's work.'[17]

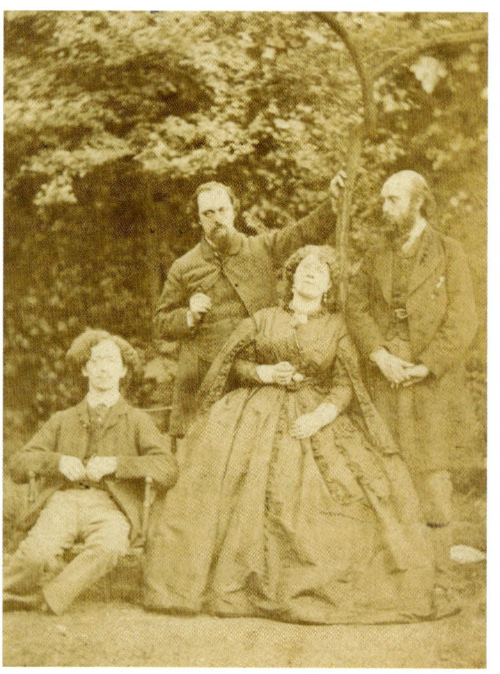

One critic to enter the Pre-Raphaelite circle – by his own admission too late to be properly part of it – was the art historian and literary biographer, Sidney Colvin (1845-1927). A product of Cambridge, Colvin began his career as a journalist in London, sending book and exhibition reviews to leading newspapers

ABOVE
11. Dante Gabriel Rossetti
1828-1882
Algernon Charles Swinburne

LEFT
9. *Algernon Charles Swinburne, William Michael Rossetti, Fanny Cornforth and Dante Gabriel Rossetti in the garden of Rossetti's home in Cheyne Walk, Chelsea.*

After much peril, friendless among friends,

Algernon Swinburne, *Atalanta in Calydon*

and journals. In 1873, aged only twenty-eight – and with the support of Robert Browning, among others – he was nominated Slade Professor of Fine Art in his *alma mater*, and continued to hold the position after becoming director of the Fitzwilliam Museum three years later. He remained at the Fitzwilliam until 1884, when he took up post as Keeper of Prints and Drawings at the British Museum.

Colvin's primary literary interests lay in the works of Walter Savage Landor and John Keats, an edition of whose letters he published in 1891, followed by a full biography in 1915.[18] Although he would come to count the formation of a cast gallery as the major achievement of his directorship at the Fitzwilliam, in literary terms at least, his greatest *coup*, post-dating his period as director, was securing the manuscript of one of Keats's finest poems, the *Ode to a Nightingale*, by persuading the Marquess of Crewe to buy it from the sale of the descendants of Keats's friend, John Hamilton Reynolds, in 1901; the manuscript – now among the greatest treasures of the collection – was given by him to the Museum in 1933 (no.2). Long after he had ceased to be director of the Fitzwilliam, Colvin continued to add, in 1912 and 1921, autograph manuscripts of correspondence he had exchanged with some of the most important literary figures of the day, among whom John Masefield, Joseph Conrad, Henry James, Robert Bridges and Matthew Arnold. As even his arch-enemy, W.E. Henley, conceded in 1892, Colvin (to whom he referred alternately as 'The Veal' and 'The Archangel'), 'can do little but log-rolling: but he can collect …'[19]

Colvin's work as a journalist in London naturally brought him into contact with many prominent artists and writers, with some of whom he developed lasting friendships. These included Swinburne, Browning, John Ruskin, George Eliot, G.F. Watts, George Meredith, Edward John Trelawney, as well as French poets and authors such as Victor Hugo and Philippe Burty, whom he saw in Paris. By far his closest association, however, was with Robert Louis Stevenson, on whose life he exerted a particularly strong (if, in later years, not always entirely positive) influence. Colvin's literary gatherings at his home in London – which Stevenson called 'the monument' – became legendary, and were celebrated in a verse written by E.V. Lucas on his retirement from the British Museum in 1912:

'How unfamiliar Bloomsbury has grown
Since Colvin left that corner house of stone
To which so many, nigh on thirty years
Have carried manuscripts, and hopes, and fears …'[20]

From the late 1860s Colvin directed much of his critical attention to the paintings and poetry of Burne-Jones and Rossetti. He was highly sensitive to the timeless quality and 'intense poetic charm' of Burne-Jones's work, and in 1869 wrote especially

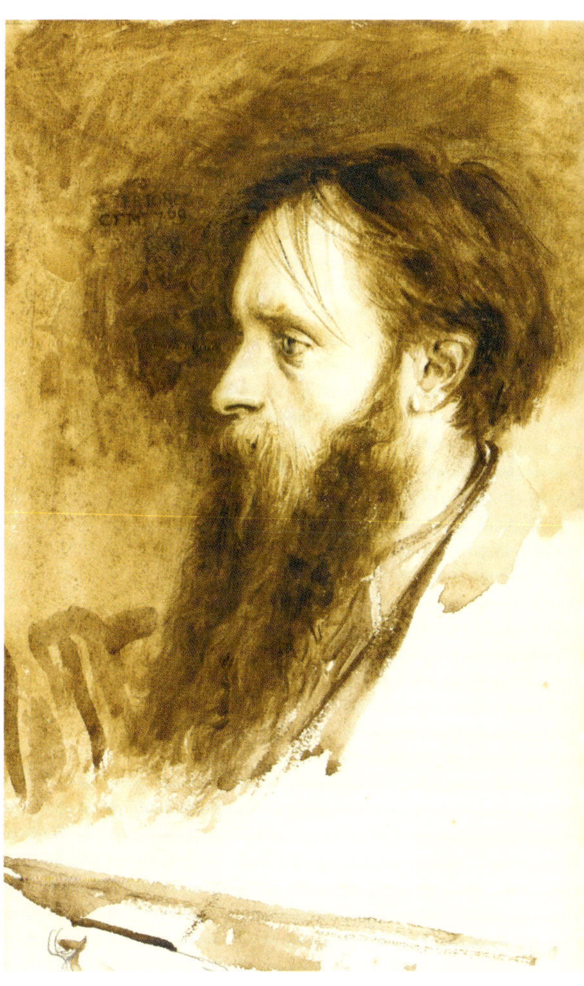

RIGHT
14. Charles Fairfax Murray
1849–1919
Sir Edward Burne-Jones

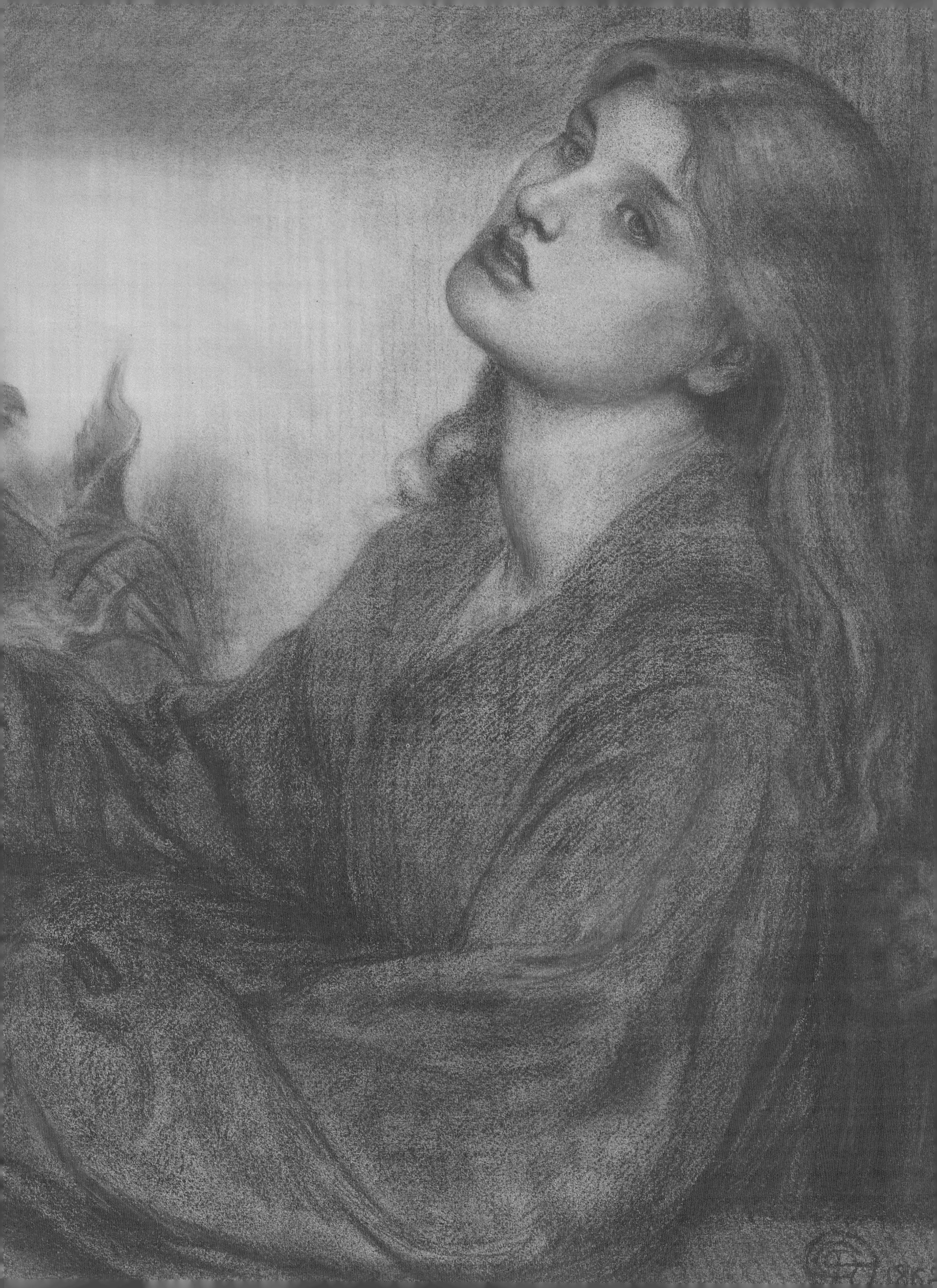

positively of his watercolours, which had for some years (Burne-Jones joined the Old Water-Colour Society in 1863) been slated by critics as being, variously, 'absolutely abhorrent', 'studiously offensive' and the work of a 'diseased imagination.'[21] Colvin took a diametrically opposed position. If his work had for some time been 'above cavil among lovers of the rarer kinds of imaginative art,' he wrote, this exhibition assured his position: 'the sentiment which informs [his work], from having been somewhat tender and exotic, is becoming hardier and more robust. If any spectator finds these things strange, startling, unaccountable, it is simply because they differ from the paltry, unbeautiful, every-day art of mere incident, whether jocose or pathetic, to which he has become accustomed …'[22] Colvin's memoirs leave us in no doubt of the affection he felt for Burne-Jones, and the 'winning sweetness' of his character.[23] Rossetti, on the other hand, of whom he saw a great deal during the 'critical and fateful' years between 1868 and 1872, was altogether tougher meat. These were difficult years for Rossetti, living in the wake of the death of both his wife and his daughter, and aggravating his depressive tendencies by a (fruitless) attempt to conquer insomnia through whisky and chloral. Anything but bohemian himself, Colvin clearly disapproved of Rossetti's 'wilful, unconventional, unhealthy habits and hours';[24] all the same, even if their personalities were emphatically at odds, he proved a loyal ally, and at a time that was critical in the formation of Rossetti's literary reputation. In 1870, after arranging for the exhumation of the manuscript poems that he had buried in the coffin of his wife Elizabeth Siddal eight years earlier, Rossetti, after some reworking, united them into a collected volume entitled, simply, *Poems* (see no. 8). Colvin was among a group of associates whom Rossetti lined up with the task of authoring positive reviews in order to counter the unfavourable reaction which he (rightly) anticipated from his 'old enemy' Robert Buchanan, although perhaps even he could not have anticipated the venom of his attack on what he termed 'The Fleshly School of Poetry.' Rossetti, Colvin wrote in his defence, was the 'poet of personal passion'; retrospectively, he added that his poetry had come at a time when the Victorian literary world thirsted for an alternative to the 'politeness' and highly-polished style of Tennyson's poetry, and found it in the 'full-blooded splendour and passionate colouring and imagery' of Rossetti's verse. In a bizarrely contradictory analogy, Rossetti's melodic 'hothouse' poetry arrived like a breath of fresh air.

Colvin, we should remember, spoke from a particularly privileged position, for he came to know a great deal of the poetry he praised, not only in published form, but also through hearing it read by its creators. His experience serves as a reminder that in addition to acting as a forum for discussion and dissemination of shared idea(l)s, a literary circle concerned itself, too, with transmission, and in particular oral transmission, through the sound of the words and the often very distinctive voice of the poet as he read his works to an assembled audience of friends and acquaintances. Colvin was especially attuned to this, and his autobiography, *Memories and Notes*, is replete with vivid – at times haunting – image-in-words of such occasions. Rossetti's voice, – 'a kind of sustained musical drone or hum with which he used to dwell on and stress and prolong the rhyme-words and sound-echoes' – was, he wrote, entirely unforgettable, and left a profound impression on all who heard him.[25] Browning, on the other hand, in stark contrast to Rossetti's and Tennyson's monotone, had an expression that was both 'flexible and dramatic'; his voice was above all things, 'virile … strong and inclining to the strident, but in passages which called for it had accents of the most moving tenderness.'[26] On occasion, however, the emotional intensity of his spoken verse proved overwhelming, so that some readings – of certain pages from *The Ring and the Book* and *Andrea del Sarto*, in particular – reduced both audience and poet to tears.

In the closing years of the nineteenth century, Colvin drew into his orbit another young writer, G.K. Chesterton (1874–1936), at the time working as a journalist and literary critic in London. Chesterton never forgot the generosity and hospitality that Colvin and his wife extended to him, but freely recognised that the only thing that they really had in common was a love of Stevenson; politically and morally, he wrote, they were poles apart: 'we differed upon every subject in earth and heaven; he was both an Imperialist in politics and a Rationalist in religion; and with all his frigid refinement, he was whatever he was with an unquenchable pertinacity. He hated radicals and Christian mystics and romantic sympathisers with small nationalities, and in fact everything that I had any tendency to be.'[27] Socially, too, they operated in very different ways. In particular, Chesterton felt remote from the passion among the generation he considered to be his elders – prime among whom, Colvin – to form themselves into distinctive literary cliques. He was, he remembered, 'puzzled by culture being cut up into sections that were not even sects. Colvin kept one court, which was very courtly; Henley kept another, which was not exactly courtly, or was full of rather rowdy courtiers; in the suburbs Swinburne was established as sultan and Prophet of Putney, with Watts-Dunton as a Grand Vizier. And I could not

LEFT
Dante Gabriel Rossetti
1828–1882
La Pia de'Tolomei

make out what it was all about; the prophet was not really a commander of the faithful, because there was no faith; and as for the doubt, it was equally common to all the rival groups of the age.'[28]

While Chesterton's *faux-naif* bewilderment clearly targets the pretensions of these 'commanders' of sectarianism, it also effectively highlights the destructive nature of such coteries. Colvin, his analogy leads us to believe, was a figure of authority in the literary world, although Chesterton was not alone in questioning whether in every case he had used his authority to good effect. Biographers of Stevenson, in particular, have criticised his unhelpfully authoritarian behaviour towards his writer-friend, and attributed his bullying actions to a glorified perception of his own literary merits.[29]

However accurate this assessment of Colvin's literary pretensions these were not accusations that could be levelled at Colvin's successor-but-three as director of the Fitzwilliam, Sydney Cockerell (1867-1962), who freely admitted to being 'not a well-read man,' though, by his own estimation, one who could 'hold [his] own in literary conversation.'[30]

Like Colvin, though the best part of a generation younger, Cockerell had known many of the Pre-Raphaelites and their associates personally, and became especially close to William Morris, through working first as a cataloguer of his books, and then as secretary to the Kelmscott Press from 1891-1896 (see no. 54). Although not always easy to like – his friend Charles Ricketts described him as a 'gruff diamond',[31] while Siegfried Sassoon found him 'really rather a *hard* man'[32] – Cockerell inspired trust by his efficiency, loyalty and persistence, and was possessed of an historical sense which enabled him to recognise and, in his role as museum director, acquire and preserve, works of art and literature of extraordinary importance. As Morris's executor and trustee, his role in tying up the affairs of the Kelmscott Press ensured the survival of material – some now in the Fitzwilliam – that would otherwise have perished, to the detriment of the history of typography and book production, while his continuing loyalty to Morris's family earned him the undying gratitude of the latter's closest associates, not least Burne-Jones.[33] Ultimately, it also earned the Fitzwilliam the better part of a collection of over 900 drawings and sketchbooks by Burne-Jones, given by his son and daughter in 1919, and his nephew-in-law, Stanley Baldwin, two years later. This is not the place to assess Cockerell's achievement as a museum director to the full. Nevertheless, it is important to note that the bulk of the Museum's outstanding holdings of Pre-Raphaelite material – whether paintings, drawings or literary manuscripts – came occasionally via an astute purchase (no. 18) or even a personal gift (no. 21), but far more frequently as a direct result of Cockerell's acquaintance with the families, friends, associates and followers of Burne-Jones, Rossetti and Morris, in particular. Chief among these was Charles Fairfax Murray, Burne-Jones's assistant from 1866, and later an expert on Old Master paintings, collector and dealer, whom Cockerell tried to flatter with an Honorary Keepership of Paintings in 1911, a role he declined. However he continued (often after preliminary discussion with Cockerell) to present the museum with almost 1300 paintings, drawings, prints, books and manuscripts of extraordinary quality and importance, many by the Pre-Raphaelite artists he had known: Holman Hunt and Madox Brown, but especially Burne-Jones and Rossetti and their intimates, Algernon Swinburne and Elizabeth Siddal.

Cockerell's own field of scholarship was in medieval manuscripts, and it is difficult not to count his purchase and solicitation of psalters, breviaries and books of hours from the thirteenth to the fifteenth century as the defining acquisitive moments of his museum career. However, he was also keenly aware of the importance of securing the present for the future when it came to the work of living authors. Like Colvin, he was a friend and advisor to many writers: Hardy and Shaw, in particular – for both of whom he acted as literary executor – but also Wilfred Scawen Blunt, Henry Yates Thompson, Lady Gregory, W.B. Yeats[34] and Tolstoy, whom he visited in 1903. In the same spirit as he sought, later in his directorship, to establish a gallery of self-portraits of contemporary artists to rival the Uffizi's in Florence,[35] Cockerell wrote to a select group of writers not long after taking up his position in 1908, to ask them for manuscripts of their published or unpublished works. He had no trouble twisting the arm of Burne-Jones's nephew, Rudyard Kipling, who, after sending his wife 'm.s. hunting' in their Sussex home, responded to Cockerell's request with the preface to his *Life's Handicap*, of 1890. From one of his closest literary friends, George Bernard Shaw, however, Cockerell succeeded in securing only his likeness by John (no. 30), one that, as far as Shaw was concerned, spoke a shade *too* grandiloquently of the author *qua* literary personality.'[36]

Cockerell may have been right to play down his personal literary pretensions,[37] but his practical abilities and organisational powers undoubtedly rendered invaluable service to a number of authors; as Siegfried Sassoon later observed, he was 'born to become … the trusted advisor of great writers.'[38]

RIGHT
24. Augustus Edwin John
1879-1961
Thomas Hardy

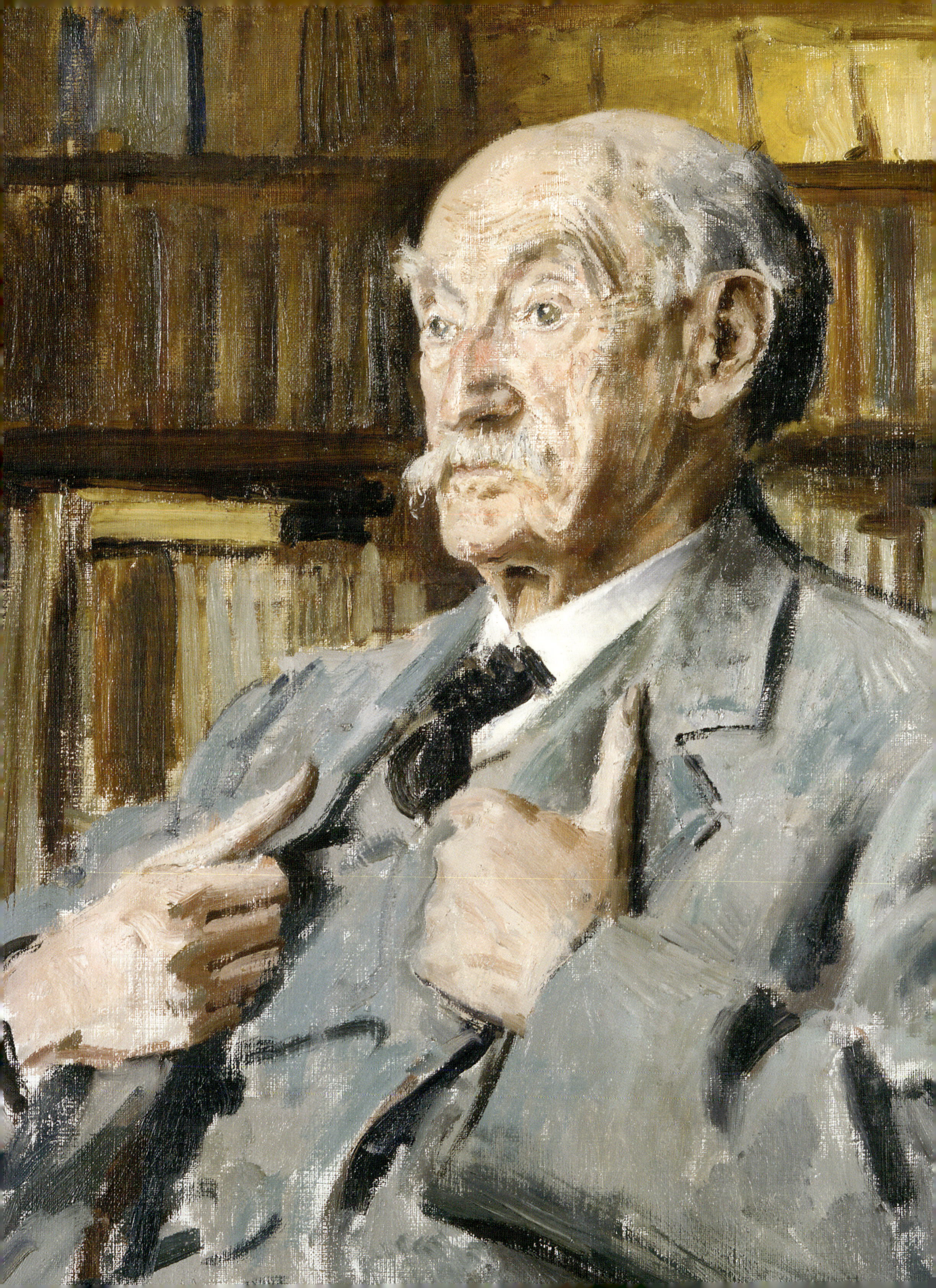

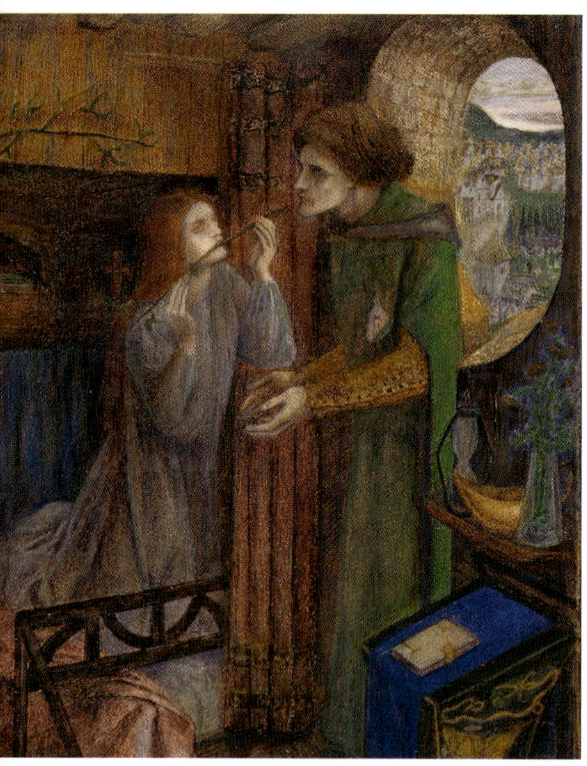

Cockerell first met one of the greatest of these, Thomas Hardy, in 1911, on a visit to Hardy's home at Max Gate in Dorset. Barely a month after they met, Hardy entrusted Cockerell with the weighty responsibility of distributing his manuscripts to libraries and institutions throughout Britain and the United States, which included the allocation to the Fitzwilliam of the manuscripts of *Jude the Obscure* (no. 26) and *Times Laughingstock* in 1911.[39] Although Cockerell's role as Hardy's executor in the management of his posthumous affairs has not been free of criticism,[40] there is no doubt that at the time, Hardy was grateful to Cockerell for 'taking him in hand', considering it 'unbecoming for a writer to send his MSS to a museum on his own judgement.'[41] At one point Hardy even suggested that Cockerell's role in the distribution be formally acknowledged in the record of their presentation, a suggestion which, in the case of the Fitzwilliam, at least, Cockerell did not take up.[42] In 1919, Hardy marvelled at Cockerell's ability to secure a cool £1000 donation for the museum over dinner,[43] but Cockerell was notoriously unabashed at asking for gifts of all sorts, and more often than not obtained them; to use Bernard Shaw's euphemism, he was 'an expert in the art of holding on to loan collections.'[44]

Given their difference in age – almost twenty years – Cockerell's relationship with Siegfried Sassoon was initially one of a more-or-less paternalistic mentor. They first met in August 1915, when Sassoon was sent to Cambridge to train for a month with the Officers' Training Corps, armed with a letter of introduction to Cockerell from Edmund Gosse. He later remembered that he emerged from evenings spent with Cockerell – 'a sort of bearded and spectacled magician' – reeling at the thrill of handling manuscripts by Rossetti and Morris, both heroes of his adolescent years, as well as superb illuminated medieval missals and psalters in which Cockerell was a recognised authority.[45] Sassoon and Cockerell remained friends and correspondents until the latter's death in 1962 (in fact, Sassoon would out-live him for less than five years). In 1924, doubtless at Cockerell's suggestion (and certainly with his sanction), he parted with his 'posterity' portrait by Philpot (no. 28), and a few months later expressed a certain gratification on seeing it hanging in the Fitzwilliam. With the gift in 1935 of a fair copy of the manuscripts of his *Fifty Poems* (no.29), Sassoon ensured that his literary remains, like his portrait, would join those of his friend, Thomas Hardy, in the Fitzwilliam.

Like Cockerell, Sassoon developed a close friendship with Hardy, but one that appears to have been of an entirely different order, borne of a sincere love of his poetry and novels, and maturing into a deeply-felt affection, bordering on adulation. Hardy, who was also a friend of Sassoon's uncle, the sculptor Hamo Thornycroft, was ever-present with Sassoon at the Front. In the trenches he read *Tess of the D'Urbervilles* and *The Return of the Native* (noting how well they suited his mood), and began *Far from the Madding Crowd* the day after being hit by a sniper's bullet in the shoulder in April 1917.[46] The previous summer, he found himself wondering what Hardy would make of his life there (the Pre-Raphaelites, he was sure, 'would have loathed it'[47]) and turned to his *Wessex Poems* so as to 'imbibe a dose of irony & Dorset landscape.'[48] Recuperating in hospital in London, he anxiously awaited Hardy's approbation of his volume, *The Old Huntsman and Other Poems*, and was thrilled when Hardy agreed to have it dedicated to him.

Sassoon did not make his first visit to Hardy's home at Max Gate until after the war had ended, but, as a stop-gap, sent him, at the beginning of 1918, a photograph of Philpot's glamorous portrait.[49] When he was eventually able to meet Hardy in person later that year, his immediate impression was of the modesty of his host and the unimposing nature of his surroundings: Hardy was, he wrote, 'a small man …. frail and rather gnome-like in the candle-shine and dim room, with his large round head, vast brow, beaky nose and pendulous grey moustache'; he was

LEFT
19. Elizabeth Siddal, later Rossetti
1829-1862
Clerk Saunders

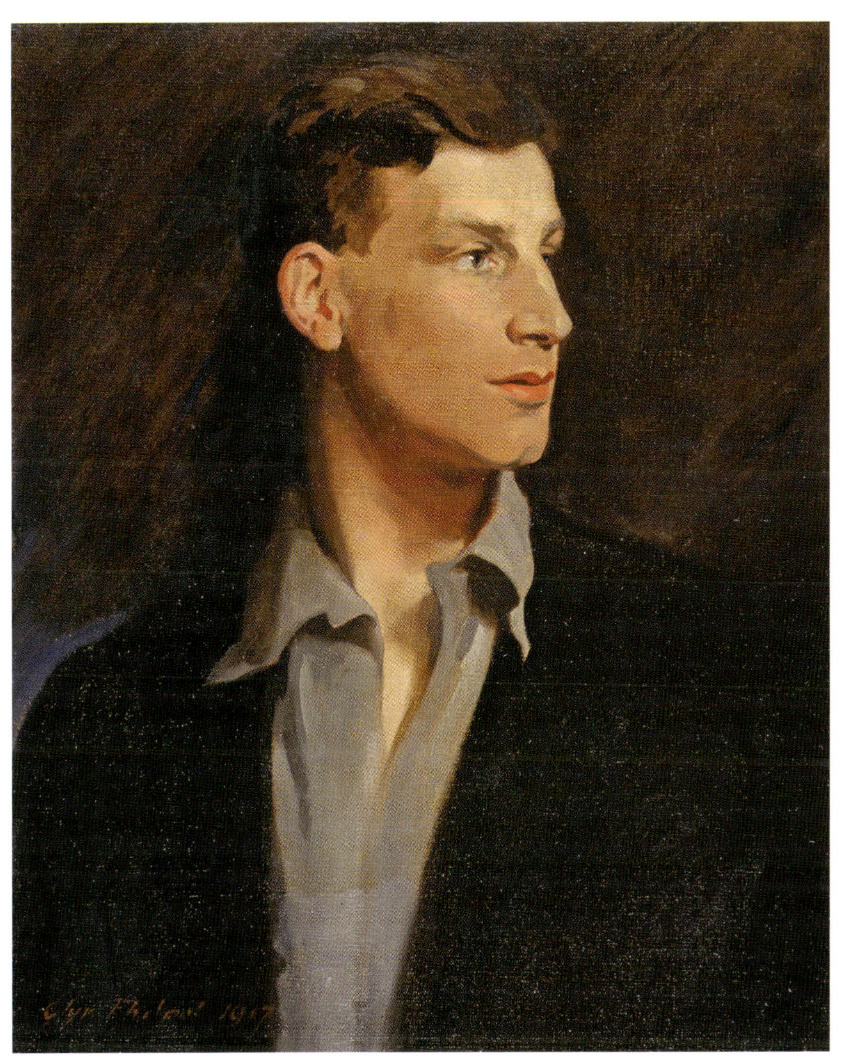

also one who, for Sassoon, 'became more loveable all the time.'[50] In subsequent years, Sassoon travelled to Dorset on several occasions, either alone, or with a posse of fellow admirers, as he did in 1919 when he and a group of young contemporaries presented Hardy with a volume of forty-three of their holograph poems in honour of his seventy-ninth birthday, or, two years later when, in the company of Virginia Woolf, James Joyce and Robert Graves, among others, he presented Hardy with a copy of a first edition of Keats's poems.

Sassoon leaves us in no doubt that he derived considerable pleasure from these shared literary pilgrimages to honour a distinguished fellow writer. In general, however, he considered himself by nature emphatically *un*clubbable, and, as he later told Cockerell, not 'the sort of man who gravitates towards social institutions.'[51] Like Chesterton, he was especially allergic to the ritualistic constraints of formal literary associations. Writing from a race meeting at Cheltenham in 1923, he drew a direct comparison between literary bores and the sporting variety: 'at a "literary gathering" I am, supposedly, in my own professional environment, for the people are interested in the things which concern my serious existence. But most of them only chatter about "the arts", in the same way as the empty-headed "sporting folk" chatter about racing and hunting'[52]; just like on the race course, the vast majority of the participants were spectators, and these only, 'a fraction of the herd which bullocks its way through a segment of a century. How small is the fraction which strives to infuse *thought* into the whole heavy lump of contemporary humanity !'[53]

It is hard not to sympathise with the creative mind that rebels at the thought of being harnessed into formal social structures of exchange. Although sometimes insidious, pretentious and vacuous – vicious, even – literary circles could also provide the conduit through which public collections were formed and developed. Those at the Fitzwilliam Museum stand as a lasting record of circles enriched by mutual respect and reward, a shared goal to protect and preserve, and – above all – by powerful bonds of affection.

You smug-faced crowds with kindling eye
Who cheer when soldier lads march by,
Sneak home and pray you'll never know
The hell where youth and laughter go.

Siegfried Sassoon, 'Suicide in Trenches' 1917, *Fifty Poems*

ABOVE
28. Glyn Warren Philpot
1884–1937
Siegfried Sassoon

1 See Rossetti's letter to William Michael Rossetti, 30 August 1848, Oswald Doughty and John Robert Wahl, eds., *Letters of Dante Gabriel Rossetti* I, 1965, no.35, 42.

2 20 August 1848, Doughty and Wahl, *ibid.*, *op. cit.*, I, no. 34, 40. Keats's letter is reproduced in Richard Monckton Milnes's *The Life, Letters and Literary Remains of John Keats*, I, 1848, 255.

3 'I do not think I ever had a greater treat out of Shakespeare. Full of romance and the most tender feeling – magnificence of draperies beyond everything I ever saw, not excepting Raphael's. But Grotesque to a curious pitch ...' Quoted Sidney Colvin, *John Keats: His Life and Poetry*, London, 1917, 42.

4 Quoted E.P. Thompson, *William Morris, Romantic to Revolutionary*, London, 1977, 10.

5 J.M.S Tompkins, *William Morris the Poet*, 1988, 45.

6 To Charles Eliot Norton, 9 January 1862, Doughty and Wahl, *op. cit.*, II, 435. Rossetti added that it was made by his friend Alexander Munro, who for the costs of the materials was happy to supply further casts to other admirers.

7 To Jane Morris, February 1880, John Bryson and Janet Camp Troxell, eds., *Dante Gabriel Rossetti and Jane Morris. Their Correspondence*, Oxford, 1976, 137.

8 Georgiana Burne-Jones, *Memorials of Edward Burne-Jones*, I, 1904 (1993 ed.), 116.

9 *c.*1785-1805, British Library; Butlin 201.

10 *Lot and his Daughters* (*c.*1799-1800, The Henry E. Huntington Library and Art Gallery, San Marino, Ca.; Butlin 381) was in Rossetti's possession by 1863, *The Infant Hercules Throttling the Serpents* (*c.*1790-3, National Gallery of Art, Washington; Butlin 253) by 1868; he also owned Blake's double-sided drawing representing on the *recto* Queen Katherine awakening from her dream and a sketch for plate 6 of Jerusalem (*c.* 1804, National Gallery of Art, Washington; Butlin 561).

11 Algernon Swinburne, *William Blake. A Critical Essay*, 1868, 90.

12 *ibid.*, 91.

13 *ibid.*, 204.

14 Martin Harrison and Bill Waters, *Burne-Jones*, London, 1973 (1989 ed.), 158.

15 Christopher Wood, *Burne-Jones*, London, 1998, 6.

16 In 1882, Swinburne wrote to Burne-Jones anxious to know when he could come to read his new poem, *Tristram of Lyonesse* to him and his wife Georgiana: 'I have been looking forward for months to the time that I should read to you 'Joyous Gard' (canto VI) – not that I am so vain of its merits ... [but] that it had something in common with your paintings in, shall we say, Tone'. ALS Swinburne to Burne-Jones, 13 July 1882, Burne-Jones Papers, Fitzwilliam Museum, I, 12.

17 ALS Swinburne to Georgiana Burne-Jones, 6 April 1886, Burne-Jones Papers, Fitzwilliam Museum, I, 24. Given the date, could he have had in mind doing just this for Burne-Jones's 'mermaid' painting, *The Depths of the Sea* (Fogg Art Museum, Cambridge, Mass.), the only painting he exhibited at the Royal Academy that year?

18 Sidney Colvin, *Letters of Keats to his Family and Friends*, London, 1891; *The Poems of John Keats*, 2 vols., 1915.

19 John Connel, *W.E. Henley*, London, 1949, 234.

20 Margery Ross, ed., *Robert Ross. Friend of Friends*, London, 1952, 227.

21 Quoted Stephen Wildman and John Christian, *Edward Burne-Jones. Victorian Artist-Dreamer*, exh. cat., New York, Metropolitan Museum of Art, 1998, 108.

22 Sidney Colvin, *Notes on the Exhibition of the Royal Academy and Old Water-colour Society, London, 1869*, London, 1869, 6.

23 Sidney Colvin, *Memories & Notes of Persons & Places 1852-1912*, London, 1921, 59.

24 *ibid.*, 62.

25 *ibid.*, 65.

26 *ibid.*, 83-84.

27 G. K. Chesterton *Autobiography*, London, 1939 (1969 ed.), 97.

28 *ibid.*, 284.

29 See, for example, Frank McLynn, *Robert Louis Stevenson. A Biography*, London, 1993, 414, who accuses Colvin of having suffered 'from the delusion, common to academics, that a critic is as "creative" as a writer of fiction.'

30 Wilfred Blunt, *Sydney Carlyle Cockerell, friend of Ruskin and William Morris and Director of the Fitzwilliam Museum, Cambridge*, London, 1964, 269.

31 J.G.P. Delaney, *Charles Ricketts. A Biography*, Oxford, 1990, 231.

32 June 1922, Rupert Hart-Davis, ed., *Siegfried Sassoon Diaries 1923-1925*, London, 1985, 182.

33 Burne-Jones told him there was 'nothing I would not do for your devotion to dear Morris.' Blunt, *op. cit.*, 63.

34 Cockerell's correspondence with Yeats, together with other documents and Yeats manuscripts, was sold at Sotheby's, 12 July 2005, lot 320. I am grateful to Nicholas Robinson for drawing this sale to my attention.

35 Between 1918 and 1928, William Strang, William Orpen, Philip Wilson Steer and George Clausen all responded to Cockerell's request for self-portraits.

36 Shaw infinitely preferred Rodin's portrait bust of himself to any of John's. See *Shaw gives himself away: An autobiographical miscellany*, Newton, 1939, 155.

37 In 1922, Siegfried Sassoon wrote that Cockerell was 'a first class factotum. But he can form no original judgements in art and literature.' Hart-Davis, *op. cit.*, 1981, 182.

38 Viola Meynell, ed., *The Best of Friends: Further letters to Sydney Carlyle Cockerell*, London, 1956, 164.

39 Cockerell may have asked for *Jude the Obscure* for the Fitzwilliam, but the suggestion that the museum receive *Time's Laughingstock*, 'said to be the best of my works in verse,' appears to have been Hardy's. See Hardy to Cockerell, 11 October 1911, Richard Little Purdy and Michael Millgate, eds., *The Collected Letters of Thomas Hardy*, IV, Oxford, 1984, 181.

40 See, for example, Norman Page's resumé in *The Oxford Reader's Companion to Hardy*, Oxford, 2000, 52.

41 Purdy and Millgate, *op. cit*, IV, 1984, 181.

42 Hardy proposed that his manuscripts be presented through Cockerell, or to him, 'to distribute as you should choose', *ibid.*, 181.

43 'How you manage to squeeze £1000 out of a dinner table passes my understanding. It is, I admit, better than big game shooting.' 15 July 1919, Purdy and Millgate, *op.cit.*, V, 213.

44 To T.E. Lawrence, 13 May 1923, Dan N. Laurence, ed. *Bernard Shaw. Collected Letters, 1911-1925*, 1985, 826.

45 Meynell, *op.cit.*, 164.

46 Hart-Davis, *op. cit.*, 1983, 156.

47 July 19 1916, *ibid.*, 96.

48 ALS to Hamo Thornycroft, April 3 (1917), private collection (from a photocopy in the Department of Manuscripts and Printed Books, Fitzwilliam Museum).

49 'That photograph! – We divined it to be you, but I was not certain ... I shall be so glad to see you walk in some day.' Hardy to Sassoon, January 8 1918, Purdy and Millgate, *op.cit.*, V., 242.

50 7 November 1918, *ibid.*, 281.

51 Xmas Day, 1941, Meynell, *op. cit.*, 86.

52 March 8 1923, Hart-Davis, *op. cit.*, 1985, 21.

53 *ibid.*

1. Joseph Severn

1793-1879

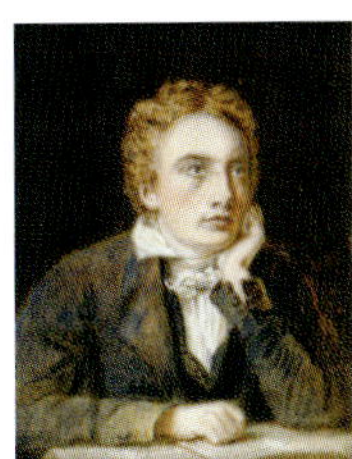

1. John Keats

Watercolour on ivory | 108 x 83 mm
Bequeathed by Charles W. Dilke, 1911 | no. 713

'Severn – S – lift me up for I am dying – I shall die easy – don't be frightened – thank god it has come ...'

Severn practiced as a painter of portraits, landscapes and history subjects, but his residing fame is as Keats's devoted friend, who nursed him as he lay dying of tuberculosis in Rome in 1821.

Severn was introduced to Keats by William Haslam around 1816, while Keats was a medical student at Guy's hospital, and he was studying at the Royal Academy schools. He became deeply attached to his friend, marvelling at his sensibility towards the natural world: 'Nothing seems to escape him,' he wrote, 'the song of a bird and the undernote of a response from covet or hedge, the rustle of some small animal, the changing of the green and brown lights and furtive shadows, the motions of the wind – just how it took certain tall flowers and plants – and the wayfaring of the clouds' (Birkenhead, 1965, 61).

Severn painted this portrait around 1818 or 1819, at the same time as others of Keats's immediate circle: Haslam, John Hamilton Reynolds, and his two brothers, George and Tom. Despite his boyish looks, Keats would have been aged around twenty-one. Severn described his friend as being small – barely more than five feet tall – but with an erect carriage and an intensity of expression, 'such as may be seen on the face of some seamen,' that gave him the presence of a man of far greater physical stature. His expression was said to have had a hawkish quality – softened in this portrait – but his most noteworthy feature was the extraordinary luminosity of his hazel eyes, which 'seemed to glow and project beams of light before them.'

This portrait was painted for Keats's beloved Fanny Brawne, and is framed with a lock of his reddish gold hair, that for Severn resembled 'the rich plumage of a bird.' It was bought from her by the donor's father, Charles Wentworth Dilke, who built the house at Wentworth Place, in Hampstead, where Keats and Fanny first met. Keats took a lock of Fanny's hair with him to his grave.

John Keats

1795-1821

2. Ode to the Nightingale

Given by the Marquess of Crewe, 1933 | MS.1-1933

Keats was inspired to write this, one of his greatest poems, on a particularly warm spring day in May 1819. It was first published in the *Annals of the Fine Arts* in July 1819, with the title slightly amended by the publishers to *Ode to a Nightingale.*

The circumstances of its composition were first documented (twenty years after the event) by Keats's friend and house-mate, Charles Armitage Brown, who wrote that Keats, on hearing the nightingale, 'felt a tranquil and continual joy in her song; and one morning he took his chair from the breakfast-table to the grass plot under a plum-tree, where he sat for two or three hours.' Brown claimed that he later recovered the 'four or five' scraps of paper on which Keats had noted down his 'poetic feeling on the song' concealing them afterwards behind books in their lodgings at Wentworth Place. Discrepancies between Brown's account (dismissed by another of Keats's friends, Charles Dilke, as 'pure delusion') and the existence of these two sheets (rather than scraps) have led a number of scholars to suggest that he may have confused this manuscript with that for the *Ode to Indolence*, now lost.

In 1901 the manuscript was put up for sale by a nephew of Keats's close friend, John Hamilton Reynolds (1769-1852). Keats's biographer, Sidney Colvin – also a former director of the Fitzwilliam Museum – wrote to the Marquess of Crewe (son of Richard Monckton Milnes, Lord Houghton), urging him to buy the manuscript in order to preserve it for the nation: 'It is a shabby enough little ms. to look at, but of almost unequalled literary interest' (4 May 1901, Fitzwilliam Museum, MS.4-1960). Lord Crewe bought the manuscript for £135.

Keats's poetry was of seminal importance to the Pre-Raphaelites (see pp. 36-45). It also inspired a later generation of writers represented in this exhibition. Sassoon kept with him in the trenches a small edition in green vellum, given to him by Lady Ottoline Morrell, while Hardy's many references to the *Ode to a Nightingale* in his own work suggest that it was one of his favourite poems. In 1887 Hardy made a pilgrimage to Keats's grave in Rome and visited the house where he died in the arms of Joseph Severn (see no. 1); in 1921, he was presented with a first edition of Keats's poems as an eighty-first birthday present by a group of his own young admirers.

Myles Birket Foster

1825-1899

3. Study for a vignette illustration to John Keats's *Ode to a Nightingale*

Pen and ink and grey wash on paper | 108 x 83 mm | Private collection

This wash drawing was made as a vignette design for the volume, *The Poets of the Nineteenth Century*, selected and edited by Robert Willmott in 1857. The volume was illustrated with what Willmott called 'Word-paintings' by almost twenty different artists, all of which were engraved on wood by the Dalziel brothers. Birket Foster was one of the main contributors to the project: in addition to this illustration, and another for Keats's *The Stream*, he also designed landscape vignettes or tail-pieces for the poems in the volume by James Beattie, Charlotte Smith, William Crowe, George Crabbe, Ann Radcliffe, Anne Letitia Barbauld, William Wordsworth, Walter Scott, James Grahame, Robert Bloomfield, John Keble, Alexander Smith and Philip James Bailey.

Birket Foster was – and remains – a highly popular landscape painter, whose vision of the countryside became synonymous with a comforting, peculiarly English rustic idyll. Trained as a wood engraver himself, he worked extensively as a book illustrator, making his name with his *Pictures of English Landscapes* (1863), with verse texts by Tom Taylor, and also engraved by the Dalziel brothers. A friend of Burne-Jones and Morris, he furnished his house at Witley in Sussex in the mid-1860s almost entirely with stained glass, tile panels and paintings produced by Morris and Company.

O pang-dowered Poet, whose reverberant lips
And heart-strung lyre awoke the Moon's eclipse,—
Thou whom the daisies glory in growing o'er,—
Their fragrance clings around thy name, not writ
But rumour'd in water, while the fame of it
Along Time's flood goes echoing evermore.

Dante Gabriel Rossetti, John Keats, 1880

John Keats
1795-1821

4. The Poems of John Keats

8o Edited by F.S. Ellis. Flower (2) paper 400 pages Golden type
Black and red ink. Limp vellum binding with silk ties 300 paper seven vellum copies. Published by the Kelmscott Press 8 May 1894.
Private collection

Keats's poetry had an enormous influence on William Morris from his student days in Oxford in the early 1850s. Sydney Cockerell, later director of the Fitzwilliam, was working as a secretary to the Kelmscott Press at the time this book was published, and remembered Morris's fury at finding that part of the text had been poorly set: 'In February 1894 the last sheets of the Kelmscott Press Keats, edited by F. S. Ellis, were being printed. A specimen of each sheet of every book was brought in to Morris as soon as it came off the press. I was with him when he happened to open the sheet on which *La Belle Dame sans Merci* was printed. He began to read it and was suddenly aware of unfamiliar words ... verses four and five transposed, and several changes in verse seven. Great was his indignation. He swiftly altered the words and then read the poem to me, remarking that it was the germ from which all the poetry of his group had sprung' (quoted, Colvin, 1917, 265).

By 1898, Cockerell noted that this had become 'the most sought after of all the smaller Kelmscott books' *(A Note by William Morris ... ;* 1898, 39; see no. 54). Although it sold for thirty shillings a copy, its price at sale five years later had rocketed to £26 (Petersen, 1991, 319).

John Everett Millais
1829-1896

5. Study for Lorenzo and Isabella

Pen and ink on paper | 236 x 314mm
Signed on the chair, left: *JEM*, and dated, lower left: 1848
Inscribed, lower centre: *They could not sit at meals but feel how well / It soothed each other to be the other by; Keats.*
Bequeathed by J.R. Holliday, 1927 | no. 1396

Fair Isabel, poor, simple Isabel !
Lorenzo, a young palmer in Love's eye!
They could not in the self-same mansion dwell
Without some stir of heart, some malady;
They could not sit at meals but feel how well
It soothed each to be the other by ...

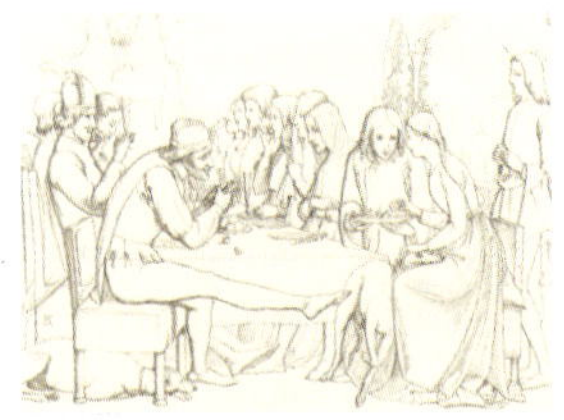

These lines, along with the following verse from John Keats's poem *Isabella ; or, The Pot of Basil* (1816), accompanied Millais's painting of the subject when exhibited at the Royal Academy in 1849; the painting is now in the Walker Art Gallery, Liverpool. The story, as Keats acknowledged, is drawn from Boccaccio, although the poem itself was consciously cast in Shakesperian manner. Isabella falls in love with Lorenzo, who works in her brothers' business. They are infuriated by the alliance, having anticipated a far more profitable marriage for their sister. They murder Lorenzo, telling Isabella that he has been called away. But Lorenzo's ghost appears and tells her the true story; she exhumes the body, cuts off the head and keeps it in a pot of basil:

She wrapp'd it up; and for its tomb did choose
A garden-pot, wherein she laid it by,
And cover'd it with mould, and o'er it set
Sweet Basil, which her tears kept ever wet.

In treating a theme from Keats's poetry, Millais followed the literary lead of his Pre-Raphaelite brethren, Dante Gabriel Rossetti and William Holman Hunt, who had exhibited his painting, *The Eve of St. Agnes* (Guildhall Art Gallery) at the Royal Academy the previous year; it may be, too, that he knew of Joseph Severn's (no. 1) painting of Isabella, exhibited in 1840.

This drawing appears to have been conceived as part of a joint project with Hunt to provide a series of etched illustrations to the poem, that was probably inspired by the publication in 1848 of Richard Monckton Milnes's *Life, Letters and Literary Remains of John Keats* (even if his edition did not include the poem). However, the project came to nothing, possibly due to the intervention of Milnes's publisher Edward Moxon, who had secured copyright of Keats's illustrations.

Dante Gabriel Rossetti
1828-1882

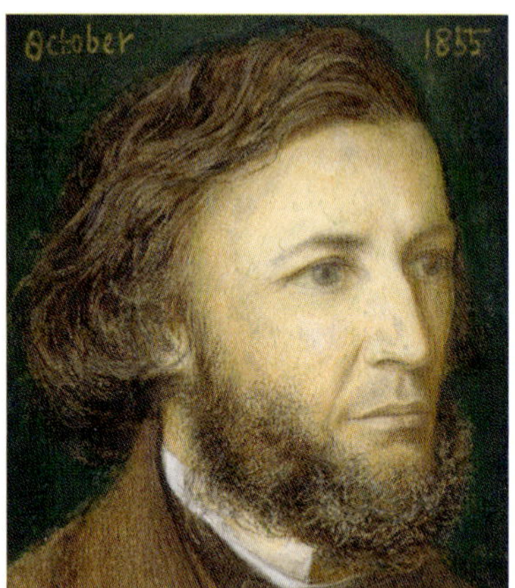

6. Robert Browning

Graphite, black chalk, watercolour, bodycolour, coloured chalks on paper
121 x 108 mm
Inscribed, upper left: *October*, dated upper right: *1855*
Given by Charles Fairfax Murray, 1909 | no. 681

Rossetti first came to know Browning's poetry in 1847 as a young man in Oxford, probably through his earlier reading of his wife's poems. He began to draw on it for themes for his painting as early as 1848, when he painted a watercolour based on Browning's poem *Pippa Passes.* He shared his enthusiasm with other members of his circle, including William Morris, Burne-Jones and his own brother, William Michael, who recorded that they would actively promote the poet's work by giving copies of Browning's poetry to their friends. By the early 1850s he was ranked 2* in the Pre-Raphaelites league of 'Immortals', only just outclassed by Christ and Shakespeare. Rossetti began to correspond regularly with Browning in 1850, and, although they met in person the following year, they became close only from 1855, the year in which he painted this portrait.

1855 was a signal year for Browning, marking the publication of his controversial volume of fifty-one poems *Men and Women.* The book provoked a storm of critical abuse, but his Pre-Raphaelite admirers were stout in its defence. Rossetti, 'drenched' in Browning at the beginning of 1856, considered it a 'magnificent series', while William Morris, in an unsigned review, defended Browning against accusations of obscurity: could not the same be said of Hamlet, he asked? (Litzinger and Smalley, 1995, 104).

Rossetti probably began to paint this portrait in October 1855, and may have finished it in Paris the following month, where he travelled with a copy of *Men and Women* for Browning to sign; by January 1856, it was hanging on the mantelpiece in his home at Chatham Place. Rossetti intended this to be a preliminary to a double portrait of Browning and his wife, but the latter was never painted. William Michael later described it as 'one of the truest extant likenesses' of the poet, accurately depicting his 'very abundant crop of finely flowing dark hair, with perhaps the first few threads of grey; hair went also around his face and under his chin, but not in the shape of a beard' (*Reminiscences*, I, 1906, 234).

At the beginning of the 1870s, the two men clashed, when Rossetti took offence at a presumed reference to himself in Browning's poem, *Fifine at the Fair* (1872). For his part, Browning's admiration for Rossetti's poetry was – at best – mixed. While he praised Rossetti heartily on receipt of his poems in 1870 – 'Go on, give us another and another' – he told a friend that they were '*scented* with poetry … like trifles of various sorts you take out of a cedar or sandal-wood box … I hate the effeminacy of his school; the men that dress up as women; that use obsolete forms, too, and archaic accentuations – fancy a man calling it a lilý – lil*iés* and so on' (Browning, 1919, 10-11).

He held no dream worth waking; so he said,
He who stands now on death's triumphal steep,
Awakened out of life wherein we sleep
And dream of what he knows and sees, being dead.
But never death for him was dark or dread;
"Look forth," he bade the soul, and fear not. Weep,
All ye that trust not in his truth, and keep
Vain memory's vision of a vanished head
As all that lives of all that once was he
Save that which lightens from his word; but we,
Who, seeing the sunset-coloured waters roll,
Yet know the sun subdued not of the sea,
Nor weep nor doubt that still the spirit is whole,
And life and death but shadows of the soul.

Algernon Charles Swinburne, On the Death of Robert Browning, 1889

7. Self-portrait

Pen, black and brown ink on paper 129 x 115 mm
Dated, lower right: *Sept 20. 1855*
Given by Charles Fairfax Murray, 1909 | no. 683

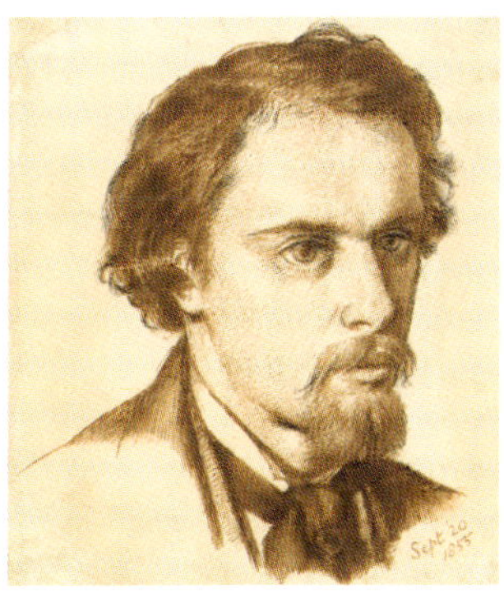

This sketch was drawn in the same year that Rossetti painted the portrait of Browning , also in the Fitzwilliam (no. 6). Over a decade later, the critic, art historian and museum curator, Sidney Colvin – also director of the Fitzwilliam Museum from 1876 to 1884 – described Rossetti in a way that suggests his appearance had altered little – at least superficially – in the intervening years. He had, he recorded, 'rich brown hair and [a] lighter brown, shortish trimmed beard, the olive complexion betraying Italian blood; handsome features between spare and fleshy, with [a] full, sensual underlip and thoughtful, commanding forehead in which some of his friends found a likeness to Shakespeare' (*Memories and Notes*, 1921, 62).

8. Dante at Verona

Autograph manuscript | Given by Charles Fairfax Murray, 1908

Of Florence and of Beatrice
Servant & sinecure from old
O'er Dante's ~~love~~ heart in youth had toll'd
The knell that gave his Lady peace;
And now in manhood flew the dart
Wherewith his city ~~stabbed~~ pierced his heart

Rossetti began his artistic career as a poet and a painter, but by the early 1850s decided to concentrate on painting, as the more potentially lucrative activity. Originally entitled *Dante in Exile*, *Dante at Verona* was begun in 1848, or possibly earlier, and was intended to act as an introduction to his translation of the *Vita Nuova*. By 1850 it was in a complete enough state to be considered for publication in the Pre-Raphaelite Journal, *The Germ*, but never actually appeared. In the years immediately following, Rossetti began to conceive of the subject in pictorial terms, specifically as an elaborate triptych, that combined in one work of art painting and poetry inspired by episodes of Dante's life; however this ambitious project never progressed beyond a single watercolour and a series of sketches.

Dante at Verona was one of a group of manuscript poems that the distraught Rossetti buried in the coffin of his wife, Elizabeth Siddal, after her death in 1862. Encouraged by Charles Augustus Howell, Rossetti famously had his manuscript poems exhumed in 1869, convinced that Siddal would have approved of his action: 'art', he wrote to his friend (and hers) Swinburne in December 1869, 'was the only thing for which she felt very seriously' (Doughty and Wahl, II, 1965, 761). Rossetti made a fair draft copy at the end of 1869, and continued to make corrections both to the manuscript – some on Swinburne's advice – and the so-called 'exhumation proofs' (Henry E. Huntington Library, California) until just before it was published as one of the *Poems*, by F. S. Ellis Strangeways and Walden in May 1870.

This is one of the lengthiest poems in the published edition. In narrative verse, it concerns events relating to Dante's second sojourn in Verona, from around 1314 to 1318, after his exile from Florence in 1302, and was intended as a revisionist corrective to received notions about the generosity of his patron there, Can Grande.

9. Algernon Charles Swinburne, William Michael Rossetti, Fanny Cornforth and Dante Gabriel Rossetti in the garden of Rossetti's home in Cheyne Walk, Chelsea. Photograph by W&D Downey, c.1863

Given by Virginia Surtees, 1993 | PH.3-1993

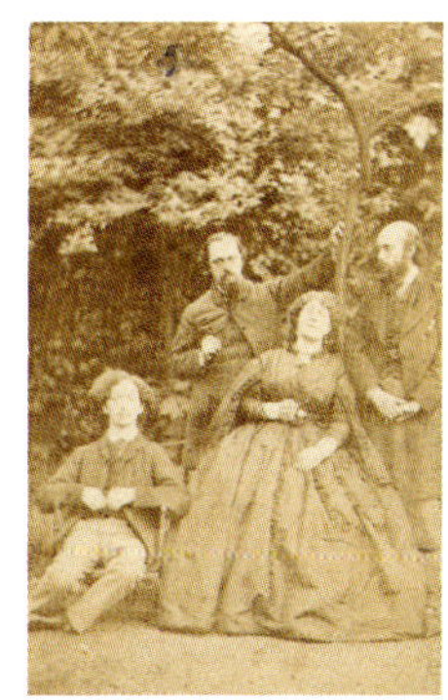

This photograph belonged to Charles Fairfax Murray, who gave it to Sydney Cockerell, director of the Fitzwilliam, in December 1916; he in turn gave it to the Rossetti scholar Virginia Surtees. Murray's inscription on the reverse records that it was taken in the garden of Rossetti's home at Tudor House, 16 Cheyne Walk, Chelsea, where he moved in October 1862, after the death of his wife, Lizzie Siddal, several months earlier. At the time, all four were resident, Rossetti assuring the £100 lease, his brother and Swinburne tenants at his request, and Fanny Cornforth a housekeeper-cum-lover.

Max Beerbohm (see nos. 113-115), to whom Cockerell lent this photograph, was thrilled to find how perfectly the 'real' Fanny in the photograph corresponded to his caricatures of her as a (frequently supine), blousy blond, listless rather than languid. In 1922, he had been arguing with Cockerell about William Michael Rossetti's being the under-rated member of the Pre-Raphaelite circle, 'because he happened to be the one (superficially) dull man in a bevy of brilliant ones.' 'Perhaps the time will come,' Beerbohm wrote, ' when he will be *over*-rated, as having been the one sane man among lunatics ! – for there was one, wasn't there? A silver thread of lunacy in the rich golden fabric of 16 Cheyne Walk' (Meynell, 1956, 30).

10. A lock of Dante Gabriel Rossetti's hair

Given by Virginia Surtees, 1993 | MS.7- 1993

According to an accompanying note in the hand of William Michael Rossetti, the artist's brother, this lock of hair was cut from Rossetti's head on the night of his death on 9 April 1882.

11. Algernon Charles Swinburne

Graphite, black chalk, watercolour, bodycolour, coloured chalks on paper
182 x 158 mm
Signed in monogram, upper right and dated: *1861*
Given by Charles Fairfax Murray, 1909 | no. 682

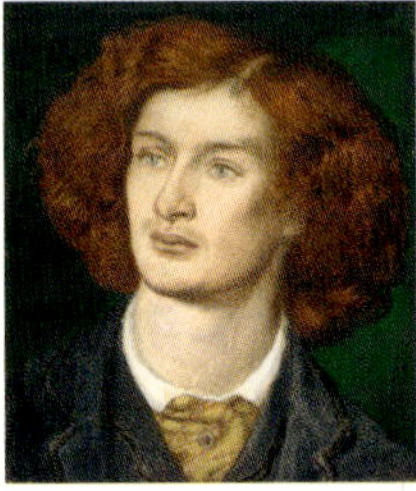

Provocative, highly-strung and given to excesses of every kind, with an explosive temper and a tongue that lashed all the harder for being gilded with erudition, Swinburne was a key figure in Pre-Raphaelite circles, much loved for his wit, loyalty and discretion. He remained a life-long friend of Burne-Jones, Morris and the Rossetti brothers, Dante Gabriel and William Michael, almost all of whom he outlived by over twenty years.

Rossetti and Swinburne first met in 1857, when Rossetti was working with other Pre-Raphaelite painters on the mural decorations for the Oxford Union building, and Swinburne was a student at Balliol College. Swinburne served as a model in several of Rossetti's paintings in the late 1850s, and at the same time introduced Rossetti – already extremely well read in several European languages – to lesser-trodden byways of Elizabethan and classical literature.

Reciprocal support and influence characterised their on-going relationship. In 1860, Swinburne dedicated to Rossetti his first poems *The Queen Mother* and *Rosamond,* describing the last as a 'verse translation of a watercolour by Rossetti.' After the death of Rossetti's wife, Elizabeth Siddal, to whom Swinburne was himself extremely attached, Swinburne moved in with Rossetti at 16 Cheyne Walk (see no. 9). In subsequent years, Rossetti helped Swinburne both to find a publisher for his *Poems and Ballads,* and to withstand the scandal and moral opprobrium unleashed by their eventual publication in 1866.

This portrait was painted as a companion piece to that of Browning (no.6), and they hung on either side of Rossetti's fireplace at Chatham Place.

Opinions as to the accuracy of Rossetti's likeness have differed. Superficially, at least, it corresponds to Georgiana Burne-Jones's recollection of his appearance as a young man, 'very unusual and in some ways very beautiful, for his hair was gloriously in abundance and colour and his eyes indescribably fine. When repeating poetry, he had a perfectly natural way of lifting them in a rapt, unconscious gaze, and their clear, green colour softened by thick brown eyelashes was unforgettable' (*Memorials,* I, 1904, 215). His biographer, Edmund Gosse, however, thought it looked nothing like; while Swinburne himself, displaying impeccable pre-Raphaelite taste, believed that his features most closely ressembled those of Niccolò Mauruzi da Tolentino (whom he took to be Galeazzo Malatesta) in Paolo Uccello's *Battle of San Romano* (1438-40), bought by the National Gallery only four years before this portrait was painted (Scott, II, 1892, 18).

Algernon Swinburne

1837-1909

12. Atalanta in Calydon

Autograph manuscript, incomplete, lacking most of the choruses
Given by Charles Fairfax Murray, 1911

Atalanta in Calydon is widely considered to be Swinburne's lyric masterpiece. It was published with a subsidy from Swinburne's father in April 1865, with a dedication to Walter Savage Landor, whom he had met in Florence the previous year, and who had recently died.

Although the goddess Atalanta has the title role, the main protagonist is Althaea, mother of Meleager, who causes his death because his infatuation with Atalanta leads him to kill his uncles in a quarrel over a dead wild boar. Swinburne described the poem as being 'all Greek', and in fact he uses the structure of Classical Greek tragedy, with formal dialogue, choruses, and semi-choruses to articulate a very personal vision that unmistakably alluded to – and challenged – Victorian attitudes to love, religion and Christianity. The choruses in particular (all but one of which are missing from this manuscript) make pronounced use of stress and alliteration, creating a distinctive musicality that his friend Burne-Jones (given to sticking burning pokers through works of literature he did *not* admire) thought 'momentous ... the rhythm goes on with such a rush that it's enough to carry the world away' (*Memorials,* II, 1904, 190). While the poem was well received in many quarters, it proved sufficiently controversial for the original publisher, Edward Moxon, to withdraw the edition; it was later re-issued by John Camden Hotten (who also published Swinburne's *Critical Essay* on Blake in 1868).

Browning had little time for the 'florid impotence' of Swinburne's verse, with its 'minimum of thought and ideas in the maximum of words and phraseology' (Browning, 1919, 4), while Bernard Shaw compared it to eating jam. Swinburne himself later confessed that 'Atalanta was perhaps too exuberant and effusive in its dialogue, as it certainly was too irregular in the licence of its choral verse, to accomplish the design or achieve the success that its author aimed at' (Stevenson, 1973, 211, n. 26).

A Kelmscott Press edition, *Atalanta in Calydon: a Tragedy,* with designs by Selwyn Image, was published in 1894; it was the only book in which Morris did not use type designed by himself.

13. Poem on the Death of Théophile Gautier

Autograph manuscript | Given by Sir Sidney Colvin, 1916

Quelle fleur, ô Mort, quel joyau, quel chant,
Quel vent, quel rayon de soleil couchant
Sur ton front penché, sur ta main avide,
Sur l'âpre pâleur de ta lèvre aride,
Vibre encore et luit ?

For Swinburne, Gautier represented 'the faultless and secure expression of an exclusive worship of things formally beautiful' (Rossetti and Swinburne, 1868, 32). This poem was commissioned as one of a series of contributions by contemporary poets to *Le Tombeau de Théophile Gautier*, Paris, 1873; Swinburne republished it in the second series of his *Poems and Ballads* in 1878. A poetic homage to Gautier, the publication included works by other – mostly French – writers, including Leconte de Lisle, Victor Hugo, Stéphane Mallarmé, Frédéric Mistral and Charles Cros.

William Bell Scott, who first met Swinburne in 1857, wrote twenty years on of how the 'Gallomania' associated with Swinburne's verse had dominated English literature in the intervening decades (1892, II, 18). Gautier's *Mademoiselle de Maupin* was a significant influence on both Rossetti (see no. 20) and Swinburne and, in particular on the latter's interest in lesbian love, as articulated in *Lesbia Brandon.* Swinburne made a number of references to Gautier in his published poems, most notably in his *Love at Sea*, 'imitated from Théophile Gautier' in the first series of *Poems and Ballads* in 1866. Reflecting on their hostile reception, Swinburne later wrote that he wished he had added, as an exergue, Gautier's lines,

J'en préviens les mères de famille
Ce que j'écris n'est pas pour les petites filles,
Dont on coupe le pain en tranches; mes vers
Sont des vers de jeune homme.

('I warn mothers of families, That what I write is not for little girls, For whom one cuts bread up into slices; my verses, are the verses of a young man')

A manuscript version of this poem in Greek was also given to the Museum by Fairfax Murray.

Charles Fairfax Murray

1849-1919

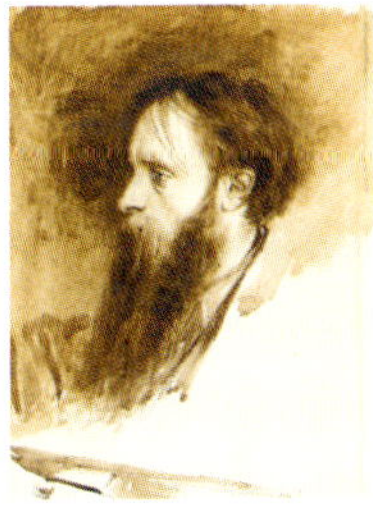

14. Sir Edward Burne-Jones

Graphite, brown ink and brown wash on paper
338 x 222 mm
Signed in initials and dated, upper left: *CFM, 7.69*
Given by Charles Fairfax Murray, 1915 | no. 778

Fairfax Murray became an assistant to Burne-Jones in November 1866, and was employed principally to help on the St George series of commissions for Birket Foster (see no. 3). He also worked as a copyist for Rossetti (see no. 42) and John Ruskin, and as both a stained glass painter and assistant at the Kelmscott Press for William Morris. Thereafter, he put his knowledge and skills to use as a collector, dealer and later advisor and donor to the Victoria and Albert (then the South Kensington) Museum, the National Gallery, Dulwich Art Gallery, and the Fitzwilliam Museum.

In Georgiana Burne-Jones's published *Memorials* of her husband, the year 1869, when this drawing was executed, barely exists. This is perhaps not unconnected with the unhappy state of their relationship at that time, when Burne-Jones's passionate three-year affair with the beautiful Maria Zambaco, a member of the wealthy Greek community in London, came to a dramatic end.

Of all the Pre-Raphaelites, Burne-Jones's paintings correspond most closely to the poetry of his friend Algernon Swinburne (see p. 14). Like Swinburne, he advocated an art that existed independently of moral and didactic purpose or fidelity to observed reality, but was instead 'a reflection of a reflection of something purely imaginary.'

Richard Doyle

1824-1883

15. *The Corsair* – a manuscript ballad illustrated by Richard Doyle before his sixteenth birthday

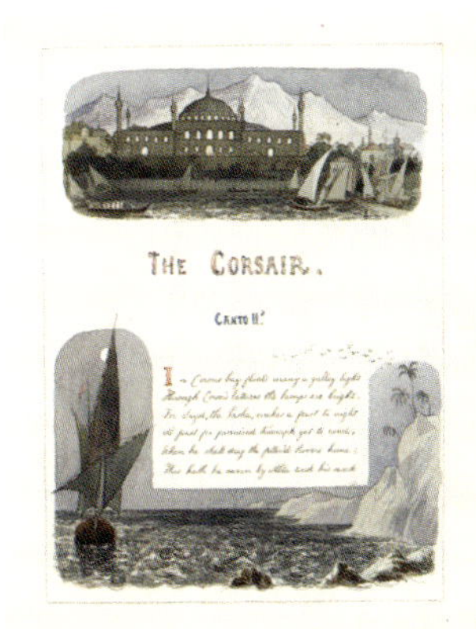

Twenty-eight sheets bound into a soft-covered book; twenty-four illustrated pages and four laid paper end pages | Graphite and watercolour on paper
253 x 200 mm | Purchased, 1886
no. 3691

The son of the political caricaturist, 'HB', Doyle himself became a caricaturist for *Punch* and is today best remembered for his paintings and drawings of fairies. His father's professional connection meant that from 1840 their home in London was filled with an array of artistic and literary figures, among them Sir David Wilkie, Samuel Rogers, Thomas Moore and William Wordsworth. The poems and novels of Sir Walter Scott and Lord Byron were favourites of Doyle's in his youth (as they were, initially, with many of the Pre-Raphaelites), although he also made juvenile illustrations to Shakespeare, Edmund Spenser and Victor Hugo.

He published his first series of drawings, representing scenes from the Eglinton Tournament, at the age of sixteen, the same year in which he painted these highly accomplished vignettes and marginal illustrations to Byron's poem, *The Corsair* (1814). Although the manuscript transcription and some of the drawings are incomplete, those that fill the album show a vigour of imagination and technical competence which are highly impressive in an artist of Doyle's young age.

In later life, Doyle became an habitué of the circle that frequented Sara Princep's literary and artistic salons at Little Holland House in the 1850s, which included her son, the painter Val Princep, G.F. Watts and Burne-Jones. Burne Jones's impish sense of fun responded enthusiastically to Doyle's delicate, imaginative fantasy; he considered his early drawings in particular 'miracles of skill – I think he never excelled them' (Lucas, 1928, 36).

In 1855, Burne-Jones produced his own 'fairy' designs, for his friend Archibald Maclaren's anthology of European fairy tales, *The Fairy Family* (1857), and with it launched a career as a book illustrator that would culminate in his collaboration with William Morris on the Kelmscott Chaucer (see pp. 48-55).

16. Dante Gabriel Rossetti to Edward Burne-Jones
Autograph manuscript, 2 May 1861

Given by Sir Philip Burne-Jones, 1923, Burne-Jones Papers, II, 2

In April 1861, Elizabeth Siddal was delivered of a still-born daughter. Nine months later, she herself died from an overdose of laudanum, whether deliberate or unintentional has never been conclusively proven.

Rossetti's and Siddal's personal tragedy is movingly conveyed in the stark brevity of this note to Burne-Jones, one of their oldest and closest friends.

Dante Gabriel Rossetti

1828-1882

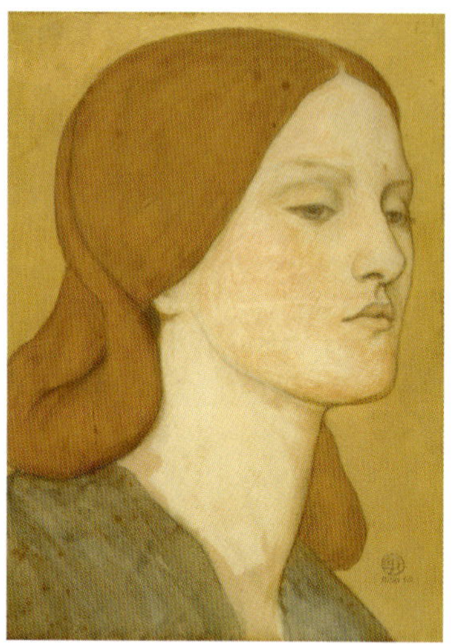

17. Elizabeth Siddal

Watercolour and graphite on paper, laid on fine linen on a stretcher
334 x 246 mm
Signed in monogram, and dated, lower right: *1850-65*
Bequeathed by J.R. Holliday, 1931 | no. 1575

Siddal's 'discovery' by the Pre-Raphaelite brotherhood, and subsequent enchantment of Rossetti, is in itself the stuff of a Victorian novel. The daughter of a cutler, she was working as a milliner's assistant near Leicester Square in London when she was spotted in the back shop by the painter Walter Deverell (1827-1854), who immediately asked her to model for Viola in his painting *Twelfth Night* (1850); soon after, she also sat for Holman Hunt and Millais. Rossetti met her shortly afterwards – possibly even the very next day – and over the next ten years, she played a central role in his life as model, mistress, and – eventually – wife.

Tall, long-limbed, with striking copper-red hair and a delicate, pale complexion, her eyes were described by Burne-Jones's wife, Georgiana, as one of her most striking features, 'golden brown – agate-coloured ... and wonderfully luminous...The eyelids were deep, but without languor or drowsiness, and had the peculiarity of seeming scarcely to veil the light in her eyes when she was looking down' (*Memorials*, I, 1904, 208). Lizzie Siddal's health was precarious throughout her short life. She suffered from both tuberculosis and neuralgia, aggravated by a nervous disposition and alleviated only by ever-increasing doses of laudanum.

In the early 1850s, she and Rossetti were seldom apart. Ford Madox Brown, who like Burne-Jones was close to Rossetti at this time, described her in 1854 as being 'thinner and more deathlike and more beautiful and more ragged than ever' (Surtees, 1981, 54), while Rossetti was all the while 'drawing wonderful and lovely "Guggums" one after another, each one a fresh charm, each one stamped with immortality'; a year on, in August 1855, Rossetti showed him, 'a drawer full of "Guggums"; God knows how many, but not bad work, I should say, for the six years he has known her; it is like a monomania with him. Many of them are matchless in beauty, however, and one day will be worth large sums.'

This portrait is thought to be one of the earliest likenesses of Lizzie Siddal, although the monogram signature is clearly later in date (Rossetti did not begin to sign in this way until 1863).

18. Elizabeth Siddal. Study for Delia in *The Return of Tibullus to Delia*

Graphite on paper | 222 x 196 mm
Given by The Friends of The Fitzwilliam Museum, 1920 | no. 985

As Georgiana Burne-Jones remembered, Rossetti's obsession with Lizzie Siddal was not simply with her physical appearance, but with her species of womanhood, and as the 'type she created in his mind' (*Memorials*, I, 1904, 216). Certainly, her features appear in those of many of the female figures in Rossetti's earliest works, whether as Dante's Beatrice, Browning's Pippa, or here, in the role of a virtuous heroine of Classical antiquity.

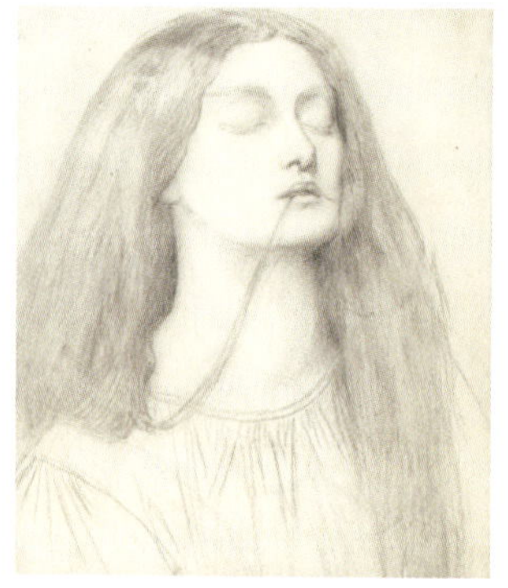

The finished watercolour of this subject (c.1853, Birmingham City Art Gallery and Museum) is inscribed on the frame with the relevant passage from Tibullus's *Elegies*, I, 3, 82-92:

Live chaste, dear love; and while I'm far away,
Be some old dame thy guardian night and day.
She'll sing thee songs, and when the lamp is lit,
Fly the full rock and draw long threads from it,
So, unannounced, shall I come suddenly,
As 'twere a presence sent from heaven to thee.
Then as thou art, all long and loose thy hair,
Run to me, Delia, run with thy feet bare.

This drawing formerly belonged to Charles Fairfax Murray, and was bought by Sydney Cockerell for the Museum in 1920.

Elizabeth Siddal, later Rossetti

1829-1862

19. Clerk Saunders

Watercolour, bodycolour and coloured chalks on paper | 284 x 181 mm
Signed and dated, lower left: *EES / 1857*
Given by Charles Fairfax Murray, 1910 | no. 680

The Ballad of Clerk Saunders was published in Scott's *Minstelry of the Scottish Border* (1802; Siddal's own copy is in the Fitzwilliam Museum) and later in William Allingham's *The Ballad Book* (1864). Like Keats's *Isabella*, the subject is one of fraternal jealousy. May Margaret is persuaded by her lover, Clerk Saunders, to sleep with him; as a result he is 'slain in his sweetheart's arms' by her brothers; and afterwards appears to his lover as a ghost:

The clinking bell gaed through the town,
To carry the dead corpse to the clay;
And Clerk Saunders stood at May Margaret's window,
I wot, an hour before the day.

"Are ye sleeping, Margaret?" he says,
"Or are ye waking presentlie?
Give me my faith and troth again,
I wot, true love, I gied to thee."

...

"And fair Marg'ret, and rare Marg'ret,
And Marg'ret, o' veritie,
Gin ere ye love another man,
Ne'er love him as ye did me.".

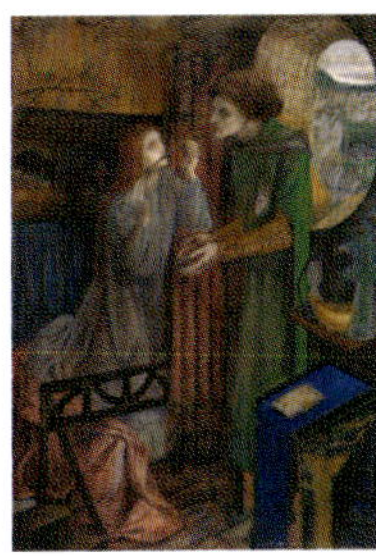

Rossetti considered this to be Lizzie's finest watercolour. In May 1854, he told Ford Madox Brown that he and Lizzie were working together on designs for engravings in Allingham's *Ballads*, and praised Lizzie's 'lovely' design for Clerk Saunders: 'her fecundity of invention and facility are quite wonderful,' he wrote, 'much greater than mine' (Doughty and Wahl, I, 1965, 200). His estimation of Siddal's talent was enthusiastically shared by John Ruskin, who is said to have been driven 'wild with delight' by her watercolours.

This watercolour was bought by an acquaintance of Ruskin, the American scholar and art historian, Charles Eliot Norton, who himself greatly esteemed Lizzie Siddal's work. After her death in 1862, Rossetti wrote to him asking for its return; by the beginning of January 1869, it was back on his wall in Cheyne Walk. It was bought by the donor, Fairfax Murray, from William Michael Rossetti in 1884.

According to a manuscript note by Murray formerly on the back of the frame, Rossetti worked on this drawing with Siddal, 'as was customary with him'; certainly the ballad was one of Rossetti's favourites, and Lizzie's fragile state of health, together with Rossetti's greater artistic experience, make collaboration at least a strong possibility.

Lizzie Siddal appears to have had no existing interest in art when she met Rossetti, but she went on to become not only an artist, but a poet in her own right. Several of her poems were published after her death by her brother-in-law, William Michael Rossetti. Many are of a melancholy cast, their titles and subjects apparently written in morbid anticipation of her early death.

Early Death

Oh grieve not with thy bitter tears
The life that passes fast:
The gates of heaven will open wide,
And take me in at last.
...
Then sit down meekly at my side
And watch my young life flee:
Then solemn peace of holy death
Come quickly unto the.

But, true love, seek me in the throng
Of spirits floating past;
And I will take thee by the hands, And know thee mine at last.'

Lord may I come ?

Life and night are falling from me
Death [and day] are opening on me.
Wherever my footsteps come and go
Life is a stoney way of woe.
Lord, Have I long to go?
Hollow hearts are ever near me,
Soulless eyes have ceased to cheer me:
Lord may I come to thee?
...
My outward life feels sad and still,
Like lilies in a frozen rill
I am gazing up to the sun,
Lord, Lord, remembering my lost one.
Oh Lord, remember me !'

Elizabeth Siddal

Dante Gabriel Rossetti

1828-1882

20. Morning Music

Watercolour and bodycolour on paper | 304 x 273 mm
Inscribed, lower left: *MORNING MUSIC*, signed in monogram and dated, lower right: *18 / 64*
Given by the Friends of the Fitzwilliam Museum, 1935 | no. 1148

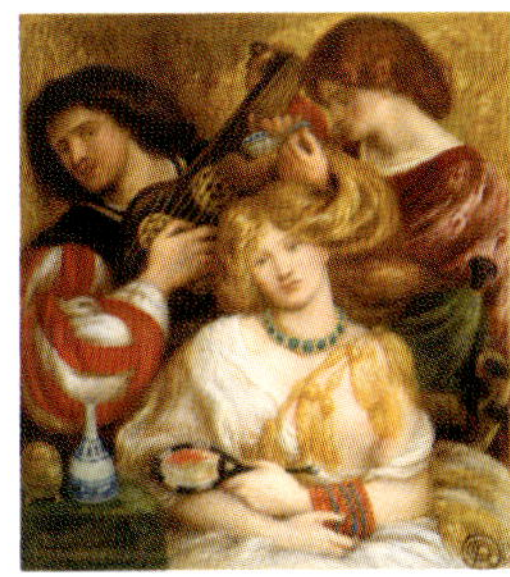

In the 1860s, Rossetti increasingly gave his paintings and drawings titles that were non-literary and self-referential. In this, they reflect the notions of 'art for art's sake' promoted by such authors as Swinburne (see p. 14) and Théophile Gautier (no. 13), and also anticipate Walter Pater's belief that all art should 'aspire to the condition of music', that is exist independently of any didactic, realistic or narrative function. In his poetry, Rossetti explores this notion most fully in *Chimes* (1871; no. 68), in which he consciously avoids a transparent narrative to allow the chant-like alliteration of the verse to create a melodic correspondence with the title.

Alastair Grieve has pointed to the recurrence of the theme of women dressing their hair in Rossetti's work in the 1860s, and highlights as a possible influence Gautier's hedonistic celebration of Sardanapalian pleasures – from good wine and women to lively horses and Angora cats – in the preface to his novel *Mademoiselle de Maupin*, as 'the end in life, the only thing useful in the world' (Parris, 1984, 298). His reading is supported by Swinburne's commentary on Rossetti's painting, *Lady Lilith* (1868; 1872-3, Delaware Art Museum, Wilmington), exhibited at the Royal Academy in 1868, which could stand for many of his so-called 'toilette' pictures of the 1860s. In it, Swinburne makes repeated references to the 'ample splendour' of the woman's hair as the dominating sensual element in Rossetti's composition: 'the heavy mass of hair like thick spun gold to its fullest length; her head leans back half sleepily, superb and satiate with its own beauty; the eyes are languid, without love in them or hate; the sweet luxurious mouth has the patience of pleasure fulfilled and complete, the warm repose of passion sure of its delight … The sleepy splendour of the picture is a fit raiment for the idea incarnate of faultless, fleshy beauty and peril of pleasure unavoidable …. Were it worth her while for any word to divide those terrible, tender lips, she too might say with the hero of the most perfect and exquisite book of modern times – *Mademoiselle de Maupin* – "Je trouve la terre aussi belle que le ciel, et je pense que la correction de la forme est le vertu"'(Rossetti and Swinburne, 1868, 46-47).

This drawing was first owned by William Graham, who from the 1860s was one of the most avid collectors of Rossetti's and Burne-Jones's work.

21. Dante and Beatrice meeting in Purgatory

Bodycolour and pen and ink on paper | 292 x 251 mm
Signed with initials, lower left: *DRG*
Given by Sydney Carlyle Cockerell, 1937 | no. 2292

Dante was a potent influence on Rossetti's literary and pictorial imagination from an early age. From the mid-1850s, he was busily engaged in translating works by early Italian poets – including Dante's *Vita Nuova*, which he eventually published 'in the original metre' in 1861, and as he did so recognised the rich pictorial potential of his verse.

This watercolour depicts Dante's reunion with Beatrice in Eden after her death, as recounted by Dante in *Purgatoria*, xxx:

... then with act
Full-royal, still insulting o'er her thrall,
Added, as one who, speaking, keepeth back
The bitterest saying, to conclude the speech:
'Observe me well,I am , in sooth, I am
Beatrice. What! and hast thou deigned at last
Approach the mountain? knewest not, O man!
Thy happiness is here?

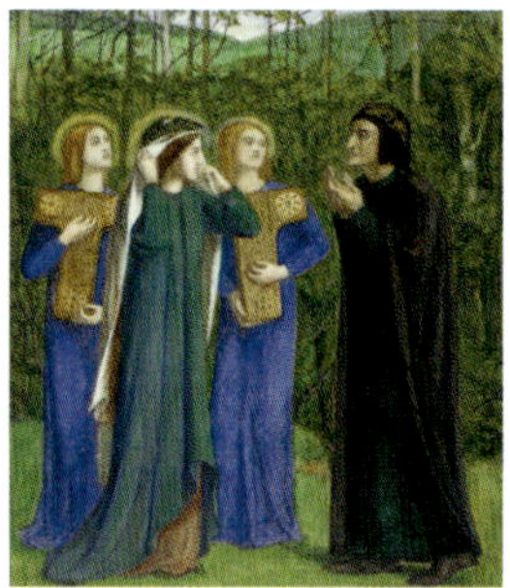

Rossetti first treated the subject as part of a diptych in 1850; he planned an independent painting later the same year, but abandoned work on it not long after he had begun. He took the subject up again in 1851, but this watercolour was finished only three years later, in the spring of 1854, for the painter G.P. Boyce. Dante's face is modelled from the supposed death mask of the poet in Rossetti's possession.

Rossetti believed that the frame was integral to the work of art, and often used it as a bearer of meaning, as here, where it is inscribed with an extract from *Purgatoria*; the same quote is one of two from the *Vita Nuova* which act as headers to his poem, *Dante at Verona* (see no. 8). It is one of his earliest frame designs to have survived.

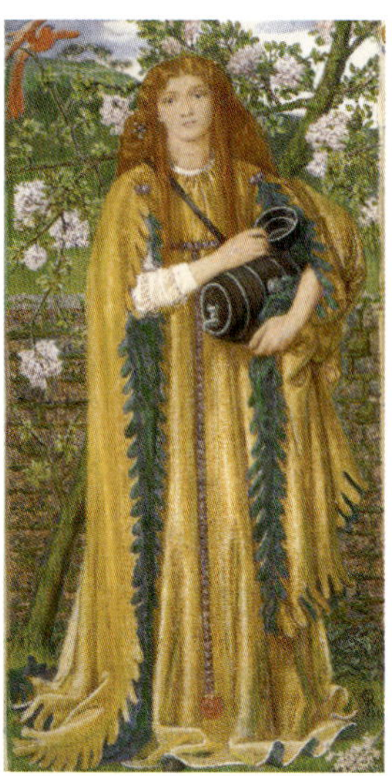

22. Princess Parizade, Golden Water

Bodycolour on paper, laid on fine linen on a stretcher | 365 x 185 mm
Signed and dated, lower right: DRG, *1858*
Bequeathed by Charles Hazelwood Shannon, 1937 | no.2148

Rossetti was drawn to the *Arabian Nights* stories from a child, and in 1840 made a group of fifteen pen and ink illustrations inspired by the scholarly translation published by the Reverend Edward W. Lane the previous year, with illustrations by William Harvey (1796-1866). These were among his first illustrations to any literary theme, and one that was infrequently represented in Victorian art outside the engraved illustrations for the many published editions of the book that appeared throughout throughout the nineteenth century.

This watercolour illustrates the last of the tales narrated by Scheherazade to the Sultan in order to postpone her death sentence, 'The Story of Two Sisters who were jealous of Their Younger Sister'. Princess Parizade – here clad in her gown of 'woven gold' – shows kindness to a mysterious old woman who in return tells her of the three things she must find to make her house 'incomparable' in beauty: the talking bird, Bulbulhezar, the singing tree, and the Golden Water, 'one single drop of which, dropped into a basin made for the purpose in any part of the garden, increases so rapidly that it immediately fills the vessel, and then rises in the middle of a sort of fountain, which never ceases springing up and falling into the basin without ever running over.' Her brothers, Prince Bahman and Prince Perviz, in turn set off to find these treasures, but both are turned to black stone by a dervish. In great distress, Princess Parizade follows, but succeeds in her quest by stopping her ears to block out the dervish's perilous voice. She scatters the Golden Water over her brothers and brings them back to life.

Rather than attempting to evoke an exotic oriental setting, Rossetti has cast the Princess in the guise of a medieval 'Blessed Damozel', an image which had dominated his literary and pictorial imagination for over thirty years.
John Ruskin, the first owner of this drawing, kept it permanently before him on his work table.

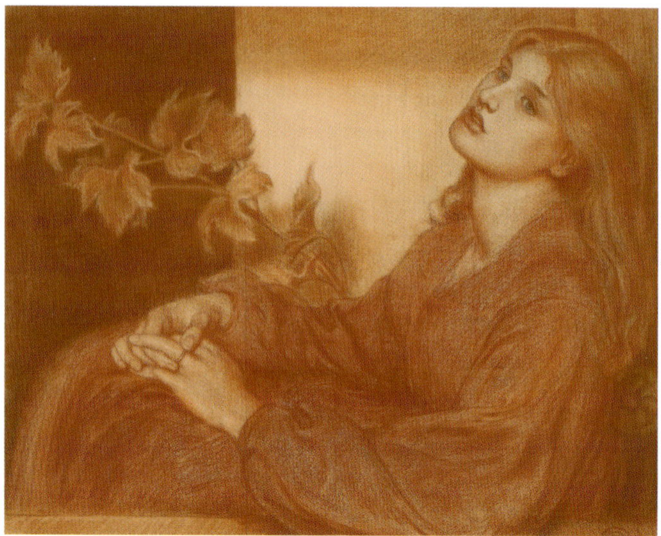

23. La Pia de' Tolomei

Red and blue-black chalk on paper | 644 x 790 mm
Signed in monogram and dated, lower right: *1868* | Private collection

This magnificent red chalk drawing is one of a number of studies for a painting in the Spencer Museum of Art, University of Kansas, begun in 1868, but completed only in 1882.

Like no. 21, the subject is once again drawn from Dante's *Purgatorio*, in this case, canto V, lines 130-136. The Italian noblewoman, La Pia, was confined to a fortress in the Maremma, a malarial district near Siena, by her husband Nello dei Pannocchieschi. She died either from malaria-induced fever, or from poison administered by her husband; unable to repent, and having died a violent death without absolution, she was one of the souls that Dante encountered in his journey through Purgatory. The relevant lines were inscribed by Rossetti on the frame, contemporary with the painting:

Remember me who am La Pia; me
Siena, me Maremma, made, unmade.
This in his inmost heart well knoweth he
With whose fair jewel I was ringed and wed

Rossetti's attention may have been drawn to the story by a play of the same title by Carlo Marenco (1837), set to music by Donizetti, in which Eleanora Duse took the leading role. His interest would have been piqued by the fact that it so closely mirrored the emotional drama of his passionate affair with Janey Morris, which was at its height at this time.

Although Jane Morris appears as the model in the finished painting, and in the preliminary drawing most closely related to the present study (Surtees,

1973, 207B), the model for this drawing was Alexa Wilding, a dressmaker whom Rossetti saw in the street one evening, and subsequently paid a weekly fee to sit for him exclusively. Another study – also depicting Alexa Wilding – is in the Fitzwilliam (no. 1782).

Referring to an 'incomplete' painting of La Pia by Rossetti exhibited at the Royal Academy in 1868, Swinburne described the 'strange look of wonder and sorrow and fatigue' in her eyes, 'without fear or pain, as though she were even now looking beyond the earth into the soft and sad air of purgatory' (Rossetti and Swinburne, 1868, 50). While this drawing powerfully evokes the mood of listless, fatalistic despair of the unloved and abandoned, the finished painting includes a number of prominently displayed additional details that enrich the reading of the image. These are painted with a high degree of realism – the ivy, for example was painted from a photograph, and the landscape from drawings of the Maremma swamps sent to Rossetti by Charles Fairfax Murray in 1880 – and were intended to be 'read' as elucidations of the story: lances pointing to the battlements of her murderous husband, the 'fair jewel' of her wedding ring which she turns, as if in a trance, a breviary and rosary beads signifying the loss of her unrepented soul at her death, and a bundle of letters, written by her once-amorous husband.

Augustus Edwin John

1879-1961

24. Thomas Hardy

Oil on canvas | 61.3 x 51.1 cm | Signed and dated, upper right: *John / 1923*
Given by Thomas Henry Riches, 1923 no.1116

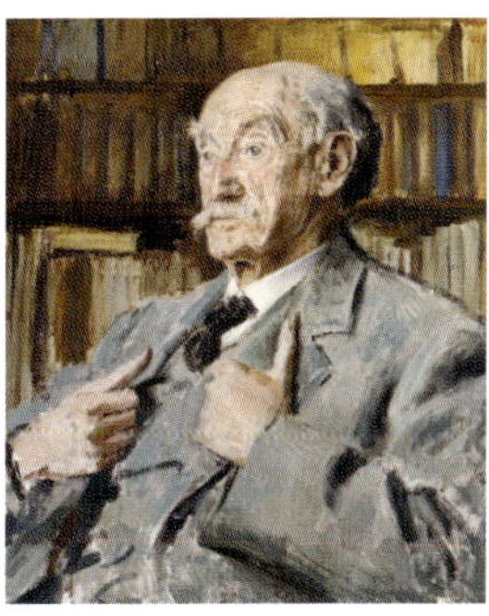

Augustus John first met Hardy in September 1923 and completed this painting by the middle of October after several visits to Max Gate. Hardy, shown at the age of eighty-three, is given the bearing of a retiring sage, his literary status alluded to by the books 'of a philosophical character' with which John surrounded him. Characteristically, he is shown sitting upright and alert, presumably in the straight-backed chair that he preferred. On seeing the finished painting, the elderly Hardy is reported to have said 'I don't know whether that is how I look or not, but that is definitely how I *feel*' (Holroyd, II, 1972, 95). The portrait was presented to the Fitzwilliam Museum by Thomas Riches, who responded to the director, Sydney Cockerell's, solicitation for funds to acquire it. Florence Hardy told Cockerell that its presence in the Fitzwilliam gave Hardy immense pleasure: 'he said he would rather have his portrait in the Fitzwilliam Museum than receive the Nobel prize: and he meant it!'

Hardy's young friend Siegfried Sassoon has left some of the finest descriptions of Hardy in old age. On their first meeting in 1918, he was fascinated by the modest, unassuming character of the author and his surroundings, sitting 'gnome-like' (Hardy was not tall) in the subdued light of a candle-lit room, but, on closer acquaintance, found his face, 'incredibly impressive. It has a beauty which can only signify the loveliness of his spirit. It is the final proof of his greatness' (Hart-Davis, 1981, 182). He remained fascinated by the contrast between his exterior signs of aging and the evident alertness of his mind: 'he is no age at all. A nimble wizard. Sometimes he seems, for a moment, incredibly aged with the rural antiquity of an old tree or house, but most of the time he is merely Thomas Hardy – eager and interested like a young man, yet so wise for all his simplicity' (*ibid.*, 42).

25. Algernon Charles Swinburne to Thomas Hardy, Autograph manuscript, 5 November 1895

Given by Thomas Hardy, 1923

In this letter, Swinburne thanks Hardy for sending him a copy of his recently published novel, *Jude the Obscure.* He writes admiringly of 'the beauty, the terror & the truth' of Hardy's 'tragedy', telling him that 'only the great & awful father of "Pierette" and "L'Enfant maudit" [Balzac] was ever so merciless to his children ... there has been no such tragedy in fiction – or anything like the same lines – since he died.' In fact, Hardy – who greatly admired Swinburne and eight years earlier had sent him another of his books, *The Woodlanders* – quotes freely from Swinburne's *Prelude* and *Hymn to Proserpine* (1866) throughout the novel.

Writing to thank him for his praise, Hardy told Swinburne in 1897 that any 'imaginative feeling' in the novel was due to his own readings of Swinburne's early poems in crowded London streets, 'to my imminent risk of being knocked down' (Purdy and Millgate, II, 1984, 158).

Swinburne, whose *Poems and Ballads* had so scandalised the Victorian public when first published in 1866, was well placed to understand the provocative nature of Hardy's novel, and the furore that was likely to ensue. Like him, Hardy rejected Christianity and highlighted the hypocrisies of contemporary mores and social institutions. When the two poets met at Swinburne's home in Putney in 1905, they were able to empathise about being the most vilified of living English writers.

Five years later Hardy wrote his poem *A Singer Asleep* as a tribute to Swinburne, while sitting next to his grave in Bonchurch, on the Isle of Wight:

From too much hope of living,
From hope and fear set free,
We thank with brief thanksgiving
Whatever gods may be
That no life lives forever;
That dead men rise up never;
That even the weariest river
Winds somewhere safe to sea.

Hardy gave this letter to the Fitzwilliam in 1923, adding to earlier important gifts of Swinburne manuscripts and manuscript correspondence given by Fairfax Murray and the children of Burne-Jones. Although delighted by the gift, Cockerell (who met Swinburne towards the end of his life), remained personally unconvinced of his literary skills as a correspondent: he was, he wrote, 'too self-centred to be a good letter-writer, or else too inhuman' (ALS to J.R. Holliday, 11 December 1923, Fitzwilliam Museum Archives).

Thomas Hardy

1840-1928

26. Jude the Obscure

Autograph manuscript
Given by the author, 1911 | MS.1-1911

First published in 1895, *Jude the Obscure* (or 'Jude the Obscene', as it was dubbed) was greeted by a storm of critical disapproval unparalleled since the appearance of Swinburne's *Poems and Ballads* over thirty years earlier. In the novel, Hardy is unflinching in his exposure of the hypocrisies of authorised religion and frank in his account of the complicated – and often tragic –

relationships between men and women. Recognising the threat it posed to social and religious institutions, the Bishop of Wakefield famously recommended that every copy of the book be burnt. Hardy later wrote in the preface to the definitive edition of 1912 that the outcry it provoked had completely cured him of 'further interest in novel-writing.'

Although the novel passed through various preliminary conceptual phases from 1887, this manuscript was written out in its present form from August 1893; the completed manuscript is dated by Hardy 'March 1895'. At the end of the following year, Hardy sent the almost-completed manuscript to the publisher, Harper's Brothers, for serial publication in their *New Monthly Magazine*, where it appeared in twelve monthly instalments between December 1894 and November 1895. Hardy had contracted himself to the serialisation at the end of 1893, but by the following April, when he realised the potentially controversial direction his novel was taking, wrote to the editor asking to withdraw. He refused, and Hardy was faced with producing a heavily bowlderized version of the novel to render it more palatable to the family-based audience that *Harper's* consciously targeted. As the inscription on the manuscript shows, Hardy highlighted the corrections he made for the serialisation – for the most part a toning down of the most explicit sexual references – in blue (and sometimes green).

This was one of two manuscripts that Hardy gave to the Fitzwilliam Museum in 1911; the other is for his 1909 volume of verse, *Time's Laughingstock*. Hardy was very preoccupied at the time with the distribution of his manuscripts throughout suitable institutions in the United Kingdom and North America, a task in which he relied heavily on the advice of the Fitzwilliam's director, Sydney Cockerell (see p. 20), whom he befriended that year, and who would eventually become his literary executor.

For a full account of the evolution of the novel from manuscript to printed state, see Ingham, 1976.

27. Wessex Poems and Other Verses

London and New York, Harper's Brothers, 1898
Private collection

Hardy's strong pictorial imagination is apparent in many of his novels, both in his highly detailed visualisation of scenes and characters, and in his frequent references to paintings, or schools of paintings (notably the Spanish and Netherlandish).

This, Hardy's first published volume of poetry, was published in an edition of 500 copies. It contains fifty-one titles, the majority of which Hardy had written in the 1860s, and is illustrated by thirty of the author's own drawings. A trained architect, Hardy had considerable skill and experience as a draughtsman, but in his preface to the volume he was dismissive of the quality of his 'rough sketches,' 'inserted for personal and local reasons rather than for their intrinsic qualities'; in every case, they postdate the poem. For the most part, they consist of vignettes or tail-pieces of landscapes, more or less topographical in nature. However, these are interspersed with townscapes and architectural detail, and with a certain number of more cryptic drawings – a procession of outline torsos descending a staircase, a pastoral landscape superimposed by a 'visionary' pair of spectacles – in which Hardy gave free play to his visual imagination.

Glyn Warren Philpot
1884–1937

28. Siegfried Sassoon

Oil on canvas | 61 x 50.8 cm
Signed and dated, lower left: *Glyn Philpot / 1917*
Given by Siegfried Sassoon, 1924 | no.1121

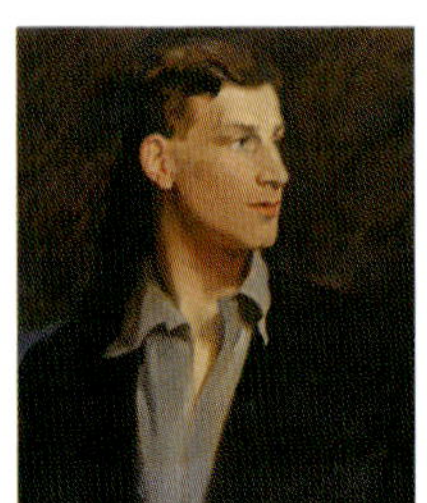

In his autobiography as a cat, *Something about Myself*, written at the age of eleven, Sassoon described himself (in pedigree cat terms) as 'very well bred for one thing: and very beautiful for another.' His finely-chiselled good looks are perfectly captured in this elegant portrait by Philpot, painted after Sassoon had returned from the Front in April 1917 to recuperate from a wound in the shoulder.

Sassoon had been introduced to Philpot, himself invalided out of active service, by the art critic Robert Ross shortly after his return; this portrait was painted within weeks of their first meeting. Philpot was possessed of what Sassoon described as a 'superbly artificial' taste for the sensuous and non-naturalistic: 'his own existence was one that consisted largely in an ultra-refined appreciation of beautiful objects,' Sassoon later wrote, 'he had what might be called a still-life temperament' (*Siegfried's Journeys*, quoted Gibson, 1984, 17). Certainly, this debonair image speaks more of an abstract sense of the exquisite than it does of personality. Sassoon nevertheless considered that Philpot had made 'rather a good job of it,' and was not displeased at being told that it gave him a romantically Byronic allure; as he joked to Lady Ottoline Morrell, it *was* 'a little popular', but as such would 'help to sell my posthumous works when sold as a frontispiece' (Hart-Davis, 1983, 194).

Philpot and Sassoon eventually became estranged. The reasons for this are unclear. One theory is that it may have been the result of complicated personal jealousies over the cultivation of a young protégé (Gibson, 1984, 18); at the same time, Philpot was an exasperating no-show on various trips to Europe in the early 1920s.

This portrait – or rather a photograph of it – was the first sight Thomas Hardy ever had of Sassoon, who sent it without an accompanying explanatory note in January 1918. Sassoon's admiration for the older writer was unbounded (see p. 20). Earlier that year he had asked Hardy's permission to dedicate to him his first book of published poems, *The Old Huntsman and Other Poems*. At the end of 1918, he made the first of several visits to Hardy's home at Max Gate in Dorset and eventually wrote a poem 'At Max Gate' in memory of his visits.

Although Sassoon's diaries suggest he was tempted to sell the portrait in 1921-1922 when 'hard-up', he gave it to the Fitzwilliam not long after that, in 1924.

Siegfried Sassoon
1886–1967

29. Fifty Poems

Autograph manuscript, 1924; rebound 1953
Given by the author, 1955 | MS.1-1955

Sassoon wrote out this manuscript anthology of fifty of his poems when making his choice for the published *Selected Poems* (1925), which contains these and nineteen other verses written between 1908 and 1923. Numerous redundant pages were removed when *Fifty Poems* was rebound in 1953, but Sassoon had intended to fill them. 'The blank pages,' he noted in the back 'are the rest of my life'. He preceded the gift of this manuscript with that, over thirty years earlier, of his 'Byronic' portrait by Philpot (no. 28). For Sassoon, there was a direct connection between the image he projected in this portrait and his war poems. 'If I looked Byronic, should I behave as such? And do something spectacular?' he asked himself, and it was in 1917 that he made his famous anti-war protest.

GB

Augustus Edwin John
1879-1961

30. George Bernard Shaw

Oil on canvas
76.5 x 46.3 cm
Signed, upper right: *John*
Given by George Bernard Shaw, 1922 | no. 1071

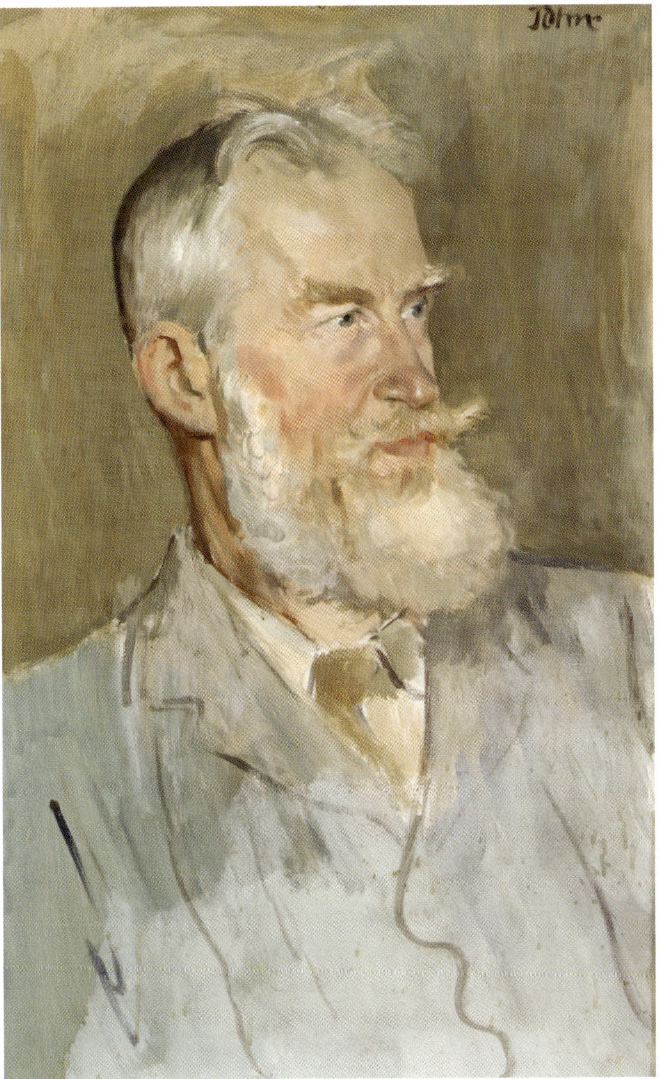

This portrait of the writer, critic and playwright George Bernard Shaw was one of three painted in May 1917 at Coole Park, County Galway, the country residence of Augusta, Lady Gregory, at whose instigation they were painted. Shaw told Frances Chesterton that John arrived a week later than expected and 'in a contrite and somewhat shattered condition … he has since painted and obliterated no less than three masterpieces. Like Penelope, he gets up early and undoes the work of the day before' (Laurence, 1985, 295). He does not appear to have much liked any of the portraits that resulted from these sittings, thinking them unduly overblown in their effort to represent him as the 'great writer': 'my vanity rebels,' he wrote, 'against being immortalised as an elderly caricature of myself.'

Bernard Shaw was a close friend of Sydney Cockerell, director of the Fitzwilliam Museum, whom he appointed as his literary executor in 1913, comparing him to the biographer John Forster (1812-1876), who acted in the same capacity for Charles Dickens (and later gave his collections of Dickens manuscripts to the Victoria and Albert Museum).

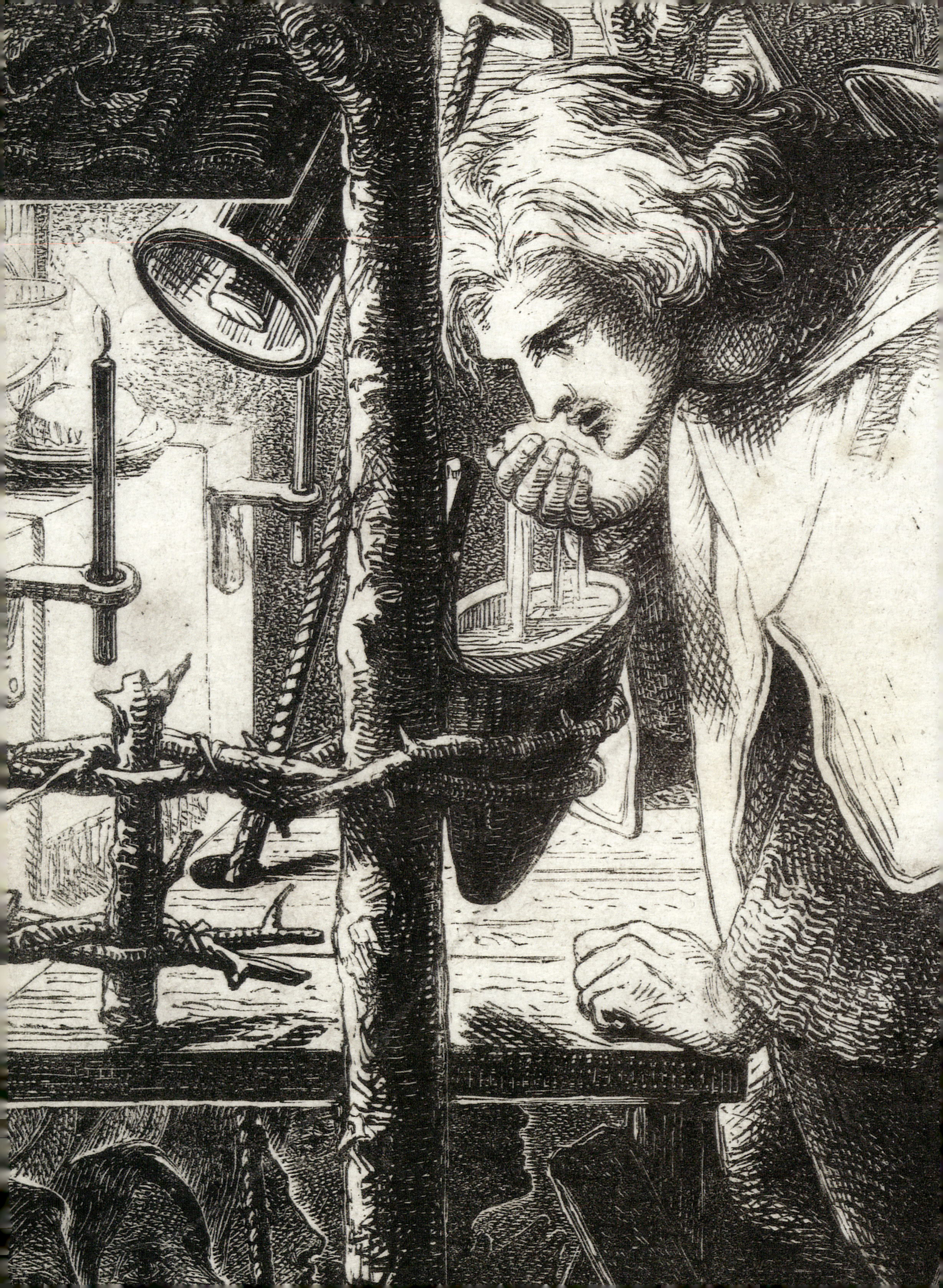

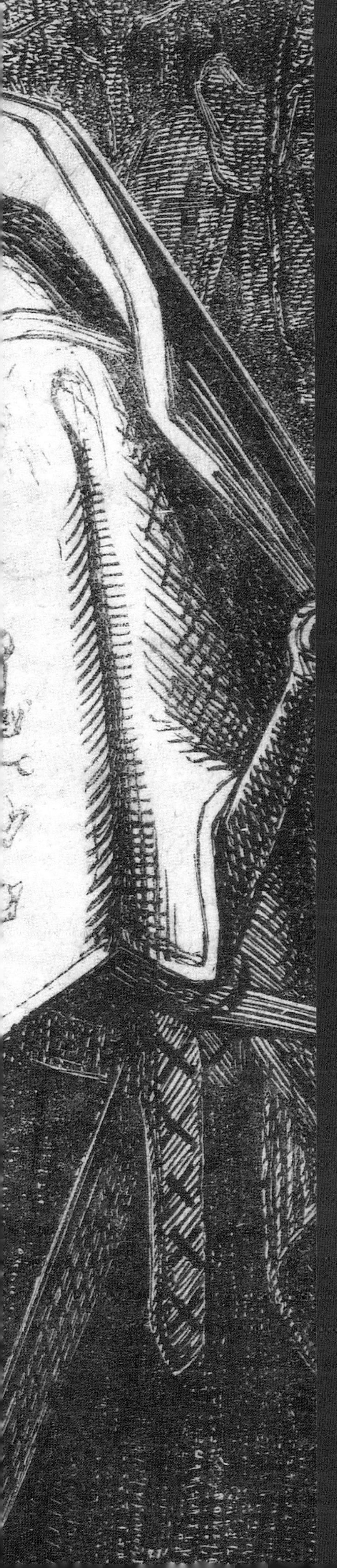

Allegorising on their own hook?

Tennyson and the Pre-Raphaelites

Linda Goddard

Allegorising on their own hook?

Tennyson and the PreRaphaelites

Linda Goddard

The 'Golden Age' of 'Sixties' illustration generated a wave of collaborations between artists and writers. From the serialised fiction of illustrated journals to the precious volumes of the private press movement, such alliances satisfied the demands of a growing readership and were potentially lucrative for all involved. With publicity and profit as guiding factors, however, they were rarely the product of an exclusive and harmonious dialogue between text and image, but involved complex relationships between artist, author, publisher and engraver. As an artist's design was prepared for reproduction, the transition from drawing to print required dedication and compromise on the part of draughtsman and engraver, but frequently resulted in dissatisfaction and frustration on both sides. As for the relationship of image to text, even when an author and artist admired each other's work, their views on the function of illustration could differ. When multiple artists and engravers were involved on a single project, as was often the case in the illustrated anthologies of the 1860s, the potential for discord threatened to overshadow the contributors' interdisciplinary ideals.

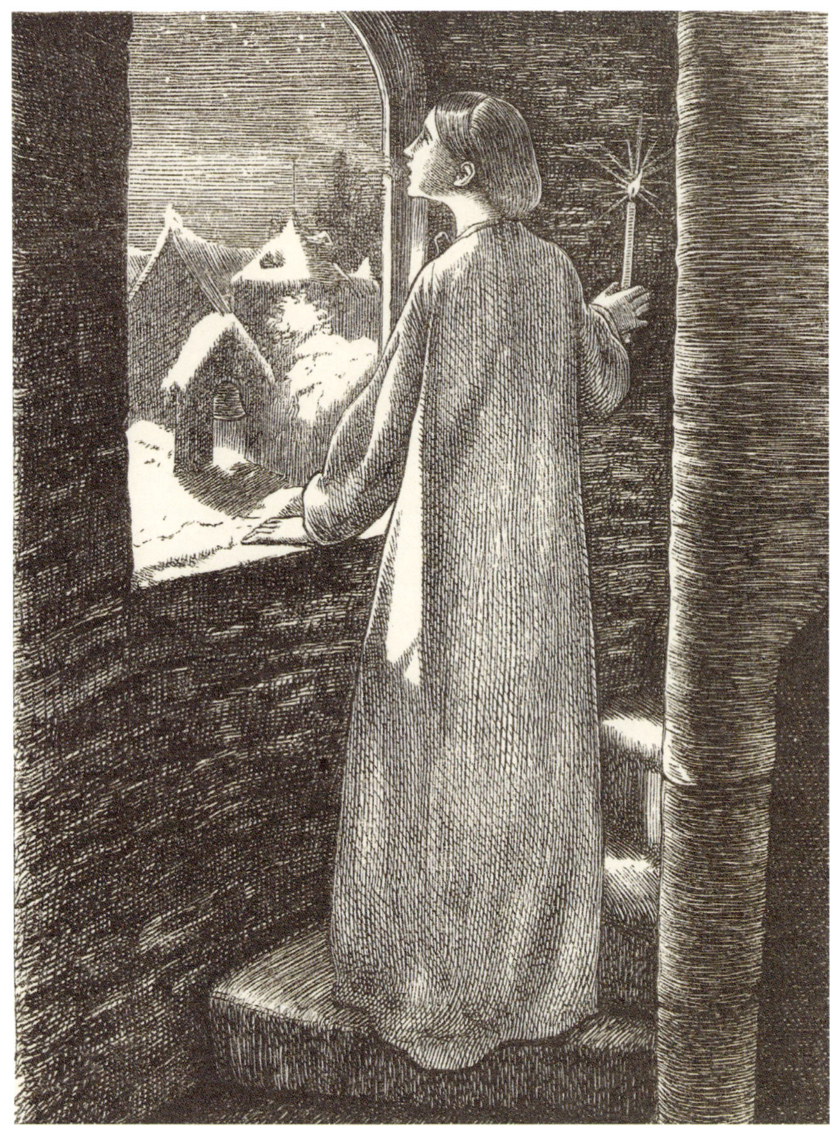

ABOVE
31. John Everett Millais
1829-1896
St Agnes' Eve

The 'Moxon' Tennyson

Stylistic diversity was a defining feature of Edward Moxon's generously illustrated 1857 edition of Tennyson's *Poems*. Known as the 'Pre-Raphaelite' or 'Moxon' Tennyson, it combined the work of Millais, Rossetti and Holman Hunt, with that of a more established group: William Mulready, J. C. Horsley, Daniel Maclise and Clarkson Stanfield. Confident of the commercial appeal of Tennyson's poetry, having already published six profitable volumes, it was Moxon who persuaded the poet and enlisted a representative sample of 'men who can draw on the wood.'[1] While the publisher chose the majority of the contributors, Tennyson himself, probably encouraged by Ruskin, proposed Rossetti and Holman Hunt. Beyond this, he took a back seat, leaving the publisher and illustrators to confer over the choice of texts, while the engravers, including the Dalziel brothers, J. Thompson and W. J. Linton, had to contend with the challenges of translating the intricately detailed designs of the Pre-

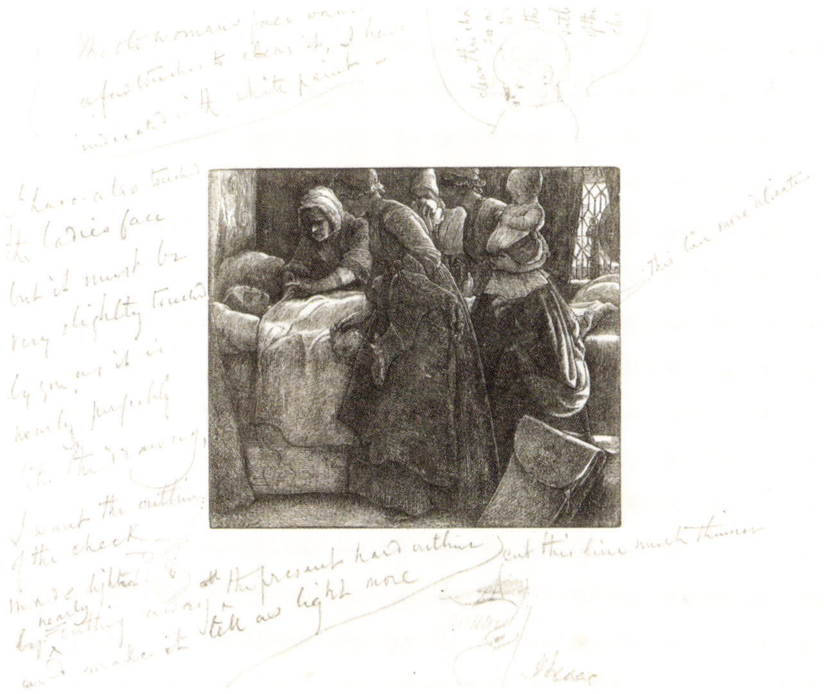

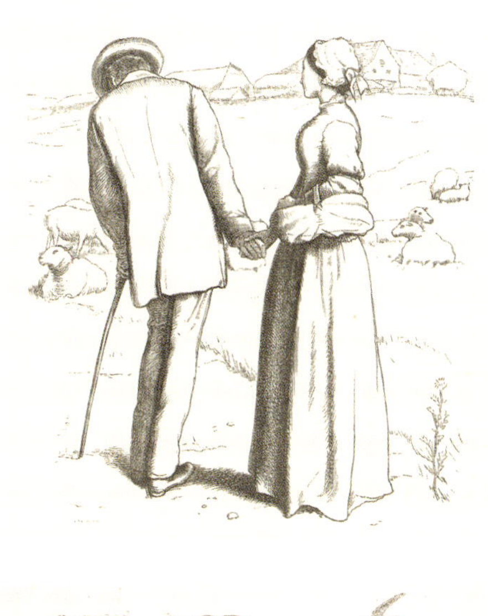

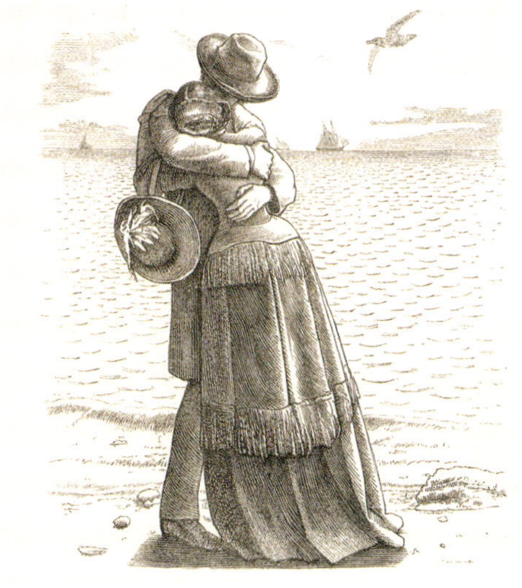

ABOVE
32. John Everett Millais
1829-1896
The Lord of Burleigh

TOP RIGHT
33. John Everett Millais
1829-1896
Edward Gray

RIGHT
34. John Everett Millais
1829-1896
Locksley Hall

Raphaelites onto the block. The resulting volume, although a landmark in Victorian publishing, was a financial failure and only a partial artistic success.[2] Ruskin judged the Pre-Raphaelite illustrations 'terribly spoiled in the cutting,'[3] while *The Art Journal* considered them 'quaint' and 'affected.'[4] Pleasing neither the Pre-Raphaelites' supporters, nor those who favoured the more conventional contingent, the overall product lacked coherence. Characterised by George Somes Layard as a 'bundle of splendid incongruities,' it not only combined artists from rival schools, but pitted the 'forcible simplicity' of Millais against the 'spirituality and sensuousness' of Rossetti. Layard's view that 'Millais has realised, Holman Hunt has idealised, and Rossetti has sublimated, or transcendentalised, the subjects which they have respectively illustrated,' highlights the complexities of the illustrator's task. Responding to the conflicting demands of text and image, the artist had to balance the 'lawful wedding of pen and pencil' with the 'brilliancy of his own imagination.'[5]

Millais

Of the eight Moxon Tennyson artists, Millais produced the greatest number of illustrations, contributing eighteen of the fifty-four designs, seven of which were engraved by the Dalziel Family. 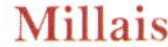 Unlike his fellow Pre-Raphaelite contributors, Millais remained committed to printmaking throughout his career, willingly adapting his style to the engraver's needs.[6] His motivations were partly financial; discouraged by the reception of his paintings at the 1859 Royal Academy exhibition, he confided in his wife Effie, 'I certainly shall have to work at small things like mad.'[7] He must also have been aware of the publicity that collaborations with figures such as Tennyson and Trollope (see nos. 62-64) would bring, and made a substantial profit by selling watercolour versions of his most popular illustrations. Contributing to over twelve periodicals, most significantly *Once a Week*, *The Cornhill Magazine* and *Good Words*, and illustrating thirty-six books, he produced 270 designs between 1854 and 1869, but his involvement with printmaking continued intermittently until the mid-1880s. His designs are notable for their stylistic diversity, in accordance with the range of literature which he tackled, from the historical novels of Harriet Martineau in *Once a Week*, to *The*

Parables of Our Lord, serialised in *Good Words* from 1862-1864 and published as a gift book by the Dalziel Family in 1864. His accurate portrayals of contemporary dress and manners moved Trollope to rate his illustrations for *Orley Farm* 'the best I have seen in any novel in any language.'[8]

Rossetti

Unlike Millais, Rossetti produced few engravings, finding 'the work of drawing on the wood particularly trying to the eyes.'[9] After an influential design, 'The Maids of Elfen-Mere,' for William Allingham's *The Music Master*, he produced five for the Moxon Tennyson and four for two volumes of Christina Rossetti's poetry, but confessed to feeling inclined to illustrate only 'once a century.'[10] Initially reluctant to contribute, Rossetti was persuaded by Millais but demanded a fee of £30 per drawing, £5 more than everyone else. In addition to two designs for 'The Palace of Art' (nos. 35 and 36), he produced three more, for 'Sir Galahad' (no. 37), 'The Lady of Shalott' and 'Mariana in the South.' Two further illustrations, another for 'Sir Galahad' and one for 'The Two Voices,' were promised but never completed. His inability to keep to deadlines and finicky corrections, as the touched proofs exemplify, caused Moxon much stress and delayed publication of the volume to such an extent that it missed the Christmas 1856 market. Rossetti was notoriously unwilling to adapt his elaborately detailed and densely linear style to the requirements of the

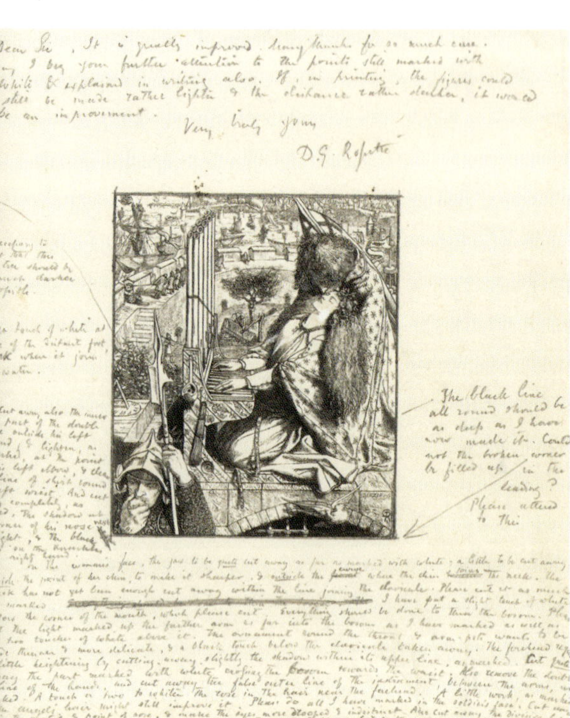

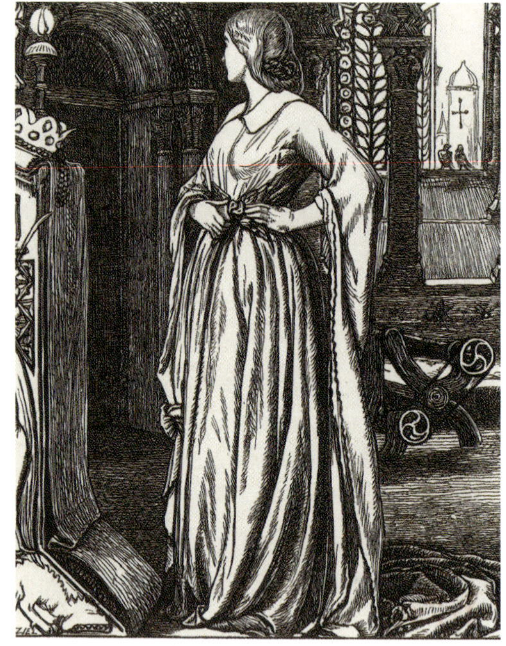

engravers, and complained bitterly about their inability to do justice to his efforts: 'after a fortnight's work my block goes to the engraver, like Agag, delicately, and is hewn to pieces before the Lord Harry.'[11] He reserved particular contempt for the Dalziel brothers, those 'ministers of wrath,' even composing a satirical 'Address':

O woodman, spare that block,
O gash not anyhow;
It took ten days by clock,
I'd fain protect it now.

Chorus, wild laughter from Dalziel's workshop.[12]

Of all the Moxon Tennyson illustrations, Rossetti's have attracted the strongest criticism as well as the highest praise. The most frequent charge leveled against his designs is their divergence from Tennyson's text. *The Art Journal* dismissed them as 'beyond the pale of criticism' and 'calculated to provoke ridicule.'[13] Rossetti himself was convinced that they had failed to please the author, writing to William Morris that Tennyson loathed them. His brother, William Michael Rossetti, however, recalled that the poet particularly favoured *King Arthur and the Weeping Queens*,[14] while his other design for 'The Palace of Art', *St. Cecilia*, was praised by Ruskin as 'the best in the book.'[15]

Although Tennyson rarely inspected the illustrations to his poems until they were finished, and in some cases, already cut on the wood, he

ABOVE LEFT
40. William Holman Hunt
1827-1910
Godiva

LEFT
36. Dante Gabriel Rossetti
1828-1882
St Cecilia

RIGHT
38. Dante Gabriel Rossetti
1828-1882
'Buy from us with a Golden Curl', *Goblin Market and Other Poems (detail)*

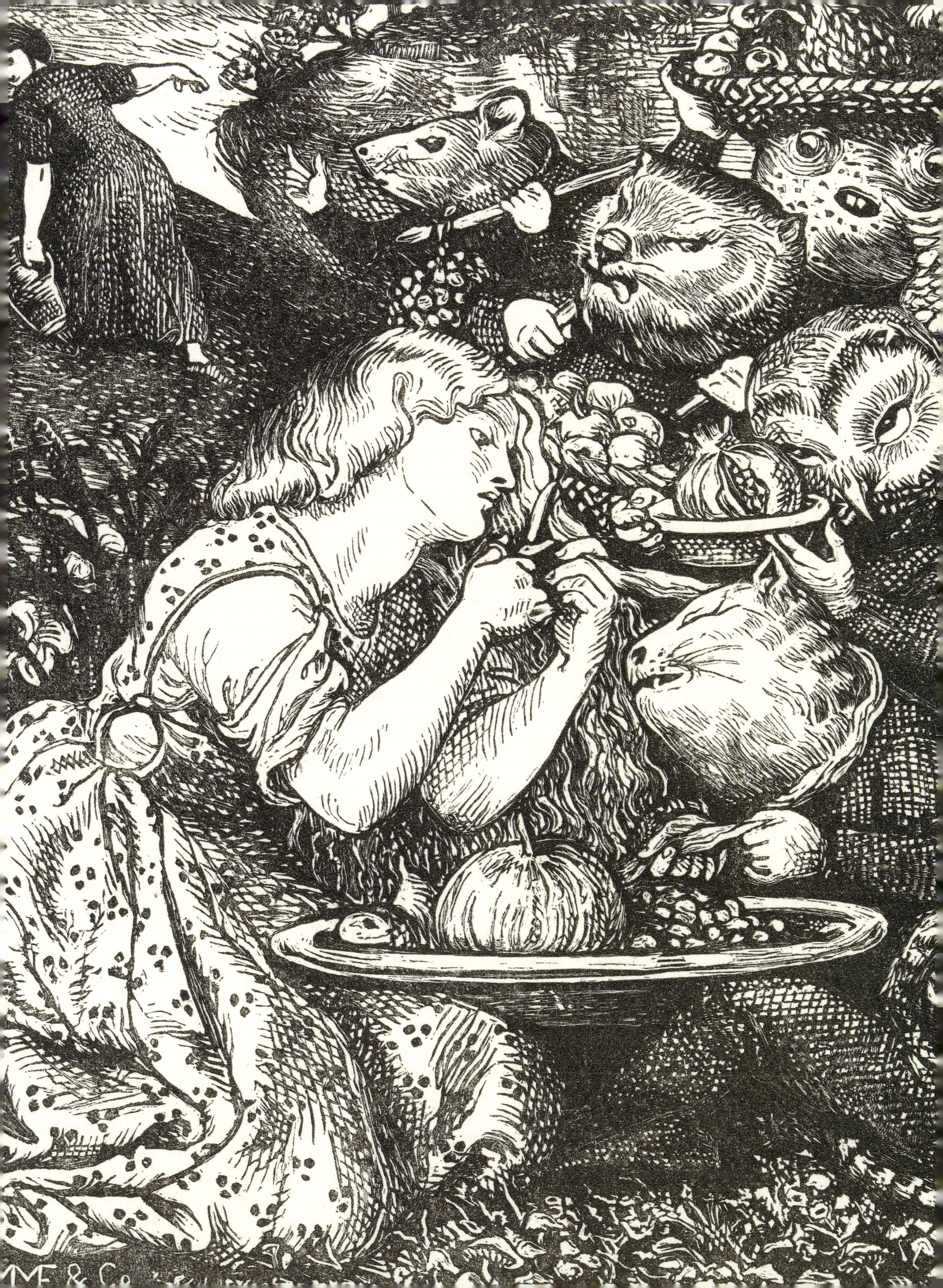
MF & Co

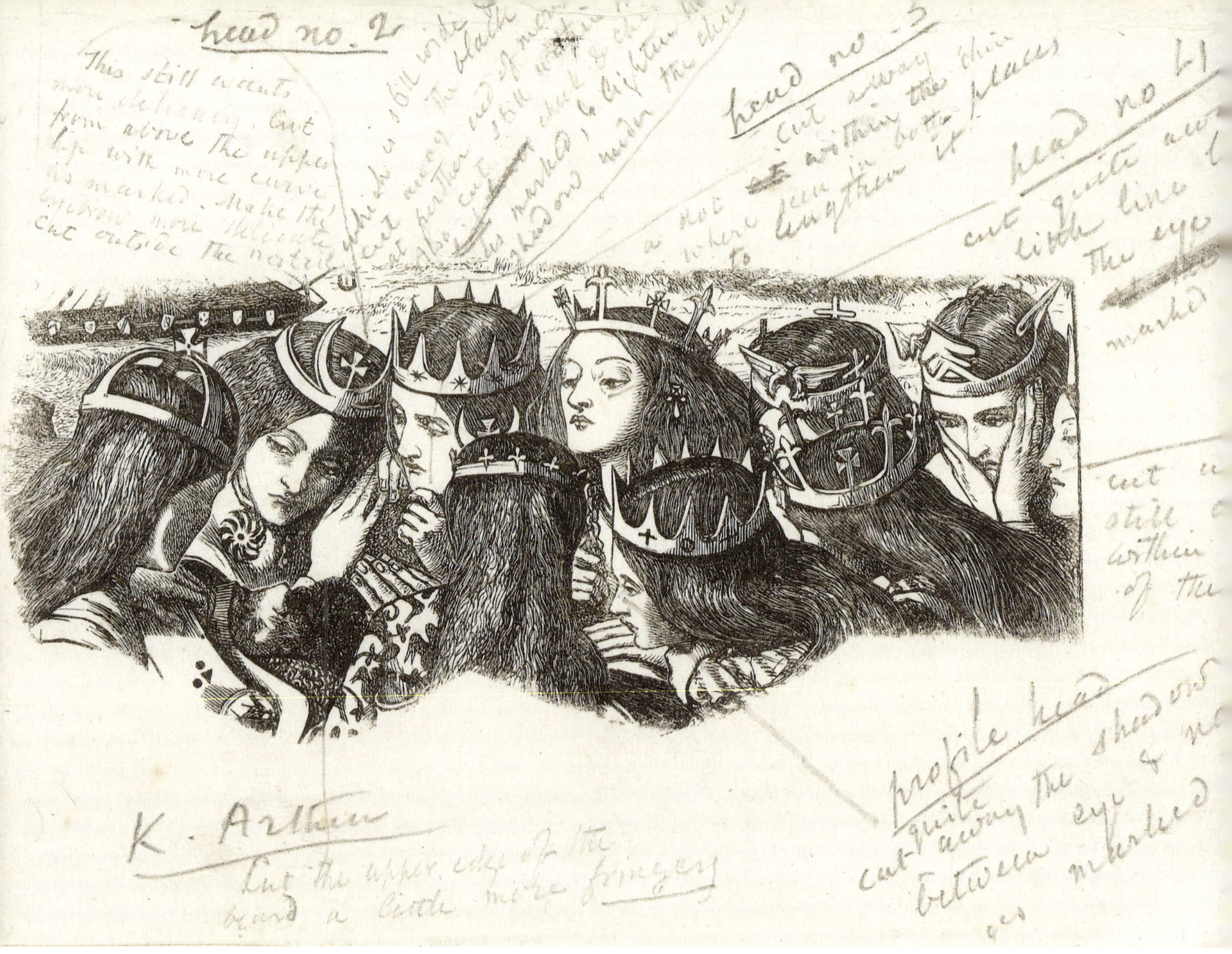

expected conformity to his words, advising Holman Hunt that, 'an illustrator ought never to add anything to what he finds in the text.'[16] Yet even Millais's interpretations, though less fanciful than Rossetti's, deviated from their source on occasion in the interests of pictorial effect. Indeed for Ruskin, the success of the Moxon Tennyson designs was inversely related to their illustrative function, as he wrote to the poet, 'Many of the plates are noble things, though not, it seems to me, illustrations of your poems. I believe, in fact, that good pictures never can be; they are always another poem, subordinate but wholly different from the poet's conception, and serve chiefly to show the reader how variously the same verses may affect various minds.'[17]

Christina and Dante Gabriel Rossetti

Rossetti's two collaborations with his sister, the poet Christina Rossetti, allowed him greater freedom as an illustrator than he had encountered on the Moxon Tennyson project. In addition to frontispiece designs for Christina's *Goblin Market* (1862) and *The Prince's Progress and Other Poems* (1866), he created the title pages and bindings. The publisher, Alexander MacMillan, had little control over the finished product, which was carefully crafted by the Rossettis in the manner of a private press book. Christina, like Dante Gabriel, was committed to the dialogue between poetry and painting. Privately, she drew sketches for her own work, and she often published in the illustrated press. As her illustrator, Christina preferred her brother 'to the world in general,'[18] and as her editor she praised his 'suggestive wit and revising hand.'[19] The siblings collaborated closely: he submitted sketches and proofs for her approval, while she consulted him on the development of *The Prince's Progress* in a substantial correspondence during the winter of 1865. This gave rise to a genuinely collaborative venture in which the visual and verbal components developed simultaneously.[20] As with Tennyson and his illustrators, Christina recognised

ABOVE
35. Dante Gabriel Rossetti
1828–1882
King Arthur in the Vale of Avalon

the prestige that her brother's name would bring, acknowledging that his 'protecting woodcuts help me to face my small public.' Such was her reliance on his contributions, which she termed 'essential to my contentment'[21] and 'too desirable to forgo' that for both editions MacMillan, like Moxon, was obliged to sacrifice the Christmas market to accommodate Rossetti's protracted delays.[22]

Through their close partnership, mutual consultation and tight authorial control over all aspects of the printing process, the Rossettis conquered some of the obstacles that had faced the illustrators of the Moxon Tennyson. The difficulty of achieving a satisfying unity between text and image when dealing with the competing demands of author, artist, publisher and engraver was recognised by Edward Burne-Jones, whose own fruitful partnership with William Morris produced their celebrated illustrated edition of *The Works of Geoffrey Chaucer*. As his wife, Georgiana Burne-Jones, remembered: 'One day in 1896, when talking of wood-engraving with reference to the Kelmscott Chaucer, he took out our old copy of the Tennyson, and turned it about and mused over it. "As a book," he said, "it's nothing. There was no command over the type and printing such as Mr. Morris has, and there were so many hands engaged on the pictures as to make it impossible as a book."'[23] By overseeing all his collaborations from start to finish, it was precisely this lack of coherence and control that Morris's Kelmscott Press was designed to overcome.

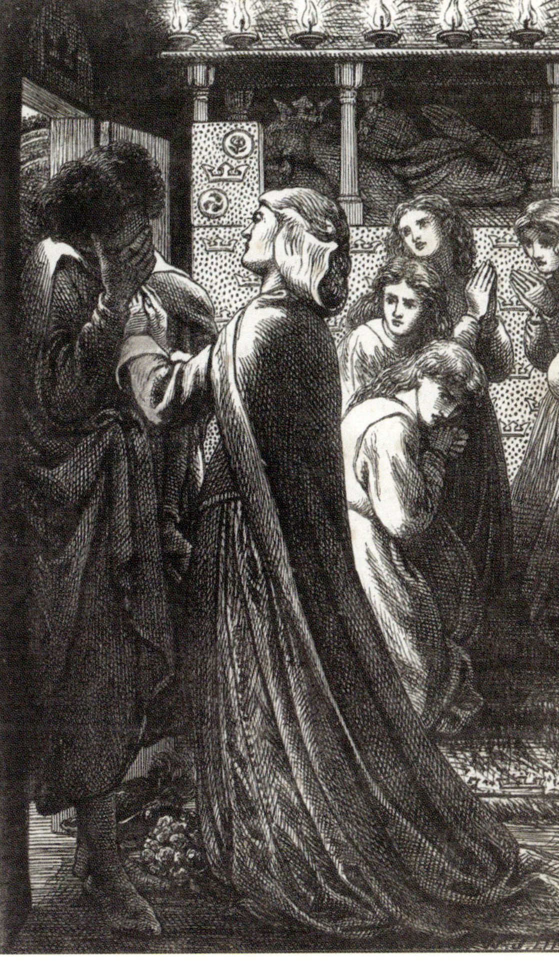

RIGHT
39. Dante Gabriel Rossetti
1828-1882
You should have wept her yesterday, The Prince's Progress and Other Poems

1 Quoted June Steffensen Hagen, *Tennyson and his Pre-Raphaelite Illustrators*, London, 1979, 102-103.

2 Ambitiously priced at a guinea and a half, it failed to cover its costs, only selling out when the publisher George Routledge bought the surplus stock in 1863 and reduced the price to one guinea.

3 Edward Cook and Alexander Wedderburn, eds., *Works of John Ruskin*, London, XV, 1904, 224.

4 Anonymous, 'Reviews', *The Art Journal*, 19 July 1857, 231.

5 George Somes Layard, *Tennyson and his Illustrators. A book about a book*, London, 1894, 9. According to Layard, Millais loyally followed the author's intentions, while Rossetti 'attempted to overpower the text.'

6 See Jane Munro, *Tennyson and Trollope: Book illustrations by John Everett Millais (1829-96)*, exh. cat., Cambridge, The Fitzwilliam Museum, 1996.

7 Quoted Michael Mason, 'The Way we Look Now', *Art History*, 1: 3, September 1978, 331.

8 Quoted Munro, 1996, 6.

9 To William Allingham, 23 January 1855, Oswald Doughty and John Robert Wahl, eds., *Letters of Dante Gabriel Rossetti*, Oxford, I, 1965, 239.

10 To William Allingham, 29 November 1860, Doughty and Wahl, *op. ibid.*, I, 385.

11 To William Allingham, 18 December 1856, *ibid.*, 310.

12 To William Bell Scott, February 1857, *ibid.*, 319. He preferred Linton to Dalziel, telling Ford Madox Brown (8 December 1856), 'Linton is the man. I have got also his second proof of *Mariana*, which is quite another thing', *ibid.*, 307.

13 *op. cit.*, at n.4.

14 William Michael Rossetti, *Some Reminiscences* ..., London, I, 1906, 254.

15 *op. cit.*, at n.3.

16 William Holman Hunt, *Pre-Raphaelitism and the Pre-Raphaelite Brotherhood*, London, 1905, 124.

17 Cook and Wedderburn, *op. cit.*, XXXVI, 264.

18 To Dante Gabriel Rossetti, 11 March 1865, Antony H. Harrison, *Letters of Christina Rossetti*, Charlottesville, I, 1997, 231.

19 Quoted Gail Lynn Goldberg, 'Rossetti's Revising Hand: His illustrations for Christina Rossetti's poems', *Victorian Poetry*, 20, Autumn-Winter 1982, 145.

20 Lorraine Janzen Kooistra, *Christina Rossetti and Illustration: A publishing history*, Athens, 2002, 75.

21 To Dante Rossetti, 15 April 1865, Harrison, *op. cit.*, 246.

22 To Alexander MacMillan, 16 December 1865, *ibid.*, 265.

23 Georgina Burne-Jones, *Memorials of Edward Burne-Jones*, London, I, 1904, 157.

John Everett Millais

1829-1896

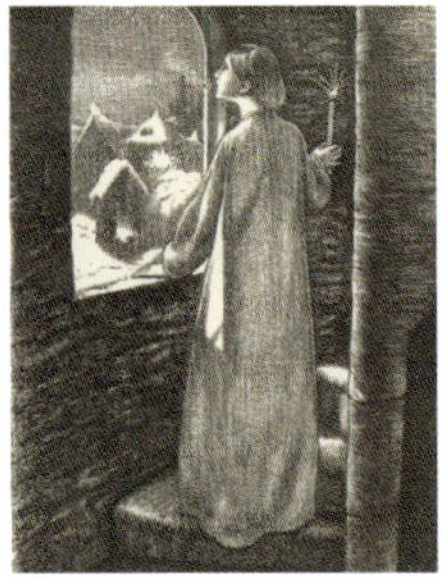

31. St Agnes' Eve

Wood engraving
Engraved by the Dalziel Family
100 x 81 mm | Bought, 1909 | P.6482-R

Millais is frequently praised, not only for his willingness to adapt his technique for the engraving process, but also for his fidelity to Tennyson's poems. According to George Somes Layard, Millais's illustrations are 'as immediately and directly inspired by the poet as Rossetti's are not' (1894, 9). However, while less eccentric than Rossetti in his choice of scene or inclusion of detail, Millais does not allow accuracy to stifle imagination. Rather than depicting the most obvious or dramatic moment, he uses composition, posture and expression to convey a mood. His style for the Moxon's illustrated edition of Tennyson's *Poems* falls into two categories: all but one of the scenes engraved by the Dalziels are highly detailed and densely hatched up to the borders, while the majority of those cut by the other engravers are linear and economic, fading towards the edges in the style of a vignette. The former technique, with which Millais is more commonly associated, allows for dramatic chiaroscuro effects which complement the mood of the poems. In *St Agnes' Eve*, the contrast between the gloomy stairwell on which the devotee to the virgin martyr stands, and the moonlit snowscape on which she gazes, conveys her desire to be united with God:

Deep on the convent roof the snows
Are sparkling to the moon:
My breath to heaven like vapour goes:
May my soul follow soon!

Millais's close attention to the text is indeed apparent in his careful rendition of the nun's ascending cloud of breath. However, his image does not simply rely on the narrative: in the absence of specific references to setting in the poem, his choice of a winding staircase and brightly-lit window aptly conveys the cloistered nun's frustration and longing, by contrasting outside and inside, light and dark: 'As these white robes are soil'd and dark, / To yonder shining ground; [...] So in mine earthly house I am, / To that I hope to be.'

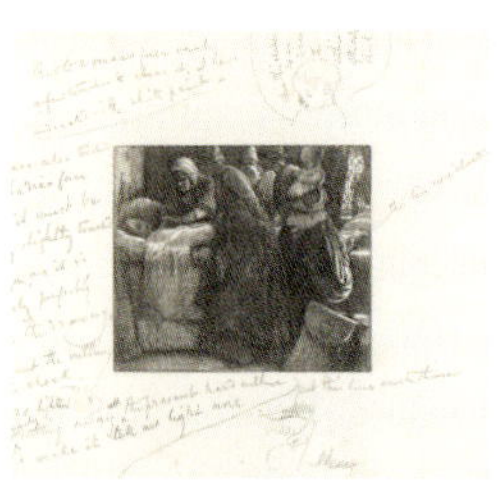

32. The Lord of Burleigh

Wood engraving, touched in graphite
Engraved by the Dalziel Family
168 x 197 mm | Bought, 1916 | P.1700-R

Millais has rendered a poignant deathbed scene for which minimum detail is provided in the poem. It shows the village maiden who married her lord, in the belief that he was a humble landscape painter, then tragically expired, unable to live with the burden of riches 'unto which she was not born':

Faint she grew, and ever fainter,
As she murmur'd, "Oh that he
Were once more that landscape-painter,
Which did win my heart from me!"
So she droop'd and droop'd before him,
Fading slowly from his side:
Three fair children first she bore him,
Then before her time she died.

Instead of three children, Millais includes only one, populating the scene with faithful servants and omitting the lord of the title to focus on the tender emotions of the devoted women. On the margins, pencil sketches and instructions to the engravers reveal the care he took in perfecting the balance of light and shade. Although he pronounces the lady's face 'nearly perfectly like the drawing,' he asks the engraver to lighten the outline of the cheek, and elsewhere indicates where shadows are to be cleared and lines made thinner and more delicate.

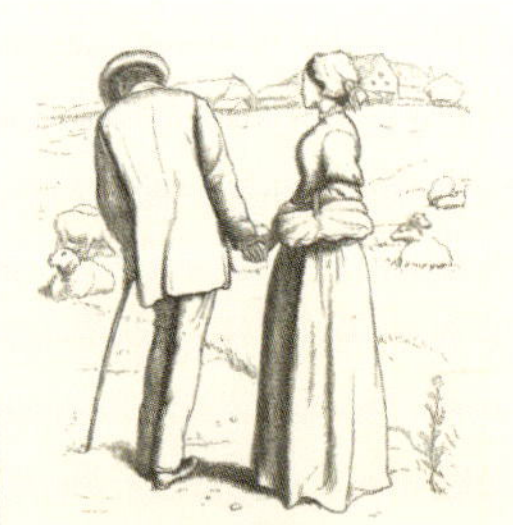

33. Edward Gray

Wood engraving | Engraved by John Thompson | 100 x 98 mm
Bought, 1909 | P.6481-R

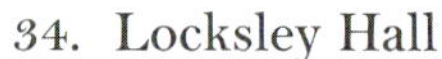

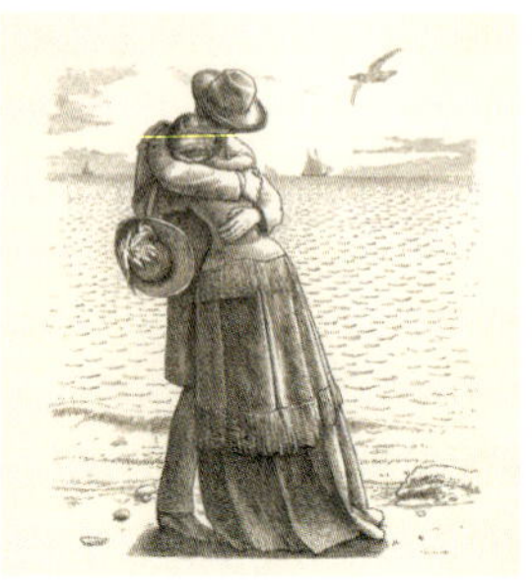

34. Locksley Hall

Wood engraving | Engraved by John Thompson | 105 x 99 mm
Bought, 1909 | P.6480-R

In contrast to the richly detailed designs cut by the Dalziel Family, those engraved by John Thompson for *Edward Gray* and *Locksley Hall* are examples of the synthetic, linear style which Millais employed for Tennyson's poems on contemporary subjects. Comparable to his 1853-1854 series of drawings on the theme of modern relationships, and like his illustrations to Trollope, they demonstrate his sensitivity to the costume and character of his times. Both illustrations pick up on the poems' theme of nostalgia for lost love and employ the device of portraying a couple from behind, or with their faces obscured, to enhance the viewer's sense of empathy with their romantic plight. Edward Gray tells in simple quatrains how he failed to recognise the devotion of Ellen Adair, who loved him against her parents' will, mistaking her shyness for pride. As he tells his kind companion, he is condemned never to love again now that she lies heartbroken in her grave:

Sweet Emma Moreland spoke to me:
Bitterly weeping I turn'd away:
"Sweet Emma Moreland, love no more
Can touch the heart of Edward Gray.

The more ambitious *Locksley Hall* is a paean to social progress as well as a lament for a doomed relationship, but Millais focuses on the idyllic memory of youthful love with which the poem opens:

Many an evening by the waters did we watch the stately ships,
And our spirits rush'd together at the touching of the lips.

While Tennyson's references to science and civilisation ('Let the great world spin forever down the ringing grooves of change') are absent from Millais's image, the expanse of sea connects the poem's wistful opening with its vigorous close: 'For the mighty wind arises, roaring seaward, and I go'.

Dante Gabriel Rossetti
1828–1882

35. King Arthur in the Vale of Avalon

Wood engraving touched with white bodycolour
Engraved by the Dalziel Family | 155 x 199 mm
Bought, 1916 | P.1980-83-R

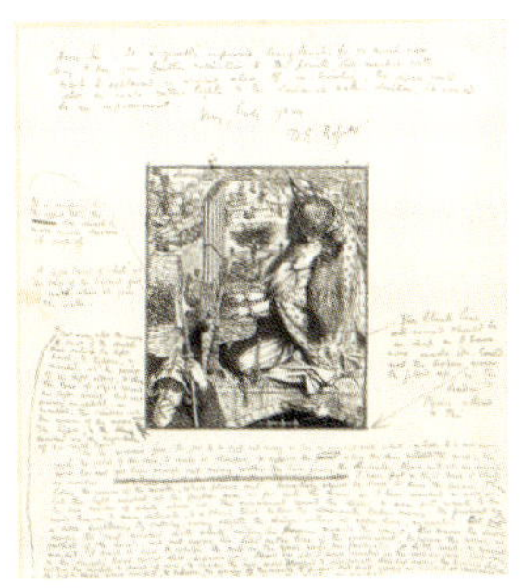

36. St Cecilia

Wood engraving, touched by the artist with white bodycolour
Engraved by the Dalziel Family
200 x 178 mm
Bought, 1916 | P.1979-R

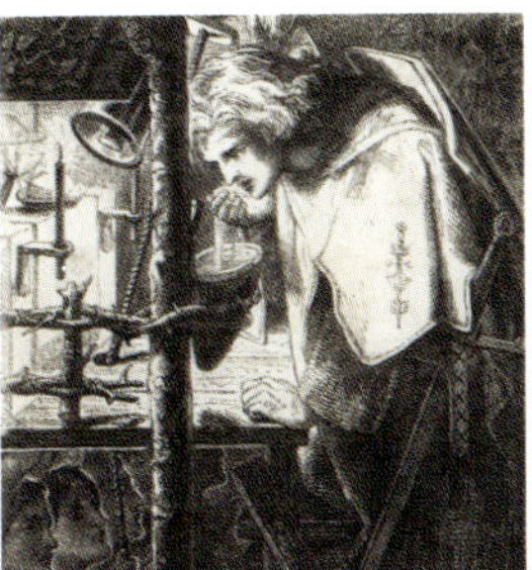

37. Sir Galahad

Wood engraving, touched by the artist with white bodycolour
Engraved by William James Linton | 104 x 91 mm
Given by Charles Fairfax Murray, 1917 | P.1987-R

Although Rossetti complained that all the best poems had been allocated before he became involved, he did identify 'The Palace of Art' as the ideal type of subject, sufficiently lacking in narrative, 'where one can allegorise on one's own hook on the subject of the poem, without killing for oneself and everyone a distinct idea of the poet's' (Doughty and Wahl, I, 1965, 239). As an allegory describing the soul's isolation in an opulent pleasure-palace of her own making, 'The Palace of Art' provides ideal material for such imaginative digression. Furthermore, the two stanzas which Rossetti has chosen to illustrate are themselves pictorial, representing scenes from a sequence of glorious tapestries of legendary subjects hung in the fantasy palace. King Arthur shows the mortally wounded knight tended by maidens in the Vale of Avalon, as described in the lines:

Or mythic Uther's deeply-wounded son
In some fair space of sloping greens
Lay, dozing in the Vale of Avalon,
And watch'd by weeping queens.

Although the illustration includes the sacred boat which conveyed Arthur to Avalon, the emphasis is less on narrative than on the poetic beauty and emotion of the queens, who dominate the composition.

St Cecilia depicts the patron Saint of music surrounded, rather like the soul in her palace, by a vast and minutely detailed cityscape corresponding to the lines:

Or in a clear-wall'd city on the sea
Near gilded organ-pipes, her hair
Wound with white roses, slept St Cecily;
An angel look'd at her.

Cecilia, who in the poem is supposed to be sleeping, reclines in a sensual swoon, while the angel, who apparently merely 'look'd at her', kisses her forehead passionately, oddly mirroring the soldier munching his apple in the bottom left corner. The divergence between image and text has often been noted, with William Michael Rossetti commenting that, 'The illustration of St Cecilia puzzled Tennyson not a little, and he had to give up the problem of what it had to do with his verses' (quoted Hagen, 1979, 103). Rossetti, who declared that he could 'get a whole city' into a sixteenth of an inch (quoted Burne-Jones, *Memorials*, I, 1904, 157), has surrounded the saint with a sundial, cannon, and bird flying free of the dungeon, against the background of ramparts, harbour and distant turrets. While such detail has no direct source in the poem, in creating a sense of spiritual and sensual excess, it is, as Laurence Housman recognised, a 'successful summing up of the drift of an entire poem within the space of a single picture' (1896, 13). Instructions on the touched proofs for both 'Palace of Art' compositions show how Rossetti repeatedly asked the engraver to refine the lines and adjust the tonal balance until he was satisfied.

While critical of his contributions, *The Art Journal* reserved some praise for *Sir Galahad*, describing it as a 'vigorous and effective study', but complaining nonetheless that it was 'without the slightest reference to any descriptive line in the poem it professes to illustrate' (1857, 231). In fact, the scene depicted clearly relates to the passage which describes the gallant knight stopping in the night at a holy shrine:

Then by some secret shrine I ride:
I hear a voice, but none are there;
The stalls are void, the doors are wide,
The tapers burning fair.
Fair gleams the snowy altar-cloth,
The silver vessels sparkle clean,
The shrill bell rings, the censer swings,
And solemn chaunts resound between.

Rossetti has faithfully represented the altar with its 'silver vessels', 'snowy altar-cloth', 'tapers burning fair', and ringing bell, while the horse seen pawing the ground in the distance and the sacred vessel from which Galahad stoops to drink are reminders of his quest for the Holy Grail. The only significant liberty which the artist has taken with the text is the inclusion of four women hidden beneath the altar, giving human form to Galahad's inner visions, where Tennyson states 'none are there.'

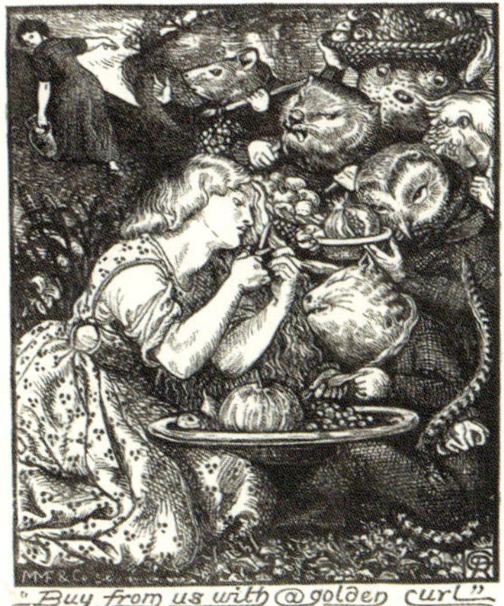

38. Buy from us with a Golden Curl, Goblin Market and Other Poems

Wood engraving | Engraved by John Faulkner
118 x 105 mm
Given by Charles Fairfax Murray, 1917
P.1986-R

39. You should have wept her yesterday, *The Prince's Progress and Other Poems*

Wood engraving | Engraved by W. J. Linton | 152 x 98 mm
Given by Charles Fairfax Murray, 1917 | P.1988-R

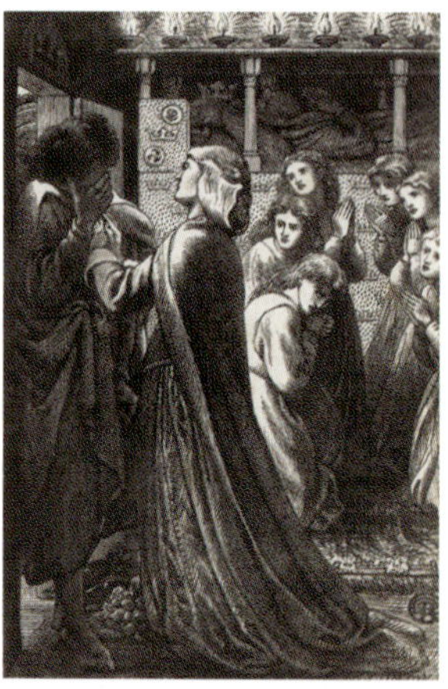

Both *Goblin Market*, which established Christina Rossetti's international reputation, and *The Prince's Progress* contrast the transient pleasures of the senses with spiritual fulfillment. Dante Gabriel's illustration to the former shows the distinction between Lizzie, dark-haired and plainly dressed, and Laura, with blond locks and a floral gown enhancing her voluptuous figure. As Lizzie flees temptation, Laura sacrifices a lock of golden hair in exchange for the succulent fruit offered by the goblins. As she has no money for the fruit, the goblins reply 'You have much gold upon your head [...] buy from us with a golden curl.' By combining two distinct moments in the poem, Lizzie's escape and Laura's surrender, Rossetti both heightens the contrast between virtue and vice, and implies, as does the poem, that the boundary between them is unstable. His design for *The Prince's Progress* similarly depicts a dramatic moment when the Prince, led astray on his journey by tempting distractions, arrives too late to claim his bride, who has wasted away, and is met with the reproach, 'You should have wept her yesterday.' Although happy with her brother's designs, thanking him for 'a most delightful pair of woodcuts,' Christina sensitively enquired whether 'two (very) small points in the frontispiece might advisably be conformed to the text? to wit, the Prince's "curly black beard" and the Bride's "veiled" face: all else seems of minor moment'(Harrison, I, 1997, 230). Having received the final proofs, in which the bride's face is duly veiled, but the prince remains without a beard (his face covered by his hands), she relents 'Never mind the Prince's beard, if you please, though I won't record his waste of time in shaving' (Harrison, I, 1997, 234). In both frontispiece designs, Rossetti has included a hand-written caption which clarifies the link to the poem and enhances the visual unity of text and illustration.

William Holman Hunt

1827-1910

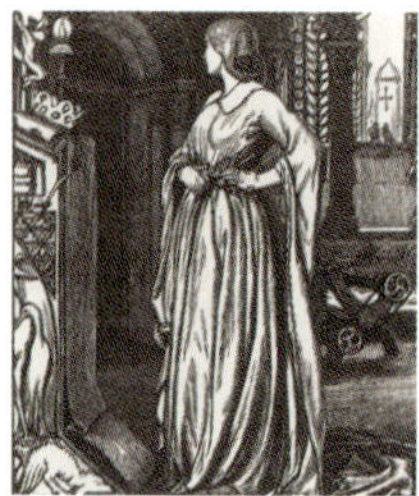

40. Godiva, Tennyson's Poems

Wood engraving | Engraved by the Dalziel Family | 138 x 132 mm
Bequeathed by Campbell Dodgson, 1951
P.188-1951

Although he occasionally contributed to the illustrated press, Holman Hunt produced relatively few illustrations overall. His seven designs for Tennyson's *Poems* were his first book engravings. Following the Moxon project, artist and poet became friends. In his memoirs, Hunt recalled how Tennyson, who admired his illustrations, challenged his decision to include certain details which did not correspond directly to the text in his designs for *The Lady of Shalott* and *The Beggar Maid*. In response, Hunt explained that the artist, unlike the poet, has to compress an entire narrative into a single frame. Tennyson accepted Hunt's defense, but reminded him that the illustrator 'should always adhere to the words of the poet' (Hunt, 1905, 125). Hunt's design for *Godiva* depicts her quiet determination as she prepares to ride naked through the streets at midday so that her tyrannical husband will lower the taxes he has imposed on the town:

> *Then she fled to her inmost bower, and there*
> *Unclasp'd the wedded eagles of her belt,*
> *The grim Earl's gift, [...]*

Alphonse Legros

1837-1911

41. Alfred, Lord Tennyson

Bronze plaque | Diameter: 118 mm
Given by Guy Knowles, 1950 | M.121-1950

French by birth, Alphonse Legros chose to settle in London, where admirers such as Dante Gabriel and William Michael Rossetti made him feel culturally at home. As a founder member of the Society of Medallists, he cast a series of portrait medallions of great Victorians of which Alfred, Lord Tennyson, which he executed in 1881, is a typical example. Poet laureate from 1850 until his death, Tennyson was also honoured as one of the Pre-Raphaelite Brotherhood's 'Immortals' (see also no. 6). An engraving of Thomas Woolner's portrait medallion of the poet formed the frontispiece of Moxon's 1857 illustrated edition of his *Poems*.

Charles Fairfax Murray

1849-1919

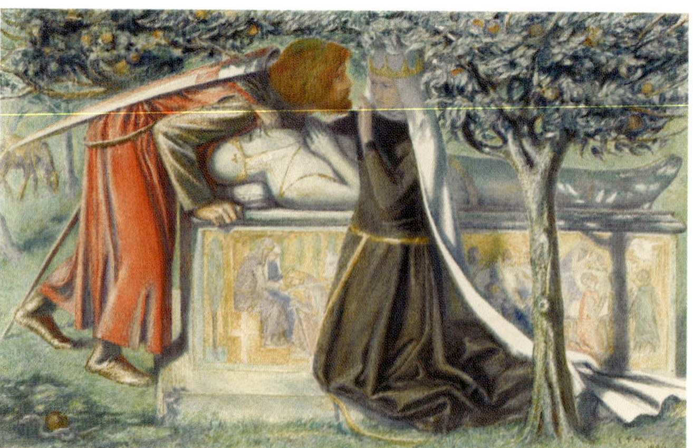

42. King Arthur's Tomb

Watercolour on paper | After Dante Gabriel Rossetti | 276 x 373 mm
Signed with initials and dated, lower right: *1964*
Given by Charles Fairfax Murray, 1908 | no. 669

An artist, collector and champion of the Pre-Raphaelites, Fairfax Murray befriended and assisted Dante Gabriel Rossetti, John Ruskin, William Morris and Edward Burne-Jones (see no. 14). Of his Pre-Raphaelite mentors, he had particular admiration for Rossetti, who encouraged his devoted study of the Old Masters, and for whom he began working as a copyist from 1869. Although an artist in his own right, Fairfax Murray, whom Rossetti nicknamed 'little Murray,' preferred to leave the limelight to his heroes. As William Michael Rossetti recalled, he was 'always ready to do any friendly and good-natured service to my brother, such as copying his poems from the original manuscript, or sending him photographs' (*Reminiscences*, II, 1906, 325). Murray's faithful copy of *Arthur's Tomb (the last meeting of Launcelot and Guenevere)* (1854, British Museum), shows Lancelot leaning over Arthur's effigy, entreating a kiss from Guinevere. A frieze on the side of the tomb depicts the knights at the Round Table, while in the left foreground a snake and an apple symbolise the lovers' betrayal. Executed in 1886, four years after Rossetti's death, it remained in Murray's possession until he gave it to the Fitzwilliam Museum in 1908. In common with other instances of pictorial and literary homage in this exhibition (see nos. 15 and 98), it serves to preserve and reinforce the influence of its model, and, in this case, to prolong the Pre-Raphaelite fascination with Arthurian themes.

Frederick Sandys

1829–1904

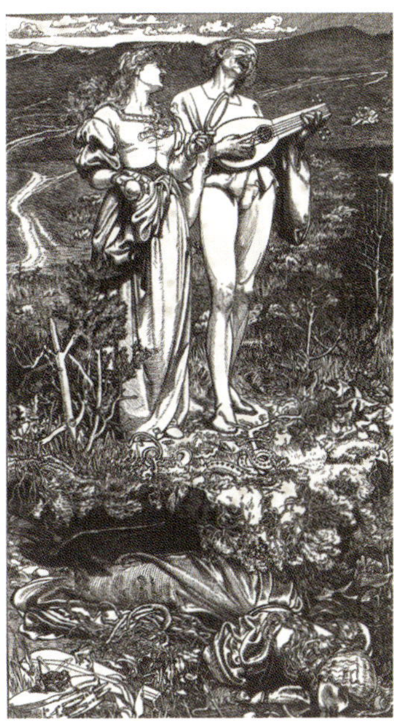

43. Amor Mundi

Wood engraving
Engraved by the Dalziel Family
253 x 163 mm
Given by Charles Fairfax Murray, 1917 | P.1995-R

44. Danaë in the Brazen Chamber

Wood engraving
Engraved by Joseph Swain
237 x 168 mm
Given by Charles Fairfax Murray, 1917 | P.2000-R

One of the least prolific, yet most distinctive, of the 'Sixties' illustrators, Sandys's reputation rests on no more than thirty designs, the majority of which were published in periodicals rather than books. Indebted in equal measure to Dürer and Rossetti, with whom he began a close personal and artistic relationship in the late 1850s, he combined a consistently solid outline with extraordinary attention to detail. *Amor Mundi*, which accompanied Christina Rossetti's poem in the May 1865 edition of *The Shilling Magazine*, depicts the irresponsible lovers straying from the righteous path:

Oh, where are you going with your lovelocks flowing
On the west wind blowing along this valley track?
The downhill path is easy, come with me an' it please ye,
We shall escape the uphill by never turning back.

Just as the couple in the poem discover the decaying corpse in the stream when it is too late to turn back, the prostrate figure in Sandys's illustration emerges only gradually from the undergrowth. Rich with symbolic detail suggestive of the vanities of earthly pleasure, such as the apple, mirror, and snake in the grass, the image reflects the passage of time in the poem by including a distant view of the couple kissing in the meadow, and suggestively juxtaposes the woman's carefree demeanour with the vision of her impending demise.

Sandys's lusty depiction of the captive Danaë potently suggests Zeus's visit to her brazen chamber. This erotically charged image was intended to accompany a poem by Swinburne published in *Once a Week* (7 December 1867); however, the depiction of the male nude on Danaë's tapestry was deemed too explicit and the poem appeared without it. Sandys has faithfully conveyed Swinburne's evocation of a dream whose 'image lingered on the loom', and Danaë's expectant pose as:

She stood, with white arm fixed in air,
And head thrown back, and streaming hair.

Detached from its literary source, it was finally published in *The Century Guild Hobby Horse* in 1888, where it accompanies an article by J. M. Gray on 'Frederick Sandys and the wood-cut designers of thirty years ago.'

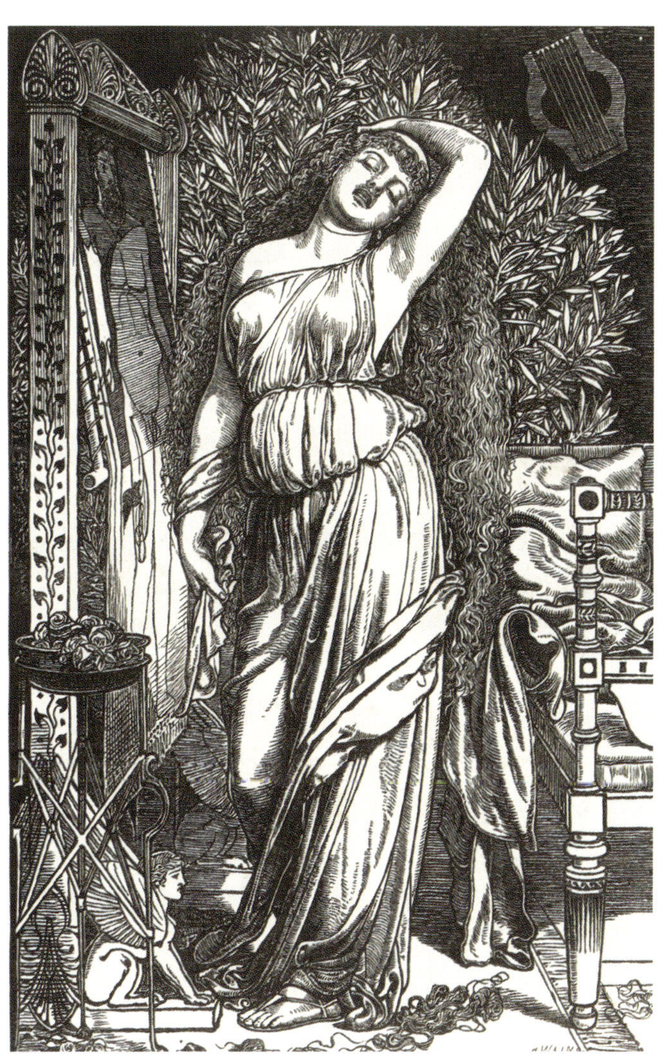

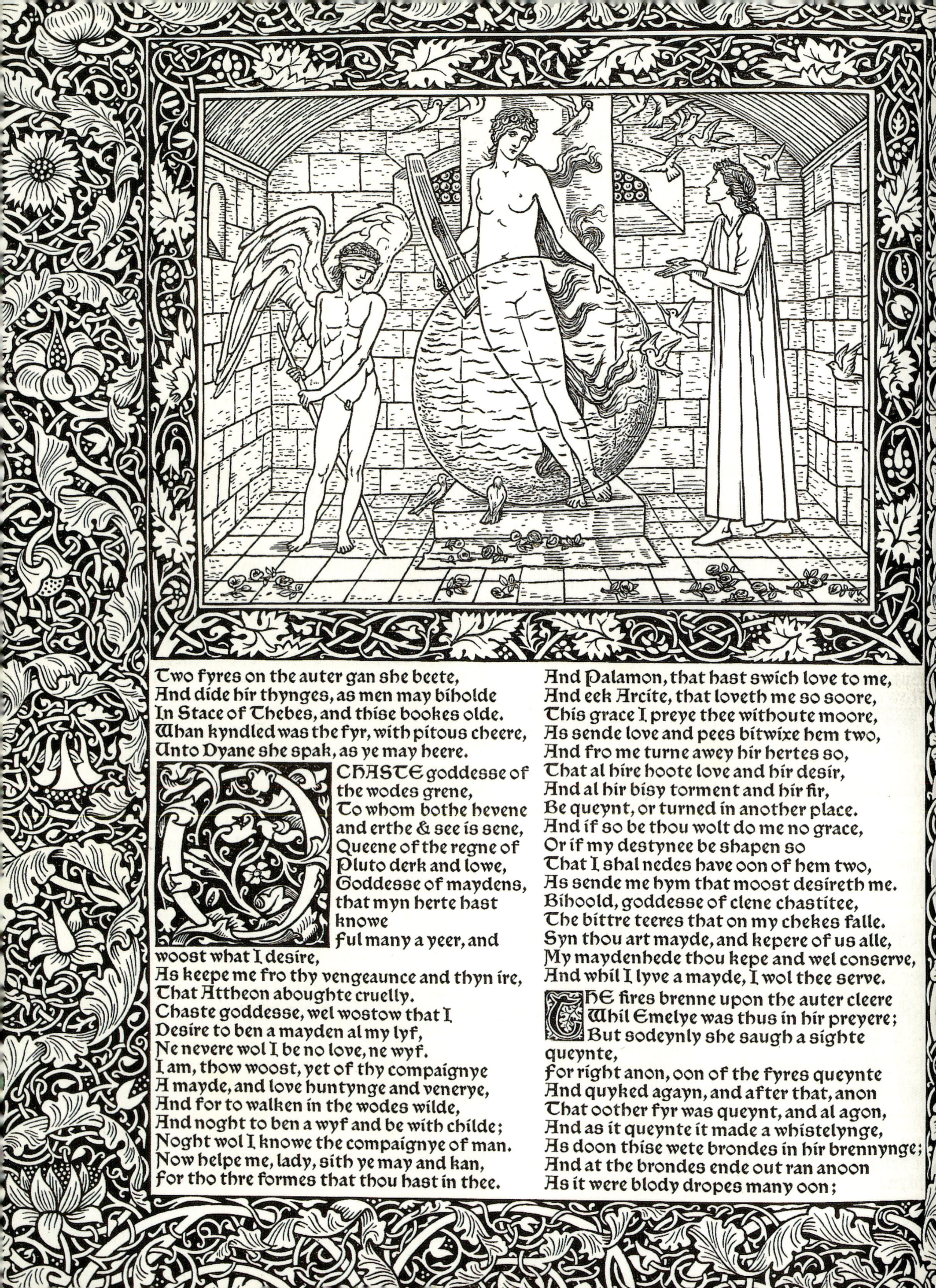

Two fyres on the auter gan she beete,
And dide hir thynges, as men may biholde
In Stace of Thebes, and thise bookes olde.
Whan kyndled was the fyr, with pitous cheere,
Unto Dyane she spak, as ye may heere.

O CHASTE goddesse of the wodes grene,
To whom bothe hevene and erthe & see is sene,
Queene of the regne of Pluto derk and lowe,
Goddesse of maydens, that myn herte hast knowe
ful many a yeer, and woost what I desire,
As keepe me fro thy vengeaunce and thyn ire,
That Attheon aboughte cruelly.
Chaste goddesse, wel wostow that I
Desire to ben a mayden al my lyf,
Ne nevere wol I be no love, ne wyf.
I am, thow woost, yet of thy compaignye
A mayde, and love huntynge and venerye,
And for to walken in the wodes wilde,
And noght to ben a wyf and be with childe;
Noght wol I knowe the compaignye of man.
Now helpe me, lady, sith ye may and kan,
for tho thre formes that thou hast in thee.
And Palamon, that hast swich love to me,
And eek Arcite, that loveth me so soore,
This grace I preye thee withoute moore,
As sende love and pees bitwixe hem two,
And fro me turne awey hir hertes so,
That al hire hoote love and hir desir,
And al hir bisy torment and hir fir,
Be queynt, or turned in another place.
And if so be thou wolt do me no grace,
Or if my destynee be shapen so
That I shal nedes have oon of hem two,
As sende me hym that moost desireth me.
Bihoold, goddesse of clene chastitee,
The bittre teeres that on my chekes falle.
Syn thou art mayde, and kepere of us alle,
My maydenhede thou kepe and wel conserve,
And whil I lyve a mayde, I wol thee serve.

THE fires brenne upon the auter cleere
Whil Emelye was thus in hir preyere;
But sodeynly she saugh a sighte queynte,
for right anon, oon of the fyres queynte
And quyked agayn, and after that, anon
That oother fyr was queynt, and al agon,
And as it queynte it made a whistelynge,
As doon thise wete brondes in hir brennynge;
And at the brondes ende out ran anoon
As it were blody dropes many oon;

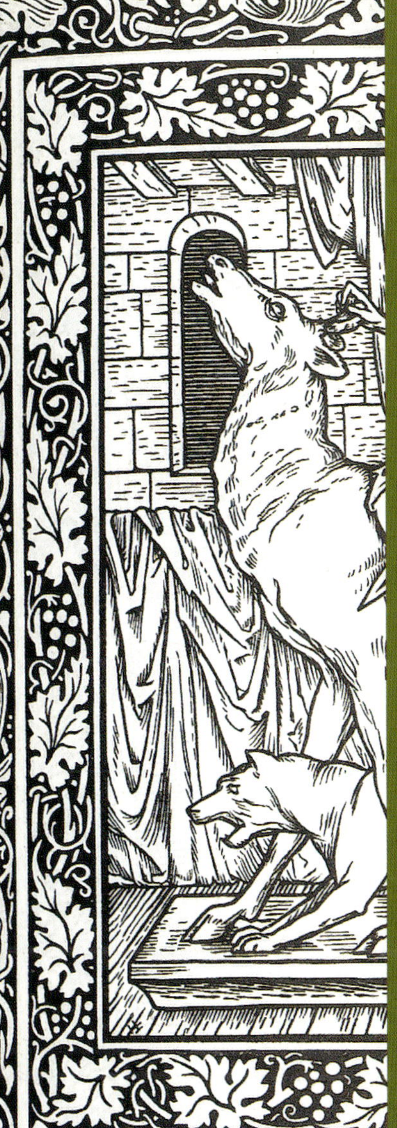

Carvers and Architects

Edward Burne-Jones, William Morris and the Kelmscott Chaucer

Duncan Robinson

Carvers and Architects

Edward Burne-Jones, William Morris and the Kelmscott Chaucer

Duncan Robinson

The illustrated edition of *The Works of Geoffrey Chaucer* published by the Kelmscott Press in 1896 marked the culmination of an artistic partnership formed by two undergraduates, almost half a century earlier. 'When Morris and I were little chaps at Oxford, we should have just gone off our heads if such a book had come out then,' Burne-Jones wrote just before its publication, 'but we have made at the end of our days the very thing we would have made then if we could.'[1]

Throughout his life Morris collected illuminated manuscripts and early printed books. His interest in them was practical, as a keen calligrapher and typographer who enlisted the help of Burne-Jones as his illustrator. In 1874 they collaborated on an illuminated manuscript of Virgil's *Æneid* (Andrew Lloyd-Webber Collection), which Burne-Jones opined 'would put an end to printing.'[2] Far from doing so, it remained unfinished while Morris embarked upon what he referred to as 'my little typographical adventure.'[3]

On 15 November 1888 Morris attended a lecture on printing given by his friend Emery Walker to the Arts and Crafts Exhibition Society. Walker's analogy, that 'type and paper may be said to be to a printed book what stones or bricks and mortar are to architecture,' cannot have failed to strike a chord with the founder of the Society for the Protection of Ancient Buildings. And, as with all of his ventures, Morris insisted on returning to original sources, in this case to the fifteenth-century type-faces designed by Jacobus Rubeus and Nicholas Jenson, and to Caxton, the father of English printing whose translation of Voragine's *Golden Legend* was projected to be the first of his own publications. Once again, Walker proved to be indispensable, with his photographic enlargements of Renaissance fonts and his critiques of Morris's own efforts. Together, the two men visited Joseph Batchelor, the owner of the paper mill in Kent from whom Morris was to obtain all of the hand-made papers for his books. Ink

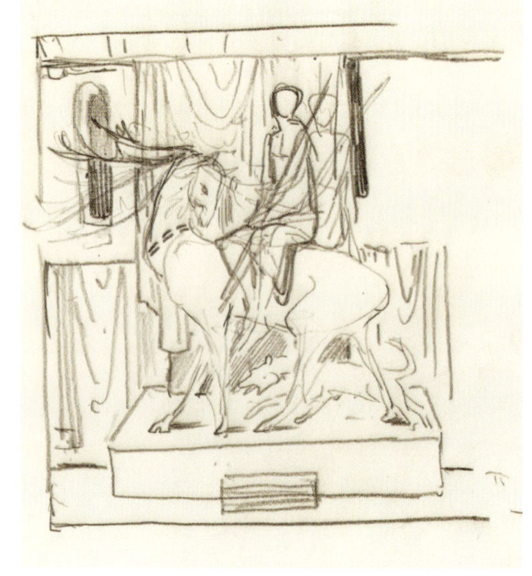

proved to be more problematic. In his determination to avoid the unstable chemistry of modern inks, Morris tested supplies from manufacturers in England and America before Walker pointed him in the direction of Jaenecke of Hanover who used the traditional ingredients of linseed oil and lamp-black to create a product which Morris found entirely satisfactory in spite of Walker's reservation that it 'was tremendously stiff and very hard work for the pressman.' The press itself was an Albion hand-press, bought second-hand. In the words of Halliday Sparling, 'Except for the change from wood to iron, and the substitution of levers for the screw, this press was essentially similar to Caxton's; indeed at the end of an hour or so, Caxton would have been comfortably at home.'[4]

Morris named his Press after his beloved manor of Kelmscott, the country house in Oxfordshire which he described as 'a heaven on earth; an old stone Elizabethan house ... and such a garden! close by the river, a boathouse and all things handy.' Discouraged by the length of *The Golden Legend*, in

LEFT
46. Sir Edward Coley Burne-Jones
1833-1898
Study for the 'Knyghtes Tale'

RIGHT
59. Sir Edward Coley Burne-Jones
1833-1898
William Morris, turning a cartwheel by moonlight

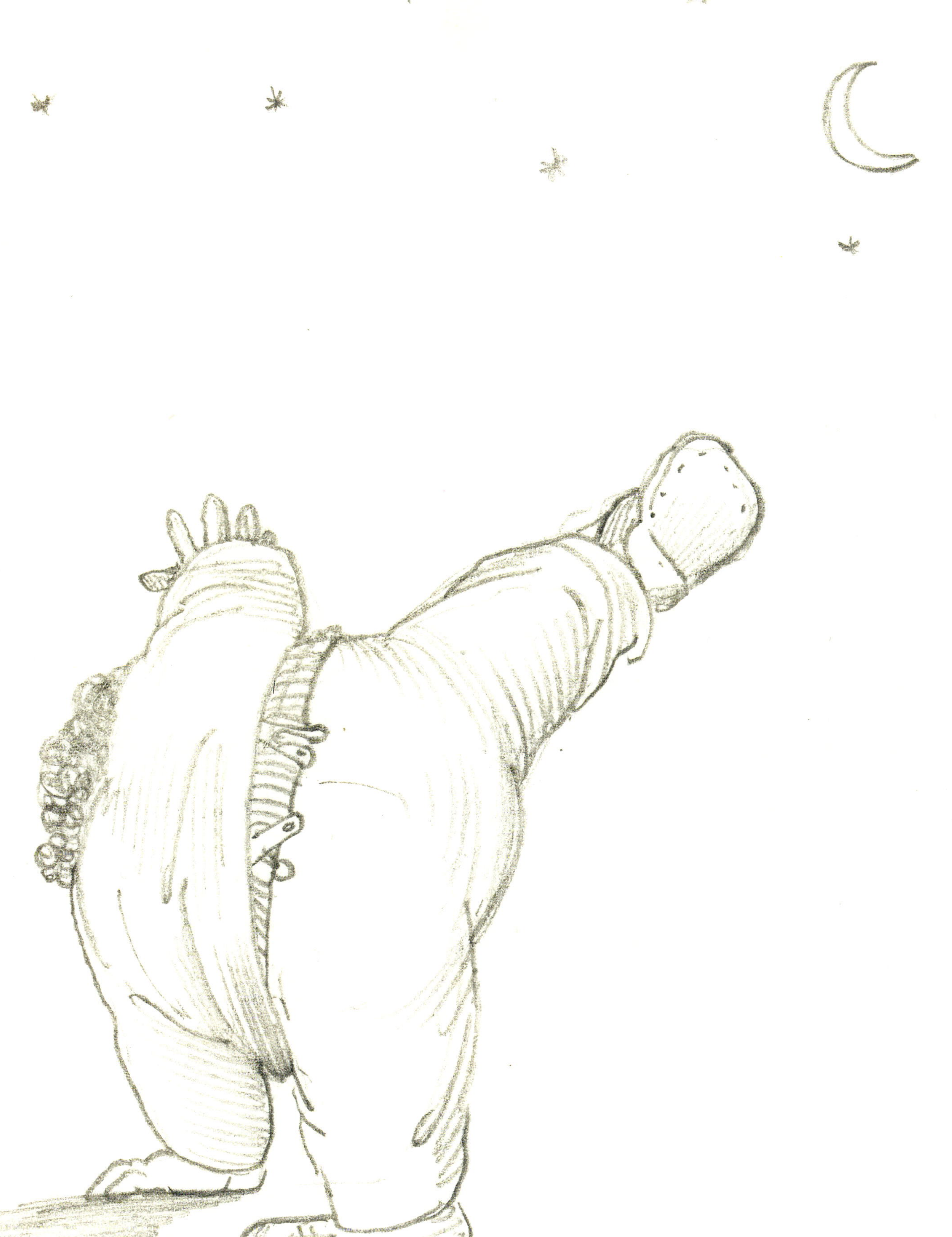

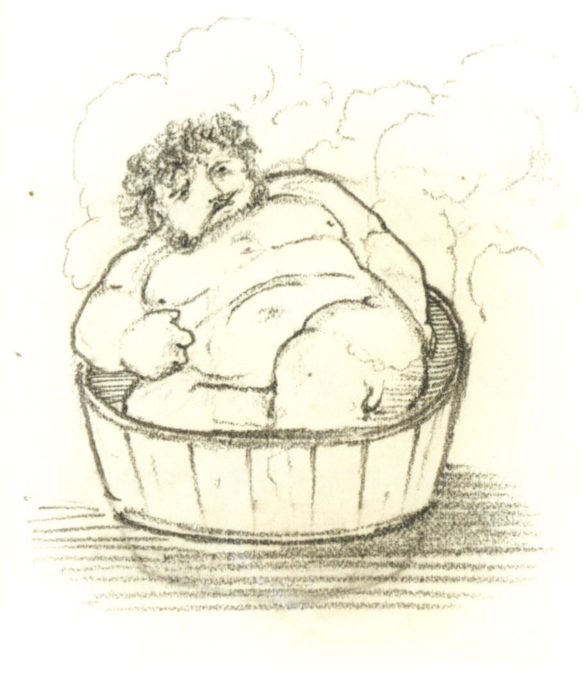

the Spring of 1891 he announced the publication of his own, much shorter, *Glittering Plain*, in small quarto. He rather nervously increased the print run from twenty copies for distribution privately to 200 of which 180 were offered for sale through Reeves and Turner at two guineas, and a further six copies printed on vellum at fifteen guineas. The edition was published on 8 May 1891 and sold out almost at once. The Kelmscott Press was, whether its proprietor liked it or not, a commercial proposition. In his choice of titles Morris revealed a clear agenda. His obligation to Caxton resulted not only in *The Golden Legend* appearing in three large quarto volumes in 1892, but it extended to a new edition of the first book printed in English, *The Recuyell of the Historyes of Troy*, and *The History of Godefrey of Boloyne and of the Conquest of Iherusalem*, 1893. *Beowulf* and Malory were complemented by Morris's friends and contemporaries: Ruskin, Rossetti, Swinburne and Wilfrid Scawen Blunt. But no book matched the size, scope and decorative detail of *The Works of Geoffrey Chaucer*.

The first announcement of the Kelmscott edition of Chaucer, illustrated 'with about sixty designs by E. Burne-Jones,' was made in December 1892. By then, according to Georgiana Burne-Jones, 'the friends (had) sat down dutifully to read Chaucer over again before beginning their work,'[5] with Morris reading aloud from the text while Burne-Jones pondered its challenges for the illustrator. To a handwritten list of contents, in Morris's hand, Burne-Jones added the number of illustrations he proposed for each section. On a rough sketchpad which contains some of his first pictorial thoughts (no.52), he noted: 'There are forty-eight planned here, but I may add to the Knight's Tale? & the early part? there may be sixty in all if I like.' Slowly the number rose; another note records 'seventy-two all and he won't have more.' Morris accepted this and further increases. In a letter to subscribers in November 1894 he informed them that, 'It has been found necessary for the due completion of the above work to add considerably to the number of woodcuts designed by Sir Edward Burne-Jones.' He also announced an increase in the print run from 325 to 425 copies. Six months later, during the summer of 1895, Burne-Jones wrote to Lady Leighton, 'Yesterday I began the last ten that will decorate the last poem, "Troilus and Cressida." Seventy I have done – ten more to do – and in three or four weeks I can breathe and look back on a longish task.' By the end of the year, the final number of woodcut illustrations had reached eighty-seven, and Morris reacted nervously to a visitor to the press who admired especially those arranged in pairs, on opposite pages: 'Now don't you go saying that to Burne-Jones, or he'll be wanting to do the first part over again; and the worst of that would be, that he'd want to do all the rest over again, because the other would be so much better, and then we should never get done.'[6]

Burne-Jones's notes betray his clear preference for the more chivalric and courtly elements in Chaucer's work. In deciding which of the Canterbury Tales to illustrate, he ruled out the more bawdy ones: 'no picture to Miller,' 'no picture to Reeve,' 'no picture to Cook's Tale,' for instance. In a letter to the poet Swinburne he confessed, 'I have abstained from decorating certain of the Canterbury Tales ... Morris has been urgent with me that I should by no means exclude these stories from our scheme of adornment – especially he had hopes of my treatment of the Miller's Tale, but he ever had more robust and daring parts than I could assume.'[7]

In matching Chaucer's text with his own images, Burne-Jones was concerned above all to respect the father of English poetry. 'In the book I am putting myself wholly aside,' he wrote, 'and trying to see things as he saw them; not once have I invaded his kingdom with one hostile thought.' On the other hand, his attempts at literal translation were occasionally thwarted by the rich ambiguities in Chaucer's text. In the dream world of the *Romaunt of the Rose*, for instance, Burne-Jones had great difficulty

LEFT
57. Sir Edward Coley Burne-Jones
1833-1898
William Morris in a bathtub

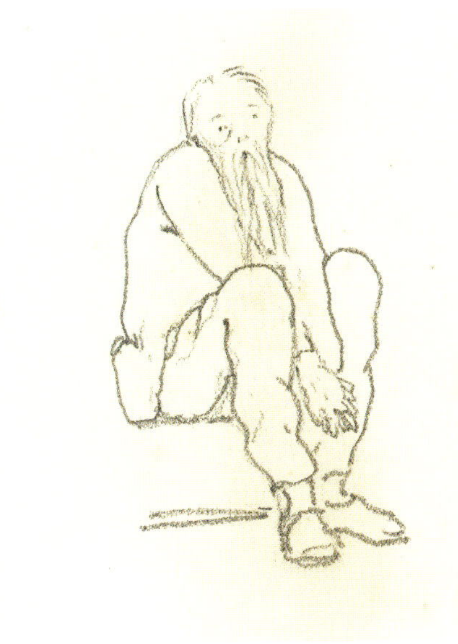

in following the poet on his imaginary journey: 'I wish Chaucer could once for all make up his unrivalled and precious mind whether he is talking of a picture or a statue.'[8] The marginal note on one of his sketches, 'Venus (make her naked never mind Chaucer),' strikes a rare note of independence.

While Burne-Jones was revising and redrawing his ideas for the woodcut illustrations, the production of the Chaucer presented Morris with a series of problems derived from its sheer size and complexity as an illustrated book. Initially he planned to set the text in his 'Troy' type, named for Caxton's *Recuyell*, which he designed in 1891, 'to redeem the Gothic character from the charge of unreadableness which is commonly brought against it.' After setting two trial pages, he realised that the point size was too large to print and bind the Chaucer in a single volume, at which point he ordered a *pica* version. Meanwhile, in spite of his failing health, Morris worked on the designs for the borders, initials and decorated capitals. Like Burne-Jones's illustrations, these had to be converted into woodblocks before they could be printed and once again the project was threatened both by the time-consuming nature of the process and by the sheer volume of material. Fortunately Emery Walker came to the rescue with his camera, persuading Morris to use electrotypes to replicate the woodblocks for the borders and devising the 'platino' or photograph of each of Burne-Jones's finished pencil sketches, over which an intermediary, Robert Catterson-Smith, worked with Indian ink and Chinese white to replace the delicate shading of the original drawings with definitive black-and-white lines. This was then re-photographed onto the wooden block to provide clear guidelines for the woodcutter.

In its final stages of production, the Chaucer became a race against time. Printing began on 8 August 1894 and in January 1895 Morris installed a third Albion press in his small printing works at No. 14 Upper Mall, Hammersmith, so that at least two machines could be dedicated full-time to the task. In May of that year there was a further setback when it was discovered that the oil in the ink had produced a yellow stain on some of the sheets. Fortunately, the solution proved to be a simple one; after exposing them to sunlight the stains faded away and have never reappeared. By January 1896 Burne-Jones was confiding that 'I am getting very anxious about Morris and about the Chaucer. He has not done the title-page yet, which will be such a rich page of ornament, with all the large lettering. I wish he would not leave it any longer.' However, on 21 March 1896 the last three woodblocks were delivered. Easter intervened, described by Morris as 'four mouldy Sundays in a mouldy row, the press shut and Chaucer at a standstill.' Printing was completed on 8 May, and less than a month later the first two copies, bound in pigskin by Douglas Cockerell at the Doves Bindery, were delivered to the two architects. On 26 June 1896 the Kelmscott Chaucer was formally issued, four months before Morris's death. It was in many ways his *nunc dimittis*, or as Burne-Jones predicted while they laboured to complete it, 'it will be a little like a pocket cathedral. My share in it is that of the Carver of images at Amiens, and Morris's that of the Architect and Magister Lapicida.'[9]

RIGHT
55. Sir Edward Coley Burne-Jones
1833–1898
Self-portrait

OVERLEAF
58. Sir Edward Coley Burne-Jones
1833–1898
William Morris, turning a cartwheel

1 Quoted Georgiana Burne-Jones, *Memorials of Edward Burne-Jones*, London, II, 1904, 278.

2 Letter to Charles Eliot Norton, quoted, *ibid*, 56.

3 William Morris, *A Note by William Morris on his Aims in Founding the Kelmscott Press*, November 11, 1895.

4 H. Halliday Sparling, *The Kelmscott Press and William Morris, Master Craftsman*, London, 1924, 60.

5 Burne-Jones, *op. cit*, 217.

6 J.W. Mackail, *The Life of William Morris*, London, 1899, II, 322.

7 Quoted Burne-Jones, *op. cit.*, 217.

8 *ibid.*

9 Burne-Jones *op.cit.*, 278.

Euston Sq:

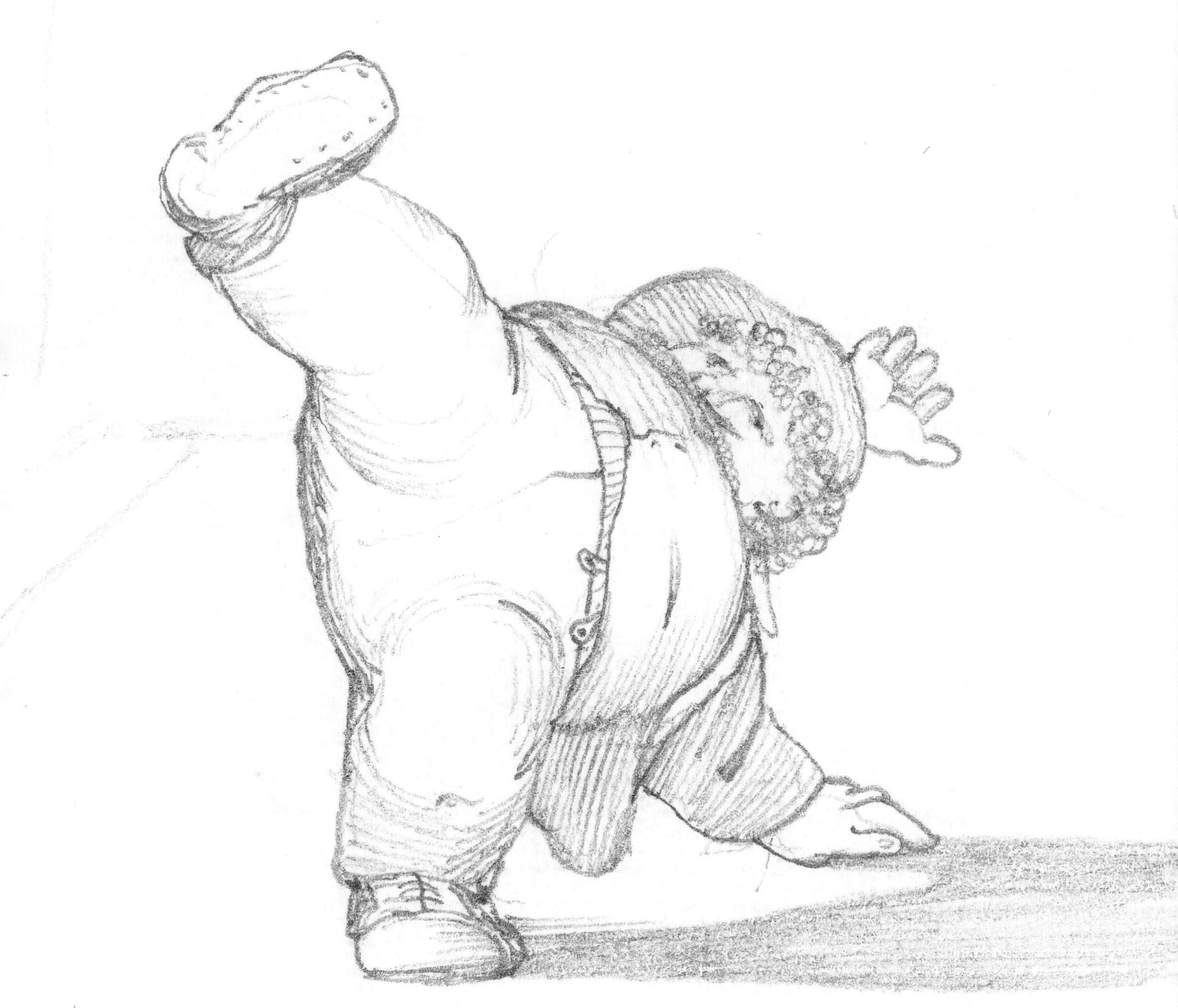

All drawings in this section are by Sir Edward Coley Burne-Jones

1833–1898

45. Preliminary study for *The Knyghtes Tale*

Graphite on paper | 159 x 200mm
Given by Stanley Baldwin, 1921 | no. 1050.6

In this illustration, for page twenty-two, Burne-Jones represents Chaucer's description of the Temple of Venus:

The statue of Venus, glorious for to see
Was naked, fletynge in the large see,
And fro the navele down all covered was
With waves grene, and brighte as any glas.
A citole in her right hand hadde she,
And on hir heed, ful semely for to see,
A rose gerland, fressh and wel smellynge,
Above hir heed her dowves flickerynge.
Biforn hire stood hir sone Cupido
Upon his shuldres wynges hadde he two;
And blynd he was, as it is ofte seene,
A bowe he bar and arwes brighte and kene.

His preliminary drawings show the difficulty he had in first visualising, and then representing, a statue surrounded by water ('fletynge in the large see'), but also his determination to include every one of the details in Chaucer's description.

46. Preliminary study for *The Knyghtes Tale*

Graphite on paper | 332 x 206 mm
Given by the Friends of the Fitzwilliam Museum, 1922 | no.1079.9

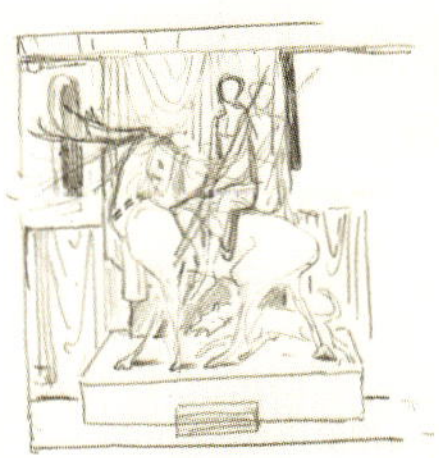

For his treatment of the Temple of Diana Burne-Jones's preliminary sketches show that at first he concentrated on the lines:

And therwithal Dyan gan appere
With bowe in honde, right as a hunteresse

Eventually, however, he decided to treat the much fuller description given by Chaucer some three hundred lines earlier in the poem:

This goddesse on a hert ful hye seet,
With smale houndes al about hir feet,
And undernethe hir feet she hadde a moone.
Wexing it was and sholde wayne soone.
. . . .
With bowe in honde, and armes in a cas,

The preliminary drawing for the hart, a mature red deer, shows the lengths to which Burne-Jones went to achieve accuracy in his representation of detail in Chaucer's description.

47. Preliminary study for *The Knyghtes Tale:* Diana's hind in profile to left, head and upper neck absent

Graphite on laid paper | 332 x 206 mm
Given by the Friends of the Fitzwilliam Museum, 1922 | no. 1079.7

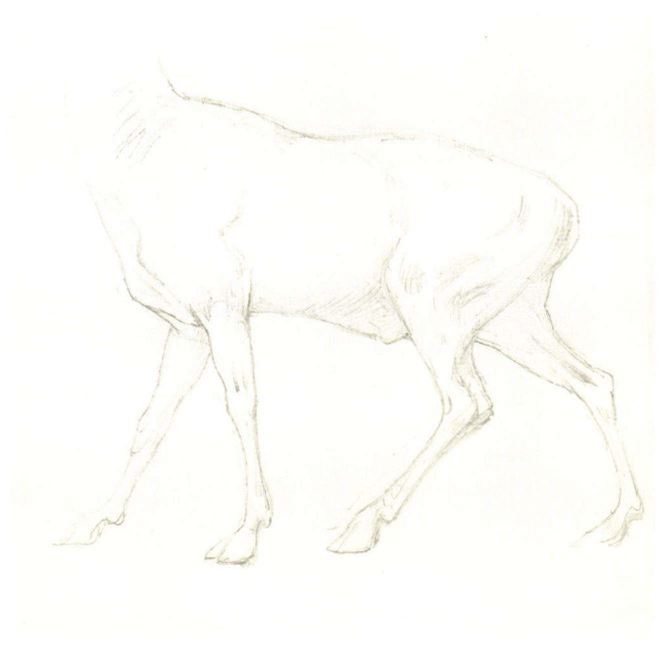

48. Two preliminary studies for *The Knyghtes Tale:* above, study of statue of Diana mounted upon deer with globe visible below; below, Emily praying before the statue of Diana

Black crayon on paper | 332 x 209 mm
Given by the Friends of the Fitzwilliam Museum, 1922
no. 1079.8

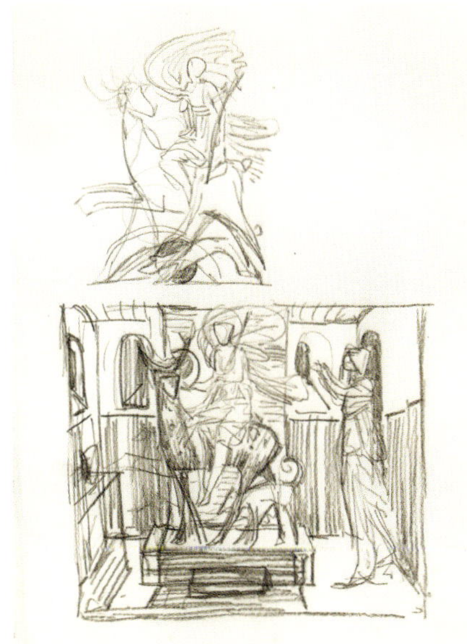

49. Intermediate study for *The Knyghtes Tale:* Emily praying before the statue of Diana

Graphite on laid paper | 178 x 252 mm
Given by the Friends of the Fitzwilliam Museum, 1922 | no. 1079.10

50. *The Knyghtes Tale:* Emily praying to Diana

Graphite on paper | 154 x 197 mm
Given by Stanley Baldwin, 1921 | no. 1050.5

51. Nine preliminary studies for *The Knyghtes Tale*

Graphite and black crayon on paper | 325 x 213 mm
Given by the Friends of the Fitzwilliam Museum, 1922 | no. 1079.12

For page 24. The Temple of Mars posed particular problems for Burne-Jones. Chaucer described it as follows:

The statue of Mars upon a carte stood,
Armed, and looked grym as he were wood;
. . . .
A wolf ther stood biforn hym at his feet
With eyen rede, and of a man he eet.

Burne-Jones's preliminary sketches show Mars standing and brandishing a sword before he decided to deviate from the text and seat the god, enthroned in a way that recalls the figure of Injustice in medieval allegories of the vices and virtues. Clearly, the detail of a wolf devouring its human victim also exercised the artist, to judge from the number of abbreviated but vigorous sketches he made of the motif.

52. Order of Chaucer

Pen and brown ink on lined paper | 323 x 202 mm
Given by the Friends of the Fitzwilliam Museum, 1922 | no. 1079.1

In this rough sketchpad, Burne-Jones noted down his first ideas for the illustrations to Chaucer. He was originally commissioned to execute 'about sixty' designs but in the end, with Morris's accord, this number rose to eighty-seven. In his role as illustrator, Burne-Jones set out to put himself 'wholly aside'. All the same, he had a distinct preference for the romantic and courtly tales, over the more bawdy passages in, for example, 'The Miller's Tale' and 'The Cook's Tale'.

53. The Works of Geoffrey Chaucer

Ornamented by E. Burne-Jones and engraved by W.H. Hooper.
One of 425 copies. Bound in pigskin by the Doves bindery.
The Kelmscott Press. Hammersmith, Middlesex, 1896
Bequeathed by Jane Alice Morris, 1935

This copy of the Chaucer was presented by Morris to his daughter, Jane, with 'best love', on 6 June 1896.

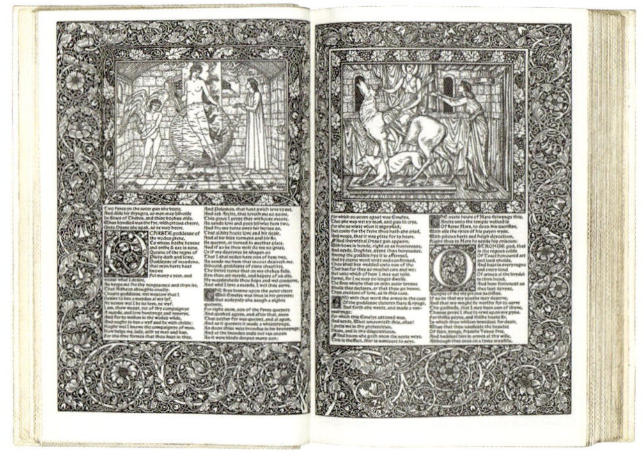

54. A Note by William Morris on his Aims in Founding the Kelmscott Press Together with a Short Description of the Press by S. C. Cockerell and an Annotated List of the Books Printed Thereat 8vo. Golden type, with five pages of the Troy and Chaucer types. Dated 4 March, issued 24 March, 1898.

The young Cockerell attracted the attention of Morris in 1886 and rapidly became indispensable to the older man. After cataloguing Morris's extensive library, he became, in 1894, the Secretary of the Kelmscott Press. In his diary for 30 August 1896 he recorded 'W.M. asked me whether I should be prepared to carry on the Press after his death, with Walker, and I said that I was in favour of it ceasing – as otherwise it would fizzle out by degrees, and the books already issued would suffer by inferior ones following them.' After Morris's death it fell to Cockerell to see to the completion of the books in press and then to wind it up. The type was deposited at the Cambridge University Press, electrotypes were destroyed, and the woodblocks for initials, ornaments and illustrations were given to the British Museum on condition that they were not used for a period of a hundred years. Ten years later, Cockerell became the director of the Fitzwilliam Museum and in due course persuaded the heirs of both Morris and Burne-Jones to give and bequeath much of the Kelmscott material the museum now holds.

Sir Edward Coley Burne-Jones

1833-1898

Five caricatures, all graphite on paper.

Each graphite on paper | Bought, as part of an album of drawings, with a contribution from the MGC / V&A Purchase Grant Fund, 1998. | PD.55-1998

Throughout his life, Burne-Jones amused his friends and his family with a constant stream of caricatures, often visual teases of his most intimate circle, and frequently used self-caricatures to cheer himself out of a gloomy mood. Rossetti paralleled this in literary terms by writing doggerel rhymes about his friends and associates (and sometimes even his enemies):

There is a young Painter called Jones
(A cheer here, and hisses, and groans):
The state of his mind
Is a shame to mankind,
But a matter of triumph to Jones

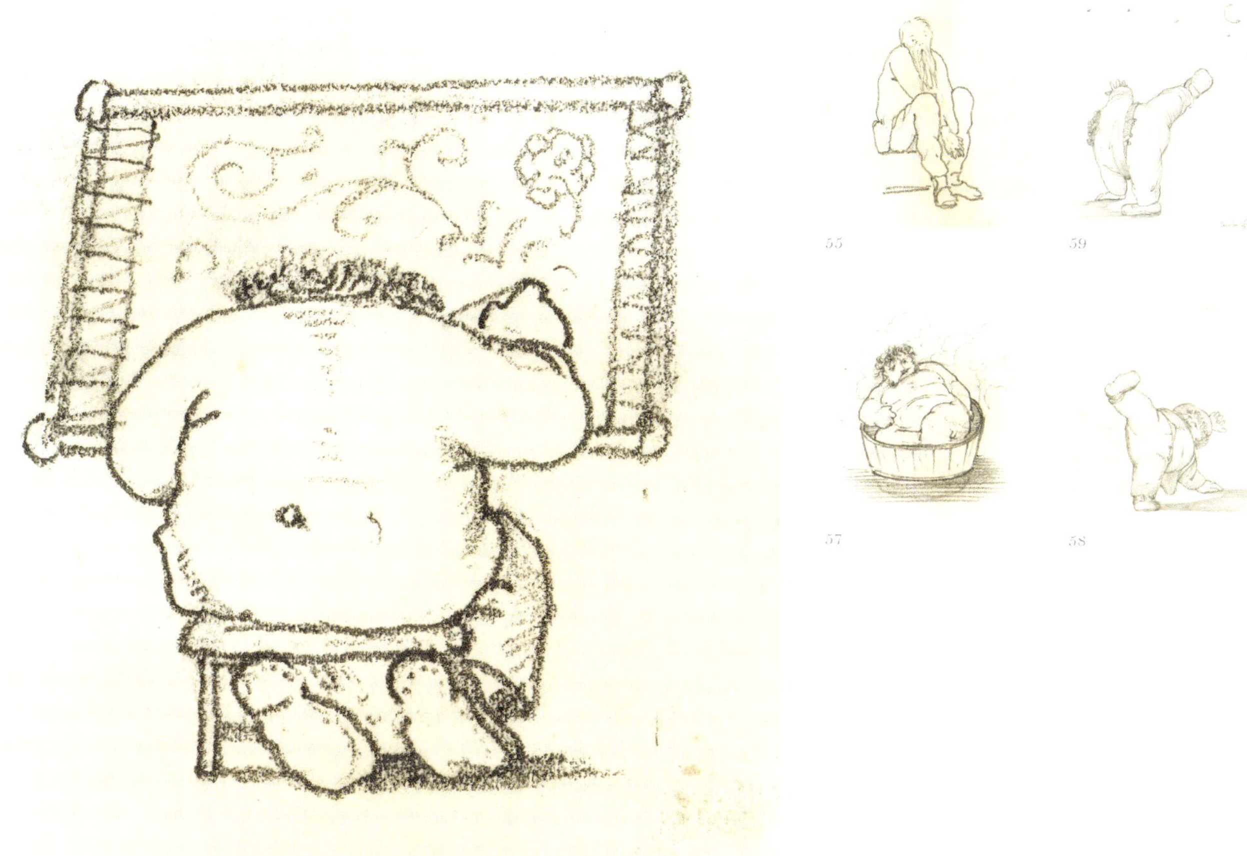

55 59 57 58

56

Literary caricature appealed greatly to him: among contemporary authors, he adored the comic characters of Charles Dickens: Sam Weller, in *The Pickwick Papers*, Mr McCawber in *David Copperfield* and Mrs Gump in *Martin Chuzzlewit* are all said to have made him 'guffaw'.

Morris's rotundity, explosive character, Falstaffian gusto and immense energy and appetites made him an especially easy target. He was, William Michael Rossetti remembered, the only member of their circle to practice any form of sporting activity, such as fishing or boating and, presumably, turning cartwheels (*Reminiscences*, I, 1906, 214). 'His frame was cast in a large mould,' he wrote, 'but he was by no means tall. ... turbulent, restless, noisy (with a deep and rather gruff voice), brusque in his movements, addicted to stumbling over doorsteps, breaking down the solid-looking chairs the moment he took his seat in them, and doing scores of things inconsistent with the nerves of the nervous. He relished a good glass of wine, and was by no means averse to a savoury dinner, and an ample one' (I, 1906, 215). 'Top' or 'Topsy' to Burne-Jones's 'Ned', he was able to counter his 'volcanic' temper with an endearing ability to laugh at himself, 'he took the chaff (in a double sense) along with the grain.'

Each of these caricatures brilliantly – and fondly – captures something of Morris's vigorous presence and personality. The willowy Burne-Jones emphasises his girth by squeezing him into a bath tub, raising his trousers to half-mast, and making him burst out of his waistcoat (in fact Burne-Jones and Charles Faulkner once played the practical joke of stitching its lining to make it smaller!). His shabby appearance was legendary; in 1949 Bernard Shaw reminded Cockerell of an occasion when Morris went to buy a manuscript valued at hundreds of pounds, but when he arrived in his usual dishevelled state the dealer found it difficult at first sight to believe 'that he was good for more than five shillings' (Meynell, 1956, 192).

To Rossetti, he looked like a veritable knight of the Round Table, while for Shaw, he was simply the 'patriarch', someone whose energies belied the fact that he always looked older than his real age '60 at 50, though a magnificent 60' (Laurence, 1972, 555). On a more sober note, Thomas Hardy could not but feel that his intelligence and force of personality had been misspent: 'what a strenuous character Morris's was,' he told Cockerell in 1917, 'My feeling is (though probably not yours) that he wasted on weaving what was meant for mankind at large. He may, however, have been helpless in the force of his tendencies' (Purdy and Millgate, V, 1985, 203).

JM

55. Self-portrait

135 x 91 mm | f.2

56. William Morris weaving

136 x 92 mm | f.4

57. William Morris in a bathtub

137 x 90 mm | f.7

58. William Morris, turning a cartwheel

181 x 126 mm. Inscribed, top right Euston Sq. | f.11

59. William Morris, turning a cartwheel by moonlight

182 x 126 mm. Inscribed, lower right: Euston Sq. | f.12

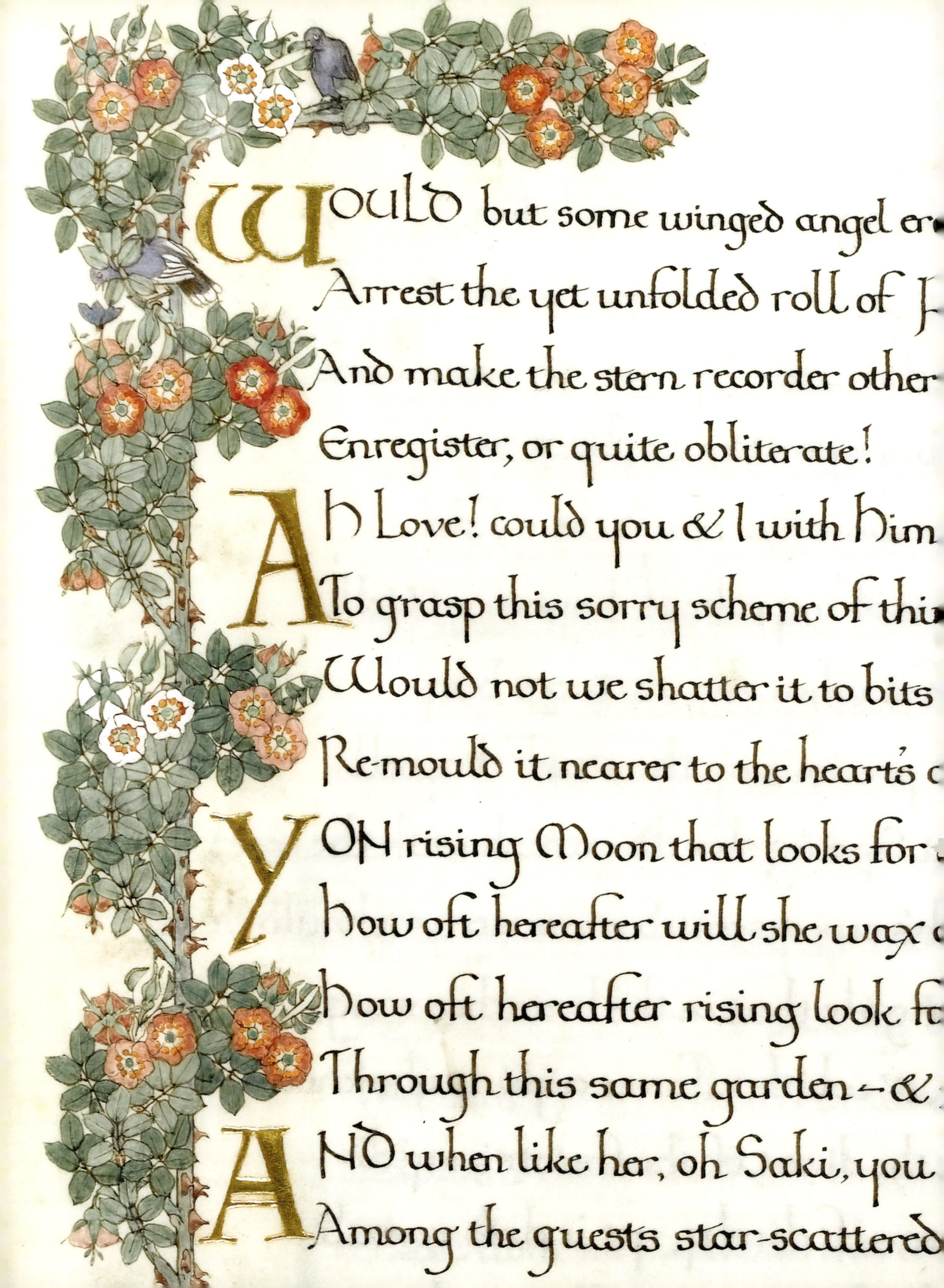

WOULD but some winged angel er
Arrest the yet unfolded roll of
And make the stern recorder other
Enregister, or quite obliterate!
AH Love! could you & I with Him
To grasp this sorry scheme of thi
Would not we shatter it to bits
Re-mould it nearer to the heart's
YON rising Moon that looks for
How oft hereafter will she wax
How oft hereafter rising look f
Through this same garden – &
AND when like her, oh Saki, you
Among the guests star-scattered

From Popular Press to Book Beautiful

Grace Brockington

From Popular Press to Book Beautiful

Grace Brockington

In the last half of the nineteenth century, British book and periodical illustration went through a cycle of artistic revival, technological transformation and aesthetic reaction, driven by, and in turn promoting, economic change, ideological debate, and a culture of creative collaboration between artists and writers. This process involved practitioners such as Dante Gabriel Rossetti, John Everett Millais, William Morris, and Lucien Pissarro, working alongside those who are now more obscure. It provided many artists with their bread and butter, but it also raised troubling questions about the status of illustration as an art, compared with traditionally more prestigious genres such as oil painting; and it generated a range of approaches to the relationship between text and image, many of which recur in different contexts throughout this exhibition.

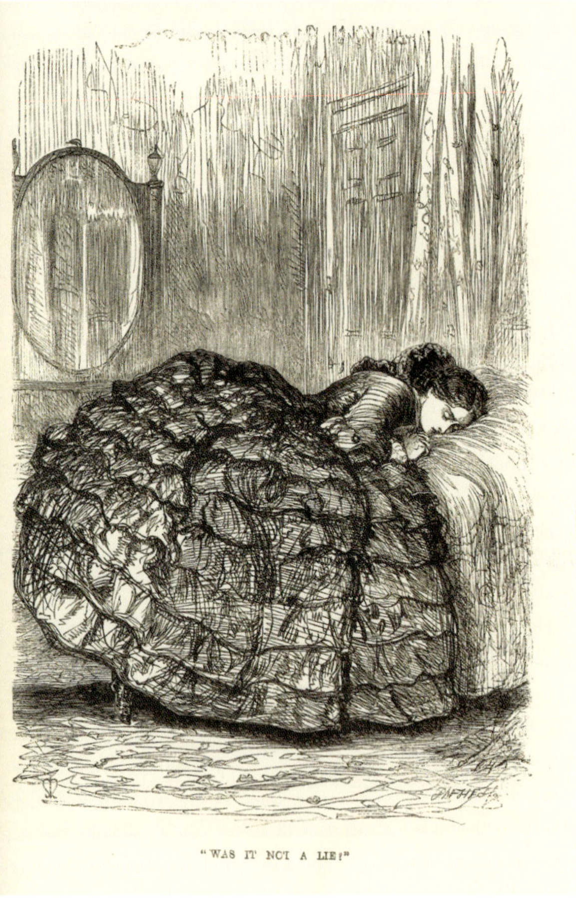

LEFT
62. John Everett Millais
1829-1896
"Was it not a lie?", Framley Parsonage

The Popular Press

During the 1850s and 1860s, renewed interest in wood-engraved reproduction coincided with a massive growth in periodical publication, leading to an apparent 'Golden Age' of illustrated magazines. Papers such as *The Cornhill Magazine* (1860-1871) and *Once a Week* (1859-1871) achieved enormous circulations (120,000 and 160,000 respectively) without exhausting the market. They and dozens of others employed the most successful artists of the day, including Millais, James McNeill Whistler and Frederick Leighton, to illustrate stories, poems and serialised novels, often by equally famous writers such as William Makepeace Thackeray, Anthony Trollope and George Eliot. The wood-engraving business expanded to meet the demand for illustrations, with companies such as the Dalziel Brothers commissioning artists and acting as middlemen between them, the authors and the publishers, as well as employing teams of engravers to interpret their work. For many artists, periodical publication became a way of earning a living, while the best among them raised illustration to the status of an imaginative art.

Various factors – economic, technical, social and aesthetic – contributed to the success of the periodicals.[1] With the near-completion of the rail network during the 1850s, distribution became simpler, cheaper and more efficient. Fiscal reform eased the tax burden for publishers, while the use of esparto (North African grass) rather than rags in the manufacturing process made paper cheaper.[2] After 1852, prices fell as the Book Sellers' Association lost its right to protect the market. At the same time, middle-class incomes rose

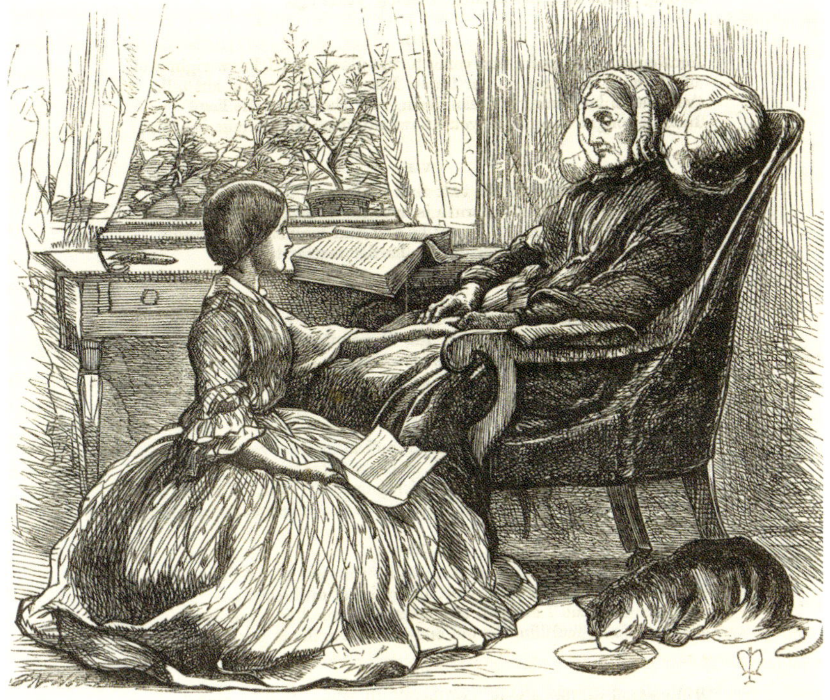

ABOVE
65. John Everett Millais
1829-1896
The Grandmother's Apology
Wood engraving

significantly compared with the cost of living, creating a new market for the magazines. Improved literacy among the working classes expanded the readership still further. Religious education programmes run by the Sunday School Movement (founded 1780), the Religious Tract Society (1799) and the British and Foreign Bible Society (1804), together with changes in primary school teaching methods, generated a hunger for reading matter. Not everyone approved of the results. In 1871, Matthew Arnold complained that 'the mighty engine of literature in the education of the working classes, amounts to little more, even when most successful, than giving them the power to read the newspapers.'[3] However, it was the seemingly ephemeral publications, like newspapers and periodicals, which facilitated a renaissance of British wood-engraved illustration.

The imaginative flair and bold execution that characterised 'Sixties' periodical illustration set it apart. Excited by the narrative possibilities of illustrative work, Pre-Raphaelites such as Rossetti, Millais and William Holman Hunt led the revival. Their images told their own story, whether or not they related directly to the given text. Millais in particular developed his illustrative technique over several decades, excelling on the one hand at the domestic dramas of contemporary novelists, on the other, at the common lore of myth and parable. His illustrations for the novels of Anthony Trollope (nos.62-64), published in various magazines, show how an artist could work with or against a text, to make a story memorable to his readership. For the most part, Trollope appreciated Millais's interpretations, calling them 'conscientious,' and true to the text.[4] Yet *Was it not a Lie?* (no.62) infuriated him. He found the woman's enormous crinoline particularly objectionable, until he glimpsed someone wearing an identical skirt, and had to concede that Millais's work was true to life, if not to his own imaginative world.

The ability of such images to stand on their own became a strength, artistically and financially, but it also made them vulnerable to criticism from those who missed a closer-knit relationship between text and image. The increasing size of wood engravings meant that they could easily be taken out of context, lifted from the magazine and framed, or reprinted in a deluxe edition. For instance, *Millais's Illustrations* (1866) reproduced the artist's book and periodical work without any accompanying text, while *The Cornhill Gallery* (1865), took a selection of illustrative gems from the *The Cornhill Magazine* and paired them with new passages of prose or verse. Printed from the wood on superior paper, rather than from metal, these reissues were often better quality than the original run. They increased the prestige of wood-engraved illustration as a serious art, but weakened the relationship with the stories and poems that ostensibly inspired the images.

After 1880, the wood-engraving industry overreached itself. The demand for illustrative work was such that new photographic and electrical techniques of reproduction superseded the labour-intensive process of engraving. Engravers had welcomed the arrival of mechanically-powered presses, replacing the slow old hand presses, and the use of photography to transfer an artist's design onto a block was cheaper and easier. Rather than drawing directly onto the woodblock, artists could now retain their original design, and sell it separately. Eventually, however, new technologies such as zincography and electrotyping rendered wood engraving commercially obsolete. Once great companies, like the Dalziel Brothers, fell into decline, leaving the craft of wood engraving open for rediscovery as an illustrative art.

The Book Beautiful

By the 1890s, the drive for quantities of cheap illustrative material had provoked a back-lash from artists who resented what they saw as the aesthetic compromise of magazine work. Led by William

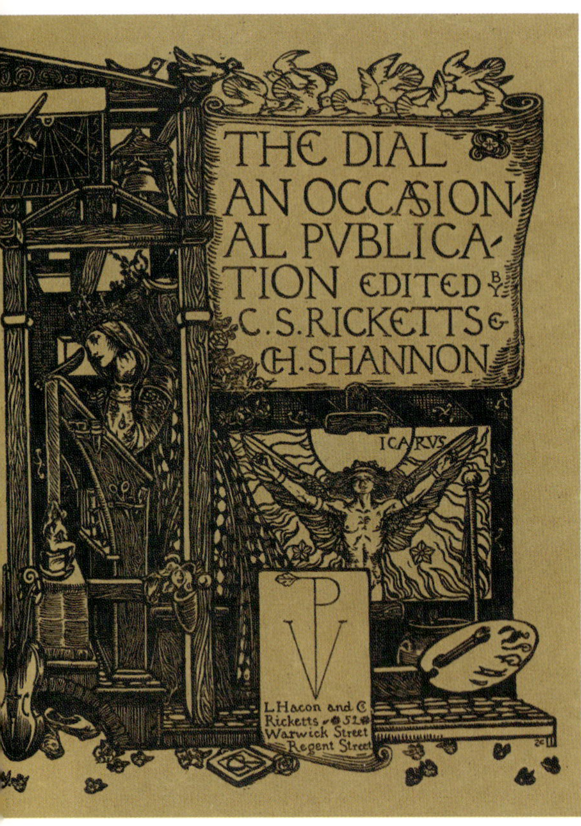

Morris at his Kelmscott Press, artist-craftsmen reacted against an industry characterised by mass-production, mechanisation and the division of labour between artist, engraver, publisher and binder. A number of presses, including the Eragny (1894), Ashendene (1895), Vale (1896), Essex House (1898) and Doves (1900) sprang up, all inspired by Morris's Arts-and-Crafts philosophy of careful workmanship and integrated design. Seeking to recover the loving labour of wood engraving and to restore the unity between word and image, they exerted a lasting influence on book illustration and production. The 1969 Circle Press edition of Rossetti's *Chimes* (no.68) demonstrates how arts-and-crafts values endured, coming full circle to reproduce and reinterpret the words of an artist who helped to initiate the revival of wood-engraved illustration a hundred years earlier.

The private presses worked to rehabilitate a relationship between artist and author, word and image, which they felt had been vitiated by the periodical press. Morris appreciated the quality of work by illustrators like Fred Walker (nos. 60, 61), but felt that its very detail and delicacy of line made his technique unsuitable for books. Burne-Jones, his collaborator at the Kelmscott Press, voiced their common frustration, when he complained that *Once a Week* was full of 'stupid, senseless rot that takes an artist half a minute to sketch and an engraver half a week to engrave,' time which, if properly used, 'might fill England with beautiful work.'[5] Taking his cue from the medieval woodcuts of the fifteenth century, Morris created simpler, firmer designs to harmonise with the solid shapes of the typescript. Moreover, he articulated a persuasive philosophy of aesthetic and social unity, based on the principle that 'illustrations should not have a mere accidental connection with the other ornaments and the type, but an essential and artistic connection.'[6] Such statements gave the Book Beautiful movement intellectual weight, perpetuating the impact of the 1890s presses after the relatively brief span of their operation.

It was perhaps the new magazines of the 1890s, rather than the Book Beautiful, that presented the most direct antithesis to the popular periodicals. Short-lived but influential journals such as *The Dial* (1889-1897) and *The Savoy* (January-December 1896) complemented the private presses in their efforts to achieve a more integrated visual effect on the printed page. Arthur Symons, writer, scholar and editor of *The Savoy*, described it as 'a new kind of magazine, which was to appeal to the public equally in its letterpress and its illustrations.'[7] *The Dial*, published by Charles Ricketts and Charles Shannon in five occasional numbers, complemented the efforts of their Vale Press to bridge the gap between design and execution. As their advertisements stipulated, 'the woodcuts and lithographs are directly from the hand of the artists and not photographic reproductions. All

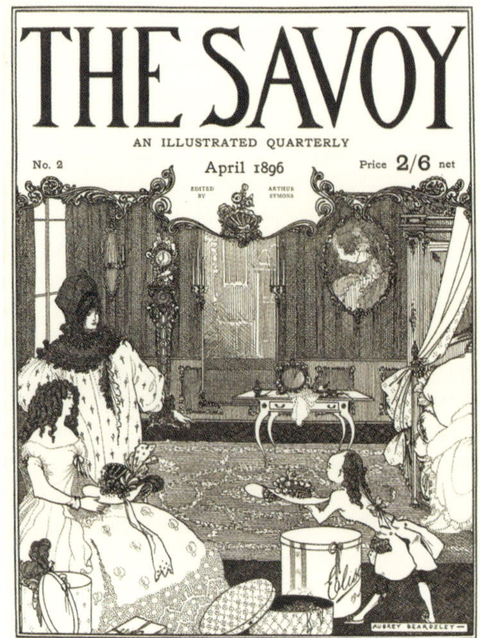

TOP LEFT
81. *The Dial: An occasional publication*
London, Vale Press, vol. 3., 1893

LEFT
83. *The Savoy*
London, Leonard Smithers. no. 2, April 1896.

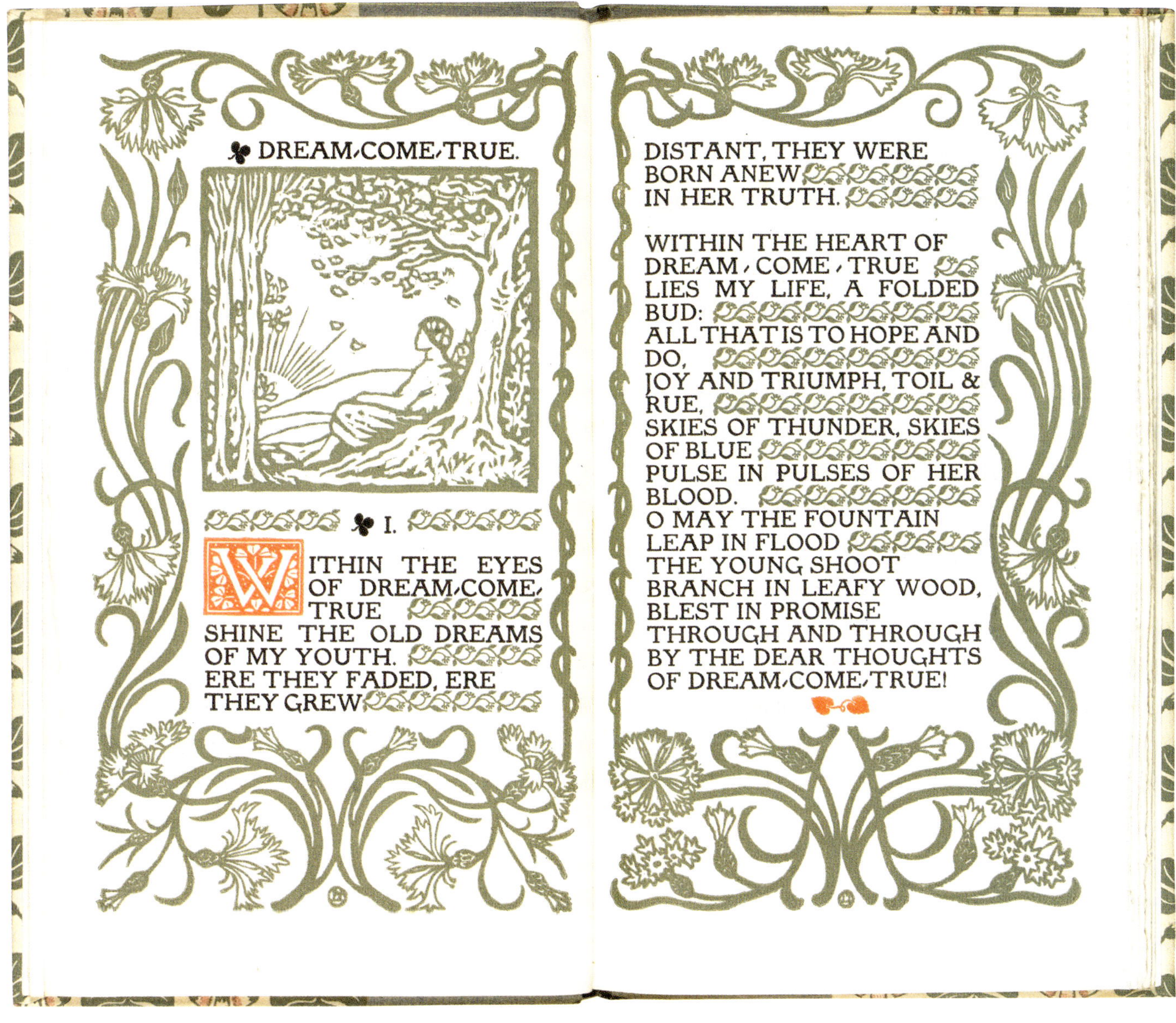

DREAM-COME-TRUE.

I.

WITHIN THE EYES OF DREAM-COME-TRUE
SHINE THE OLD DREAMS OF MY YOUTH.
ERE THEY FADED, ERE THEY GREW
DISTANT, THEY WERE BORN ANEW
IN HER TRUTH.

WITHIN THE HEART OF DREAM-COME-TRUE
LIES MY LIFE, A FOLDED BUD:
ALL THAT IS TO HOPE AND DO,
JOY AND TRIUMPH, TOIL & RUE,
SKIES OF THUNDER, SKIES OF BLUE
PULSE IN PULSES OF HER BLOOD.
O MAY THE FOUNTAIN LEAP IN FLOOD
THE YOUNG SHOOT BRANCH IN LEAFY WOOD,
BLEST IN PROMISE THROUGH AND THROUGH
BY THE DEAR THOUGHTS OF DREAM-COME-TRUE!

ABOVE
74. Laurence Binyon
1869-1943
Dream-Come-True

the woodcuts have been printed from the wood to ensure the greater sweetness in the printing.'[8] In terms of profit and circulation, it would be misleading to compare such experimental magazines with the mass-produced periodicals. *The Dial* was deliberately limited to 200 copies per issue, while *The Savoy* folded within a year. In terms of literary and aesthetic innovation, however, they made themselves known far beyond their immediate readership.

The Book Beautiful, as developed by Morris, Ricketts and their circles, embodied the ideal of good living and working which also motivated their ventures in architecture and interior design. As Morris stated, 'to enjoy good houses and good books in self-respect and decent comfort, seems to me to be the pleasurable end towards which all societies of human beings ought now to struggle.'[9] However, the fate of the private presses and periodicals also demonstrated the economic flaw that weakened the Arts and Crafts movement, undermining its claim to offer an alternative to the industrialised, urban misery of late nineteenth-century Britain. Despite his socialist principles, Morris's Kelmscott Press relied on substantial investment, high prices, and a coterie of friends and supporters, to survive financially. An astute businessman, Morris employed engravers and printers to execute his designs. While the resulting books were aesthetically beautiful and crafted to the highest standard, the process of production compromised the holistic model of the Artist-Craftsman. When Lucien and Esther Pissarro

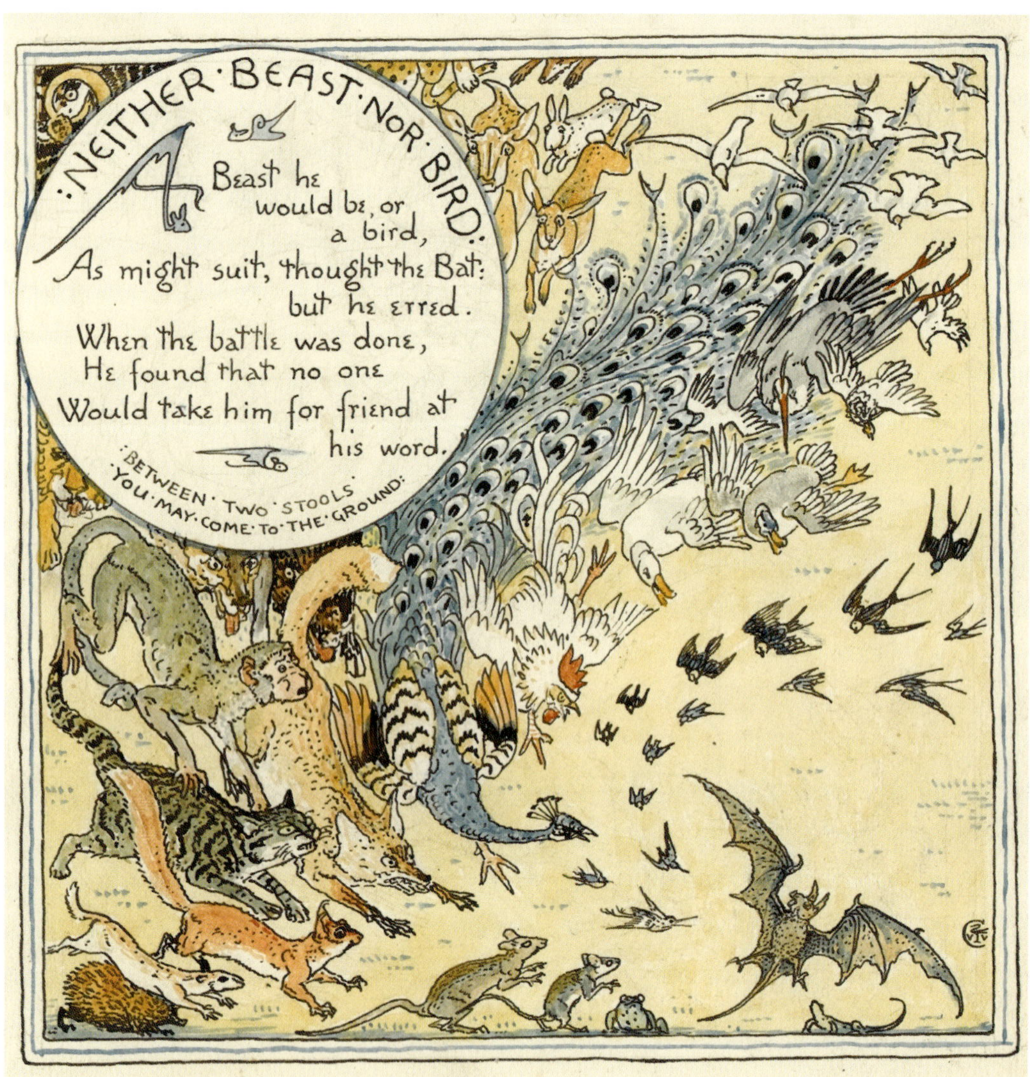

founded the Eragny Press in 1894, they believed they could emulate the Kelmscott success, combining art and commerce to make a useful living. Yet without capital, connections, or any division of labour between artist and craftsmen, the Eragny struggled financially, and produced disappointingly few books – thirty-two in twenty years, compared with Morris's fifty-two in seven.[10] As, one by one, the presses of the 1890s revival closed (the Eragny in 1914, Ashendene in 1915, Vale in 1904, Essex House in 1910 and Doves in 1916) it became clear that the Book Beautiful could never replace the periodical press as an item of daily life. Instead, it created an enduring market for luxury books that has more in keeping with the French *livre d'artiste* than with Morris's socialist aspirations. The tension between the needs of artist, author and producer, text and image, art and economics, that characterised book and periodical illustration during the second half of the nineteenth century, remained unresolved.

ABOVE
71. Walter Crane
Baby's Own Aesop Being the Fables Condensed in Rhyme with Portable Morals

1 Paul Goldman, *Victorian Illustrated Books 1850–1870: The heyday of wood-engraving*, London, 1994, 33–44.

2 In 1855, compulsory stamp duty ended. In 1861, paper duty was abolished.

3 Matthew Arnold, *Reports on Elementary Schools*, London, 1871, 129, 157.

4 Quoted in *Life and Letters of Sir John Everett Millais, by his Son*, London, I, 1899, 282–288.

5 Georgiana Burne-Jones, *Memorials of Edward Burne-Jones*, London, I, 1904, 254–255.

6 William Morris, *The Ideal Book: Essays and lectures on the arts of the book*, ed. William S. Petersen, Berkeley and Los Angeles, 1982, 40.

7 Karl Beckson, ed., *The Memoirs of Arthur Symons: Life and art in the 1890s*, London, 1977, 170.

8 Advertisement for second issue of *The Dial* (1892).

9 Morris, *op. cit*, 1.

10 Marcella D. Genz, *A History of the Eragny Press 1894–1914*, London, 2004, 43–44.

Frederick Walker

1840-1875

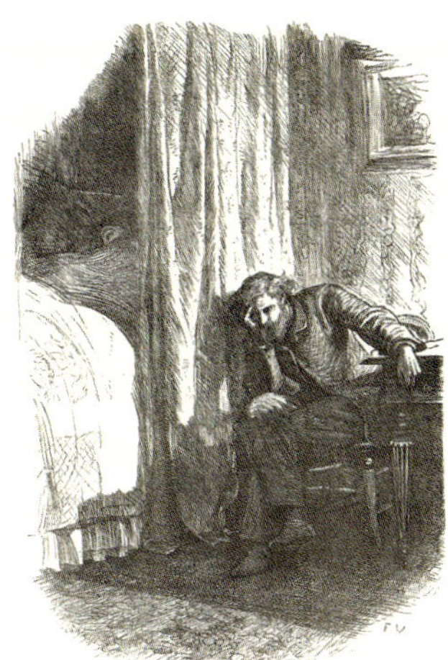

60. Paterfamilias

Wood engraving | Engraved by Joseph Swain | 228 x 145 mm
Bequeathed by Henry Scipio Reitlinger, 1991 | P.1456-1991

61. Nach Zehn Jahren (After Ten Years)

Wood engraving | Engraved by Joseph Swain | 240 x 161 mm
Bequeathed by Henry Scipio Reitlinger, 1991 | P.1474-1991

A key member of the 'Idyllic School' of illustrators, which specialised in realistic yet palatable scenes of everyday life, Walker contributed regularly to the periodical press from 1860. These designs for *The Cornhill Magazine* and *Once a Week*, engraved by the Dalziel's chief competitor, Joseph Swain, both deal with the popular Victorian themes of family relationships and domestic drama. Walker's illustrations to Thackeray's last finished novel, *The Adventures of Philip*, serialised in *The Cornhill Magazine* from 1861-1862, established his reputation. He acquired the commission after approaching the publisher, George Smith, who invited him to interpret Thackeray's sketches for his novel. Boldly, he insisted on creating his own designs instead, with which the author was fortunately satisfied. *Paterfamilias*, a scene from chapter thirty-five (May 1862), shows Philip hunched disconsolately at his wife's bedside as she sleeps next to their baby daughter. Having quarreled with his boss, his career as a journalist is under threat and he realises that he is failing in his patriarchal duty to provide for his family.

Illustrating a translation of 'Nach Zehn Jahren' by the German poet and playwright Emmanuel Geibel (1815-84), *After Ten Years* (*Once a Week*, 28 March 1863) depicts an emotional reunion between brother and sister. Faithful in spirit to the verses printed beneath, Walker has adapted certain details, choosing not to show the boys 'climbing up to kiss' their uncle, or the smallest child who 'put out its little hands to feel for me.' He also obscures the uncle's 'great beard,' muting the encounter between youth and age which leads in the poem to a reflection on the passing of time and the inevitable approach of death.

LG

John Everett Millais

1829-1896

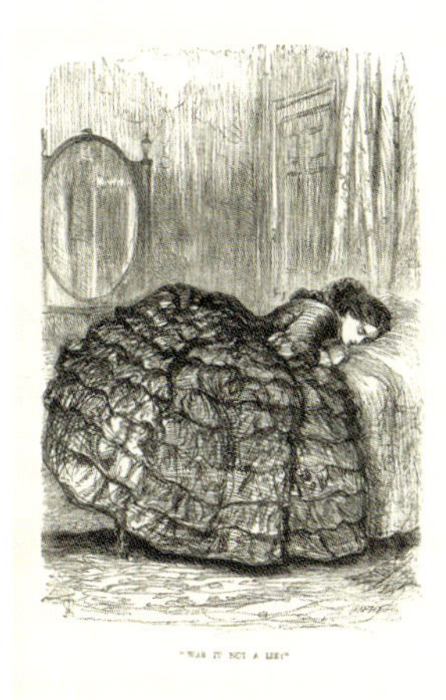

62. 'Was it not a lie?', Framley Parsonage

Wood engraving | Engraved by the Dalziel Family | 215 x 138 mm
Bequeathed by Henry Scipio Reitlinger, 1991 | P.1081-1991

The serialisation of *Framley Parsonage* in *The Cornhill Magazine* marked the start of a unique partnership between Trollope and Millais, who went on to produce a further eighty-six illustrations for the author. Published in sixteen installments (1860-1861), with six works by Millais, the hugely popular *Framley Parsonage* was Trollope's first piece of serialised fiction. *Was it not a Lie?* (June 1860), Millais's second illustration for the novel, depicts the dramatic moment when the humble Lucy Robarts, having denied her love for Lord Lufton and rejected his marriage proposal, flings herself on the bed and asks, 'Was it not a lie — knowing as she did that she loved him with all her loving heart?'As in all but one case, the subject was selected by Millais, with the publisher, George Smith, requesting a caption from Trollope. Heavily overworked, the artist forgot the assignment and was obliged to complete it in a rush, leading to a rare complaint from Trollope, who declared the picture 'simply ludicrous' and asked for it to be omitted, but was later consoled when he saw a lady wearing the exact same style of dress.

LG

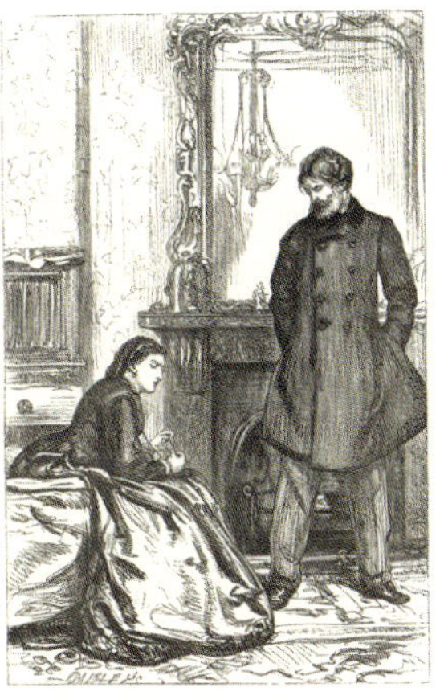

63. 'Why, on earth, on Sunday?', The Small House at Allington

Wood engraving | Engraved by the Dalziel Family |219 x 138 mm
Bequeathed by Henry Scipio Reitlinger, 1991 | P.1098-1991

The Small House at Allington marked Trollope's third collaboration with Millais, who produced eighteen full-page illustrations and nineteen chapter-heading vignettes to accompany the serialisation in *The Cornhill Magazine*. *Why on Earth, on Sunday?* (December 1863) was used as the frontispiece for the second part of the two-volume book edition, published by Smith and Elder in 1864. In contrast to the procedure for *Framley Parsonage*, this time it was Trollope who instructed Millais in the choice of subjects for illustration. Although he was flexible, assuring the publisher, George Smith, that 'If [Millais] chooses to change the subject I shall not complain,' he nonetheless emphasised the writer's authority, insisting that 'the author can select the subjects better than the artist – having all the feeling of the story at his fingers' end' (quoted Hall, 1980, 56). Both narrative and illustration use a trivial domestic exchange to convey the lack of intimacy between Adolphus Crosbie and his aristocratic wife Lady Alexandrina de Courcy, for whose wealth and social standing he foolishly rejected the young heroine Lily Dale. As punishment for his betrayal of Lily, to whom he was previously betrothed, Crosbie has to endure the company of his new relatives. Dismayed at the prospect of visiting his tiresome inlaws, the Gazebees, he weakly protests 'Why on earth, on Sunday?,' to which he receives the dispiriting reply 'Because Amelia asked me for Sunday. If you are asked for Sunday, you cannot say you'll go on Monday.' Although there is a humorous element to the dialogue and illustration, the reluctant couple's frozen postures and averted eyes painfully reveal the self-inflicted despair of Crosbie's loveless marriage.

LG

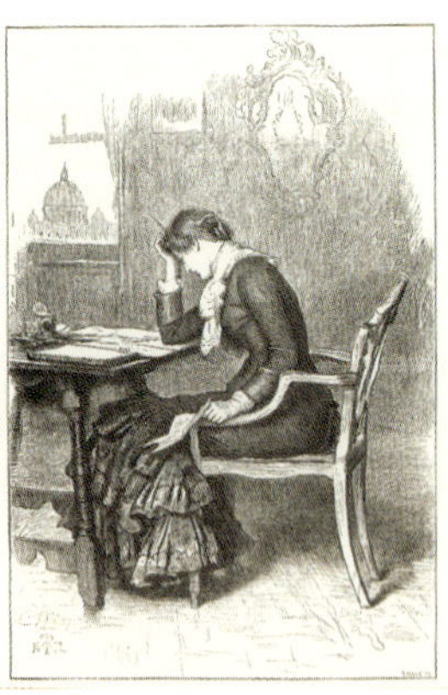

64. 'When the letter was completed she found it to be one which she could not send'

Wood engraving | Engraved by Joseph Swain | 169 x 117 mm
Bought, 1909 | P.6483-R

Millais's single illustration for *Kept in the Dark*, serialised in *Good Words* from May to December 1882, resumed his collaboration with Trollope for the final time after a gap of thirteen years. Preferring to concentrate on his increasingly successful painting career, Millais cut back on illustration work from 1869, refusing Trollope's requests to illustrate *Can you Forgive her?* (1865) and *The Last Chronicle of Barsetshire* (1867). Published in the author's final year, *Kept in the Dark* is a comedy of manners conveying the anxiety and jealousy caused by the weight of a guilty secret. 'When the letter was completed…' (*Good Words*, June 1882) depicts the scene in chapter five when Cecilia Holt, having accepted George Western's proposal of marriage, prepares to admit that she terminated a previous engagement to the selfish baronet Sir Francis Geraldine. As George himself has recently been jilted by Cecilia's successor in the baronet's affections, she is reluctant to confess for fear of suggesting unwelcome comparisons. As she attempts to reveal the truth, Millais accurately depicts her despair at 'finding that the story, when told, extended itself over various sheets of paper.' Pride prevents her from sending a letter which, in defending her actions, seemed only to cast greater suspicion: 'She had done nothing which she ought not to have done, nothing which she could not have acknowledged to him without a blush. When the letter was completed, she found it to be one which she could not send.'

LG

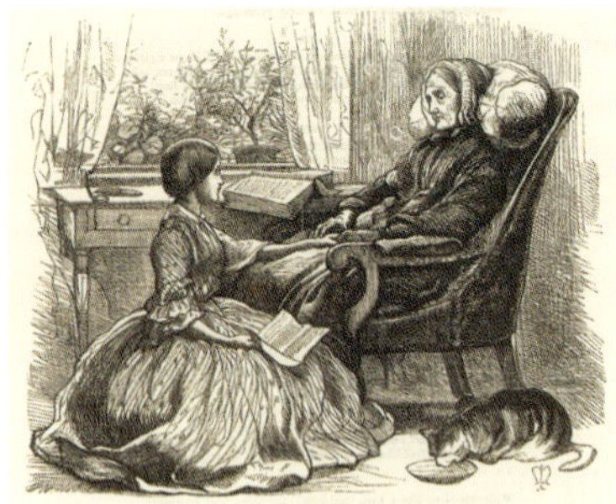

65. The Grandmother's Apology

Wood engraving | Engraved by the Dalziel Family | 106 x 133 mm
Bequeathed by Henry Scipio Reitlinger, 1991 | P.1109-1991

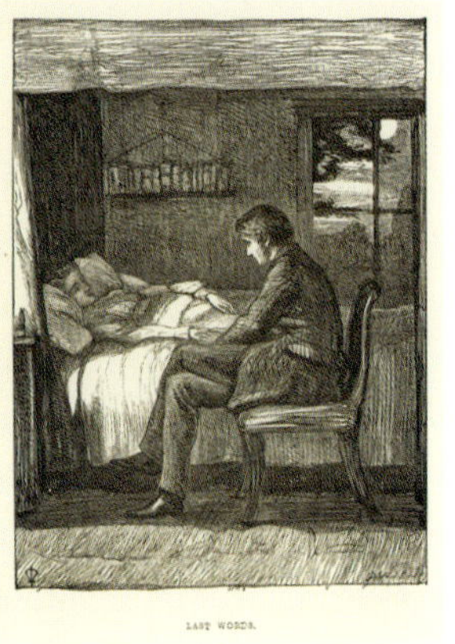

66. Last Words

Wood engraving | Engraved by the Dalziel Family | 224 x 142 mm
Bequeathed by Henry Scipio Reitlinger, 1991. | P.1082-1991

Millais was a regular contributor to *Once a Week* and *The Cornhill Magazine*, illustrating a wide range of poetry and prose by figures both celebrated and obscure. *The Grandmother's Apology*, accompanying a poem by Tennyson (*Once a Week*, 16 July 1859) and *Last Words*, illustrating a poem by the statesman and poet Robert Bulwer-Lytton (pen-name Owen Meredith) (*The Cornhill Magazine*, November 1860) both deal with the common Victorian themes of the passing of time and the approach of death. In Tennyson's poem, the grandmother, who has survived all her offspring, feels her time is near as her eldest son has just died. Millais's portrayal of the tender communication between the woman and her granddaughter highlights the contrast between youth and age:

I cannot weep for Willy, nor can I weep for the rest;
Only at your age, Annie, I could have wept with the best.

'Last Words' describes an ailing poet on his deathbed, beseeching his faithful friend to 'burn every book I have written.' Published as 'Last Words of a Sensitive Second-Rate Poet' in Meredith's *Chronicles and Characters* (1868), it was the subject of a cruel satire by Swinburne, who mocked Meredith's prolixity and pretentiousness in 'Last Words of a Seventh-Rate Poet,' the fifth parody in *The Heptalogia*, published anonymously in 1880.

LG

Dante Gabriel Rossetti

1828–1882

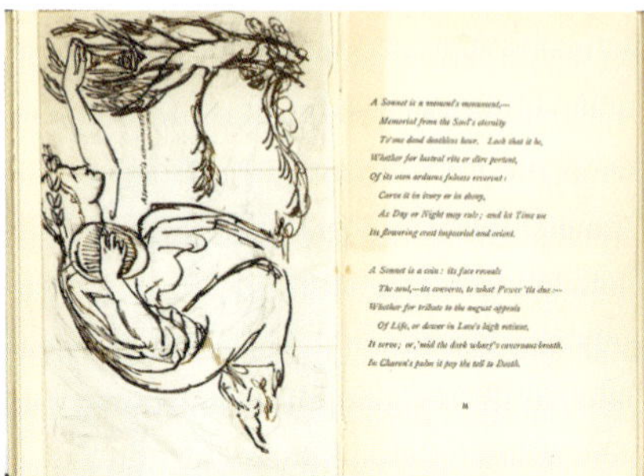

67. Ballads and Sonnets

London, Ellis and White / Chiswick Press, 1881
Tipped in on verso of title-page for 'The House of Life': Drawing of 'The Sonnet' by D. G. Rossetti. Annotated by Dante Gabriel Rossetti, Christina Rossetti and Sydney Cockerell. Bound in green cloth with pattern of flowers stamped in gold.
Given by Virginia Surtees, 2005 | PB. 71-2005

Dante Gabriel Rossetti published *Ballads and Sonnets* a year before his premature death in 1882. Many of the poems included were written in response to works of visual art, or to complement his own paintings. Some had even been incorporated into a canvas, or inscribed around the frame. Yet the relationship between his work as painter and as poet troubled Rossetti, and he alternated between confidence that the arts are essentially one, and anxiety that they are irreconcilable, and that he had failed at both. The pen drawing inserted into this book copy of the *Ballads and Sonnets* demonstrates one attempt to weave together poem and picture into a unified design.

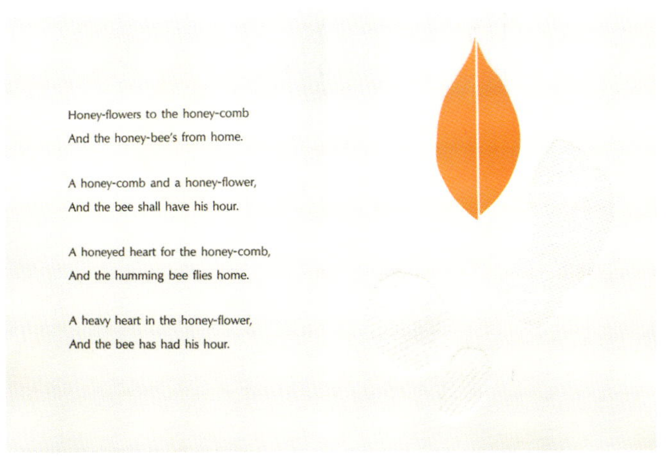
Honey-flowers to the honey-comb
And the honey-bee's from home.

A honey-comb and a honey-flower,
And the bee shall have his hour.

A honeyed heart for the honey-comb,
And the humming bee flies home.

A heavy heart in the honey-flower,
And the bee has had his hour.

68. Chimes

Guildford, Circle Press, 1969
Etchings in relief by Birgit Skiöld.
No. sixty-four in an edition of seventy-five copies signed by the artist. With ten artist's proofs, each with seven original prints. Binding by David Collins.
Bought, 1971

Birgit Skiöld's 1969 interpretation of 'Chimes', a sequence of poems lifted from *Ballads and Sonnets*, builds on Rossetti's apprehension of an intimate relationship between painting and poetry. As the title suggests, 'Chimes' also evokes the idea of music as a model of aesthetic autonomy which Rossetti increasingly applied to his own media of word and image (see no.20). Enlarged, generously spaced, hand-printed on mould-made paper, and bound in an award-winning limited edition of seventy-five signed copies, the text becomes itself a work of visual art. The decision to leave unstitched the folio sheets which make up the book enhances this effect of rich materiality, as each poem-picture pair can be lifted out and displayed on its own. Skiöld (1923-82), a Swedish-born printer, paper-maker, painter and photographer, was a founder member of the acclaimed Circle Press, formed in 1967, and played an important role in the development of British printmaking from the 1950s until her death in 1982.

Walter Crane

1845-1915

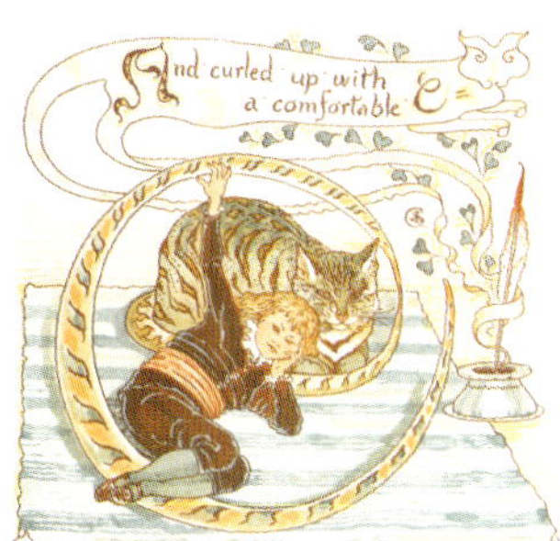

69. Pothooks and Perseverance: or, the A. B. C—Serpent, penned and pictured by Walter Crane

London: Marcus Ward & Co., 1886

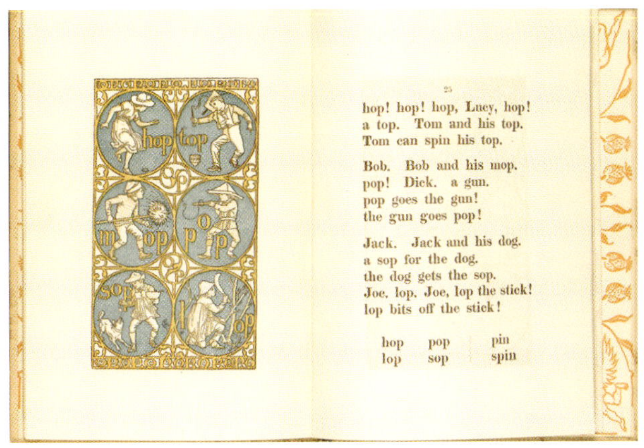
25

hop! hop! hop, Lucy, hop!
a top. Tom and his top.
Tom can spin his top.

Bob. Bob and his mop.
pop! Dick. a gun.
pop goes the gun!
the gun goes pop!

Jack. Jack and his dog.
a sop for the dog.
the dog gets the sop.
Joe. lop. Joe, lop the stick!
lop bits off the stick!

hop pop pin
lop sop spin

70. The Golden Primer by J. M. D. Meiklejohn

London, Edinburgh: William Blackwood & Sons, 1884
Engraved and printed by Edmund Evans
Bought, 1914

71. Baby's Own Aesop being the Fables condensed in rhyme with portable morals pointed by Walter Crane (1887)

Twenty-eight leaves, bound in a cardboard cover
Watercolour, pen and ink on paper | 185 x 187 mm
Given by the Friends of the Fitzwilliam Museum, 1931 | no. 1606

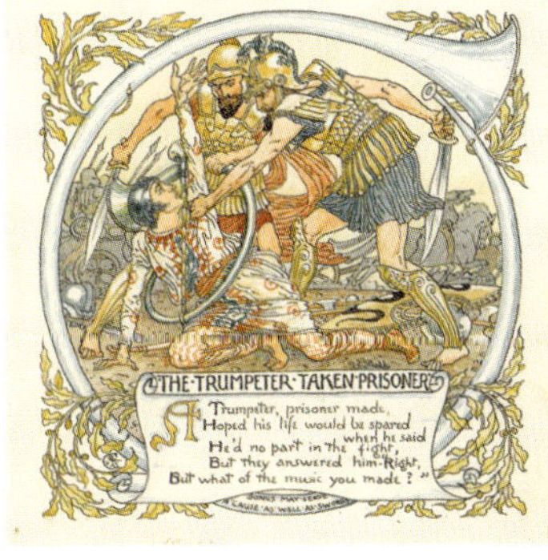

In the public mind, Walter Crane formed one of a trio of illustrators, including Kate Greenaway (nos. 72, 73) and Randolph Caldecott (1846-86), who transformed children's books during the 1880s. However, he was keen to differentiate his work, pointing out that he had begun to draw and write for children much earlier, in the mid 1860s, and claiming a sense of educational purpose which his rivals lacked. These three books demonstrate his underlying seriousness, as well as his visual wit. *The Golden Primer*, for instance, combines words and pictures so as to ease the chore of learning to read, while *The Baby's Own Aesop* brings the fables to life as limericks. Crane's children's books were commercial ventures, published in bulk and selling cheaply. However, as a friend of artist-craftsmen such as William Morris and Edward Burne-Jones, he valued good printing, and the expressive eloquence of a well-designed page. Together with Edmund Evans, his printer, he worked to increase the range of colours used in children's illustration, and the complexity of designs. He found imaginative ways of incorporating the text into his image, framing it in scrolls, or disguising it as monumental inscription so that the letters became a function of the image, rather than a commentary upon it. The manuscript copy of *The Baby's Own Aesop* exhibited here shows how he would write the script himself, in an elegant, calligraphic hand, following the rhymed version of the Fables which, in a prefatory note, he attributes to his 'early friend,' W. J. Linton. A signature crane's-feather quill is a recurring motif in his work, underlining the intimate exchange between Crane the artist, and the written words he illustrated and often wrote. The book was engraved and printed in colour by Edmund Evans, and published in London and New York by George Routledge & Sons, 1887.

Kate Greenaway

1846–1901

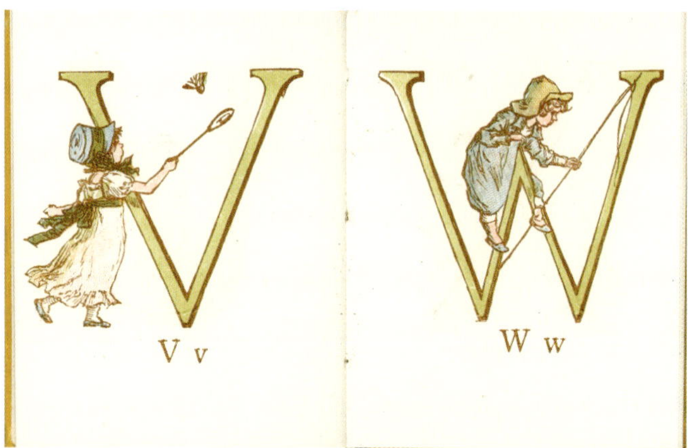

72. Kate Greenaway's Alphabet

London and New York, George Routledge & Sons, 1885
Bequeathed by John Charrington, 1933

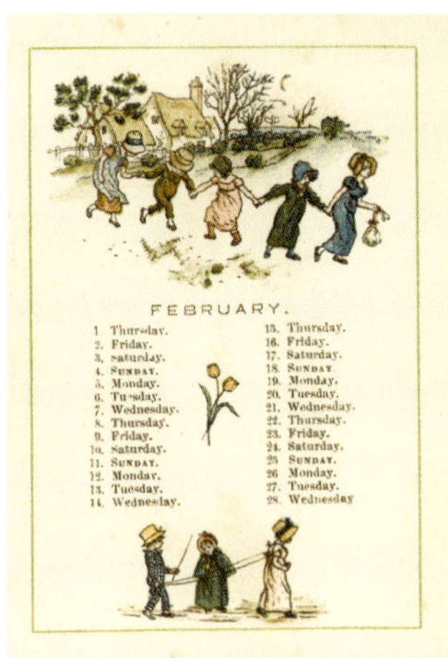

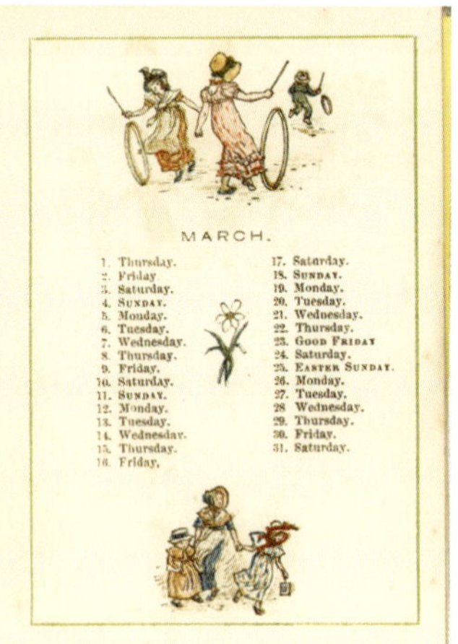

73. Almanack for 1883

London, George Routledge & Sons, 1882
Bequeathed by John Charrington, 1933

One of the most enduringly successful children's illustrators, Kate Greenaway produced finely wrought images for the mass market. Like Walter Crane, she worked with Edmund Evans, a printer who specialised in children's books, and prided himself in the accuracy of his colouring and engraving. Greenaway began her career designing greeting cards, but her first commercial success, *Under the Window* (1879), was an illustrated collection of her own verses, and she soon established a reputation as a writer for children. Reproduced and imitated across Europe, her images of happy children appeared on tea sets, samplers, and as china dolls, as well as in books. The *Almanack* was the first of a series produced between 1883 and 1897. Priced at one shilling, it sold 90, 000 copies in England, America, France and Germany. The tiny *Alphabet* (1885) was likewise successful, selling 24, 500 copies, although its contents had to be salvaged from Greenaway's unsuccessful edition of William Mavor's *The English Spelling-Book* (1885). John Ruskin had written highly of the speller, calling it 'one of the most inspiring school-books ever published for children.' However, it was Ruskin who encouraged Greenaway to break with her career as a popular illustrator, and fashion herself as a serious artist. Just as he had influenced artists of the Pre-Raphaelite Brotherhood, and female associates, such as Elizabeth Siddal (no.19), so he had a profound impact on Greenaway's work after 1883, encouraging her to draw realistically from nature, learn perspective, and take up watercolour and oils. The results were unsuccessful. Her exhibited paintings sold badly. On the other hand, her illustrated books have become collectors' items, evolving in the century after her death from beautiful but commercially-driven publications to the exclusive status of the Book Beautiful.

Laurence Binyon

1869–1943

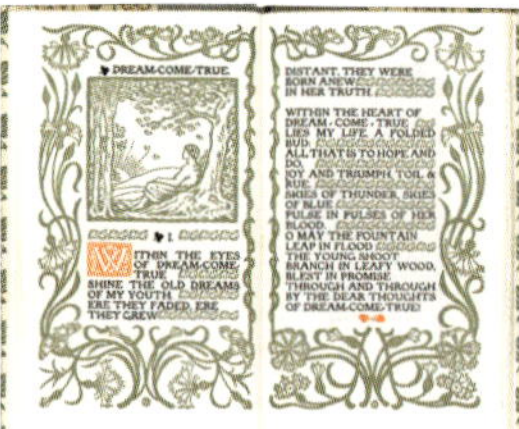

74. Dream-Come-True

Hammersmith, London, Eragny Press, 1905
Frontispiece designed and cut in wood by the author. Decorations designed by Lucien Pissarro and cut in wood by Esther Pissarro. Edition limited to 175 paper copies and ten vellum. Bound in 'Daisy' printed paper-covered boards, and printed with Pissarro's own 'Brook' fount.
Given by Sir Herbert Thompson, 1920

It was Laurence Binyon, poet and art historian, who approached his friends Lucien and Esther Pissarro with the idea that they might publish a selection of his love poems. The Eragny Press put into practice the idea that a book should embody unity: the unity of word and image, and of artist and craftsman. Here, Binyon went a step further, designing and cutting the frontispiece illustration to his own text. *Dream-Come-True* is a private book, celebrating his betrothal, honeymoon, first year of marriage, and first experience of fatherhood, and it was made by one of the smallest of the private presses. The publisher's prospectus emphasised its rarity, promising the potential purchaser that there would be no second edition, and that the frontispiece engraving would never be used again. Thanks to Binyon's many friends and connections, however, the book made a profit. Encouraged, the Pissarros planned a whole series of contemporary English poets, but only produced one other, *The Little School* (1905), a collection of children's poems by Thomas Sturge Moore.

75. Rubaiyat of Omar Khayyám

Translated by Edward Fitzgerald, written out by Graily Hewitt, finished London, May 1902. Illuminated by Florence Kingsford, finished at Assisi, May 1904. Bound in green pigskin by Katherine Adams at Broadway, Worcestershire.
Bought with contributions from the Cockerell family, and other benefactors, 1974 | MS. 9-1974.

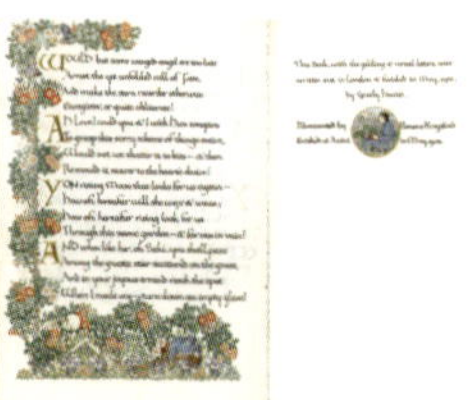

Edward Fitzgerald (1809–83) made the most influential English translation of the *Rubaiyat*, a collection of over 1000 poems attributed to the Persian mathematician and astronomer Omar Khayyám. Fitzgerald's version was famously free, even inventive, and a great success, running to five editions between 1859 and 1889. Swinburne particularly admired his work, remembering in later life how Rossetti had introduced him to the poem, and how they had bought up cheap copies of Fitzgerald's first edition, before prices soared from one penny to thirty shillings a book. The copy displayed here is a selection of verses illuminated by the artist Florence Kingsford. It was owned by Sydney Cockerell, who married her in 1907.

William Strang

1859-1921

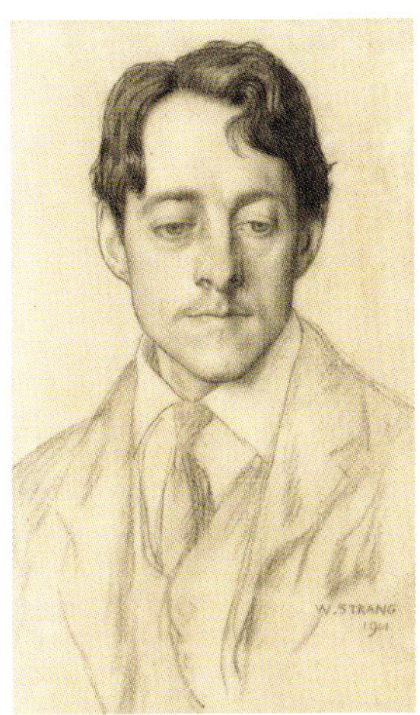

76. Laurence Binyon

Black chalk on laid paper | 305 x 185 mm
Signed and dated in black chalk, lower right: *W. Strang 1901*, and lower left: *W. Strang* | Given by John Charrington, 1933 | no. 1671

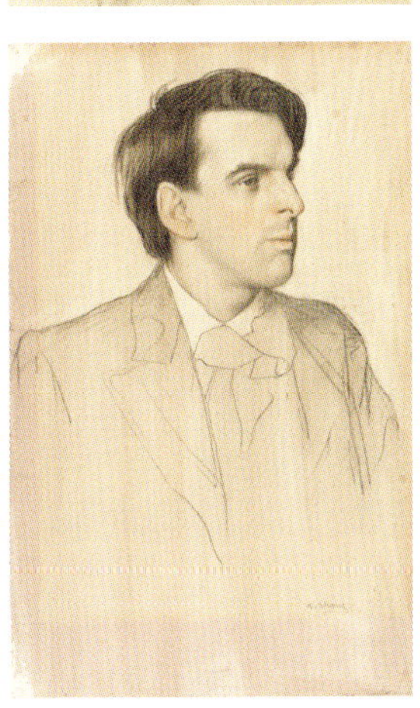

77. William Butler Yeats

Red and black chalk with white highlights on laid paper, prepared with a pinkish wash. | 405 x 261 mm
Signed in graphite, lower right: W. Strang
Given by William Strang, 1910
no. 704

A student of Alphonse Legros (who drew the portraits of Ricketts and Shannon exhibited here), William Strang specialised in etched portraits of leading literary and artistic figures, many of whom he knew personally. He made several likenesses of Binyon in various media, including this 1901 drawing. A published poet and historian of Asian art, Binyon came to know Strang, as he knew so many other artists, through his work as curator in the Print Room of the British Museum. In 1896, Strang taught Binyon wood engraving, and Binyon became an advocate of the idea that artists should cut their own wood blocks, rather than relying on photography, or a professional engraver. He therefore designed and cut illustrations for his own books (see no.74), and in 1904 edited *Artist Engraver*, a short-lived quarterly which published etchings, engravings, woodcuts and lithographs, by contemporary artists such as Strang, Charles Shannon and William Nicholson. Binyon and Strang also collaborated on books. Together they produced *Western Flanders* (1899), a collection of prose meditations by Binyon, illustrated with etchings by Strang, and Binyon chose to engrave Strang's design *The Dryad* as a frontispiece for his *Odes* (1901).

Yeats's fame as a poet and striking looks made him a favourite subject for artists. As well as this 1903 portrait by William Strang, he was painted by Augustus John (1907) and Charles Shannon (1908), and caricatured by Max Beerbohm and Edmund Dulac. The son and brother of artists, he was closely involved with the visual arts and, as a writer, took an active interest in the private press movement, contributing to avant-garde periodicals such as *The Yellow Book* and *The Savoy*. In 1905, he was thrilled to receive a copy of the Kelmscott Chaucer as a collective birthday present from his friends. Writing to Sydney Cockerell (then working with Emery Walker, engraver and typographer), he declared that 'it is a book I have longed for for some years; indeed ever since it was made. To me, it is the most beautiful of printed books.'

Alphonse Legros

1837-1911

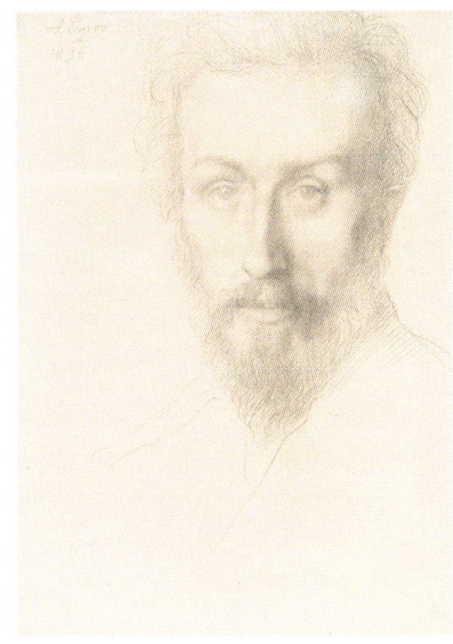

78. Charles Ricketts

Silverpoint on pink prepared ground, on paper
276 x 219 mm
Signed and dated, upper left: *A. Legros / 1896*
Bequeathed by Charles Hazelwood Shannon, 1937
no. 2095

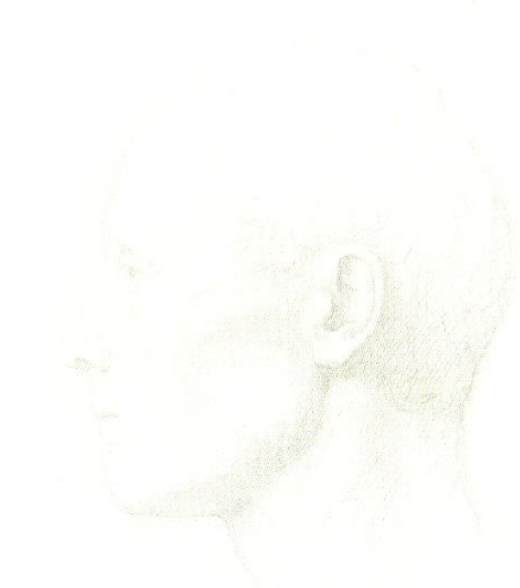

79. Charles Shannon

Graphite on paper
314 x 229 mm
Signed and dated, top right: *A. Legros / 1897*
Bequeathed by Charles Hazelwood Shannon, 1937
no. 2096

Max Beerbohm

1872-1956

80. Mr Ricketts and Mr Shannon in the Enjoyment of Popular Success

Pen and watercolour on paper | 323 x 406 mm | Signed and dated, centre right: Max '07; and, in ink, lower edge: *Mr Ricketts and Mr Shannon, in the / Enjoyment of Popular Success.*
Given by the Friends of the Fitzwilliam Museum, 1952 | PD.24-1952

Beerbohm's double caricature of Ricketts and Shannon (1907), and Legros's more dignified portraits (1896 and 1897), celebrate key figures of the *fin-de-siècle* literary and artistic world. Life-long partners, Ricketts (1866-1931) and Shannon (1863-1937) worked together as artists, illustrators, fine-press publishers and collectors. Beerbohm shows them here in their studio, surrounded by works of art. The deliberately shapeless sculpture on the

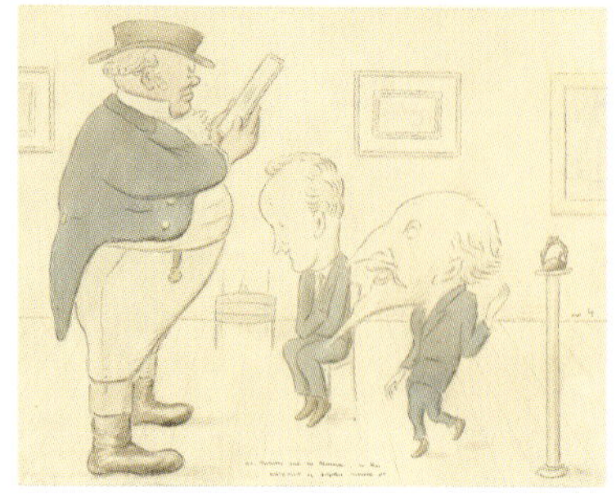

pedestal is Ricketts's bronze *Orpheus and Euridyce* (c. 1905-1906). Shannon, the quiet one, sits shyly, while the more gregarious Ricketts explains a painting to a stolid John Bull.

Ricketts and Shannon met at the City and Guilds Art School, Kennington, where they learned drawing and wood engraving. At the beginning of their joint career, they arranged that Ricketts should earn money as a popular illustrator, while Shannon developed his talents as a painter. However, they soon found ways of bridging the divide. Between 1896 and 1904, they ran their own private press, the Vale Press, which specialised in beautiful editions of canonical English poetry. Like William Morris at the Kelmscott Press, they aimed to restore the visual integrity of the book, and to involve the artist in every stage of its production. Rejecting recent technological changes, such as the photographic reproduction of illustrations, they returned to wood-engraving, even cutting their own designs onto the wood. In 1899, fire destroyed their stock and workshop, and the Press closed five years later. While Shannon returned to painting and lithography, Ricketts turned his hand to a variety of crafts, most notably theatre design. One of the most innovative and prolific designers of his day, he was involved in many important productions, including Oscar Wilde's *Salomé* (1906), W. B. Yeats's *The King's Threshold* (1894), and George Bernard Shaw's *St Joan* (1924).

The Vale, Chelsea, where Ricketts and Shannon lived between 1888 and 1894, became a centre for their circle of artists and writers, as well as providing a name for their press. They knew most of the artists and writers who feature in this exhibition: Beerbohm and Legros were close friends, as were Shaw, Thomas Sturge Moore, William Rothenstein, W. B. Yeats and Sydney Cockerell. It was Cockerell who persuaded them to leave most of their extensive collection of French, English, and old master drawings and paintings to the Fitzwilliam Museum, including the two Legros portraits/

81. The Dial: An occasional publication

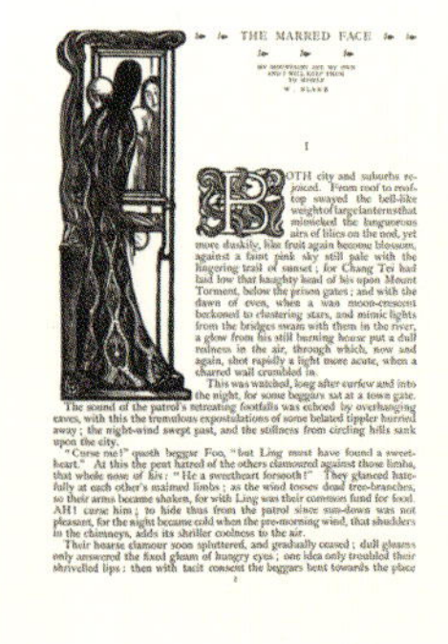

THE MARRED FACE

W. BLAKE

I

BOTH city and suburbs rejoiced. From roof to roof-top swayed the bell-like weight of large lanterns that mimicked the languorous airs of lilies on the rod, yet more duskily, like fruit again become blossom, against a faint pink sky still pale with the lingering trail of sunset; for Chang Tei had laid low that haughty head of his upon Mount Torment, below the prison gates; and with the dawn of even, when a wan moon-crescent beckoned to clustering stars, and mimic lights from the bridges swam with them in the river, a glow from his still burning house put a dull redness in the air, through which, now and again, shot rapidly a light more acute, when a charred wall crumbled in.

This was watched, long after curfew and into the night, for some beggars sat at a town gate. The sound of the patrol's retreating footfalls was echoed by overhanging eaves, with this the tremulous expostulations of some belated tippler hurried away; the night-wind swept past, and the stillness from circling hills sank upon the city.

"Curse me!" quoth beggar Foo, "but Ling must have found a sweetheart." At this the pent hatred of the others clamoured against those limbs, that whole none of his: "He a sweetheart forsooth!" They glanced hatefully at each other's maimed limbs; as the wind tosses dead tree-branches, so their arms became shaken, for with Ling was their common fund for food. AH! curse him; to hide thus from the patrol since sun-down was not pleasant, for the night became cold when the pre-morning wind, that shudders in the chimneys, adds its shriller coolness to the air.

Their hoarse clamour soon spluttered, and gradually ceased; dull gleams only answered the fixed gleam of hungry eyes; one idea only troubled their shrivelled lips: then with tacit consent the beggars bent towards the place

2

The Marred Face, woodcut by Charles Ricketts, no. 2, 1892
London, Vale Press | 5 vols, 1889-1897
Private collection

Published as an occasional magazine by Charles Ricketts and Charles Shannon. *The Dial* (1889-1897) became an important conduit for European Symbolism. In its pages, contemporary French and Belgian Symbolists mingled with British late Pre-Raphaelites, facilitating the close connections between the two movements. Rejecting the miscellaneous appeal of the popular periodicals, Ricketts and Shannon paid fastidious attention to the design of the page. Their determination to create their own wood-engraved and lithographic illustrations invoked the example of William Blake, and set a precedent for the revival of these media. Reactions were mixed. *The Athenaeum* predicted that the first number would be the last (in fact, five appeared at irregular intervals). While Oscar Wilde admired his complimentary copy, and befriended Ricketts and Shannon, William Morris identified what he called equal proportions of 'talent and the aberration of the talent' in the magazine (Lewis, 1939, 20). Critical reviews (proudly reproduced in the prospectus for the second number) likewise emphasised *The Dial*'s esoteric, whimsical quality. As *The Spectator* put it, 'We cannot conceive its becoming generally popular; we can easily conceive its being adored by a small section of artist and art-lovers, who admire beauty in execution and do not object to extravagance and even absurdity in style.'

Arthur Rackham

1867-1939

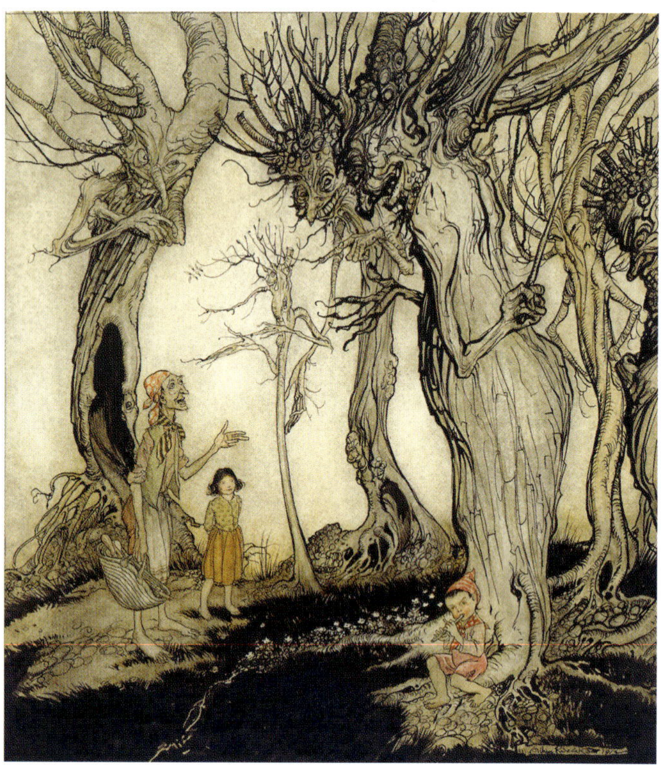

82. The Trees and the Axe (from Aesop's Fables)

Pen, black ink and watercolour on paper, laid down on card | 312 x 268 mm
Signed dated in black ink, lower right: Arthur Rackham 1912
Bequeathed by Harris Rackham, 1944 | no. 2710

A master of the genre of fantasy illustration, Rackham cut his teeth illustrating for the periodical press. He published his first book illustrations in 1893, but his reputation soared with the success of *Rip Van Winkle* in 1905. From then on, he continued to illustrate numerous editions of fairy tales and fables, including the 1912 edition of *Aesop's Fables* published by William Heinemann. This illustration to the tale of 'The Tree and the Axe', in which the aged trees sacrifice a sapling to satisfy the woodman's request for an axe handle, only to be slain by that very instrument, displays Rackham's signature gnarled, anthropomorphic trees. Among his contemporaries, Beardsley and Dadd were his greatest influences.

LG

Aubrey Beardsley

1872-1898

83. The Savoy

London, Leonard Smithers | 8 vols., 1896 Front cover, no. 2, April 1896.
Bequeathed by Henry Scipio Reitlinger, 1991 P.482-1991

Beardsley joined *The Savoy* at the invitation of Arthur Symons, scholar, writer and editor of this short-lived periodical. Beardsley had been sacked from *The Yellow Book* because of his friendship with Oscar Wilde (recently disgraced), and *The Savoy* was intended to replace *The Yellow Book* as publisher of the best contemporary writers. At first, Symons feared that the artist was too close to death to take on the job, but he found him full of ideas and enthusiasm, and it was Beardsley who came up with a name for the new magazine – possibly a facetious reference to the hotel where Wilde was meant to have committed sodomy. With Beardsley's illustrations, and contributions by new and established writers, including Yeats, Shaw, Conrad and Beerbohm, *The Savoy* began well. But after six months sales dropped, and within the year, all was over. The last issue, appearing in December 1896, was written entirely by Symons, and illustrated by an ailing Beardsley. The difficulties were mostly financial, but exacerbated by acrimony between the two men. In this instance, poor relations between artist and author put paid to their attempts at collaboration.

84. How Morgan le Fay Gave a Shield to Sir Tristram

Pen and black ink with black ink wash on paper | 275 x 212 mm
Bequeathed by G. J. F. Knowles, May 1959 | P.D. 52-1959

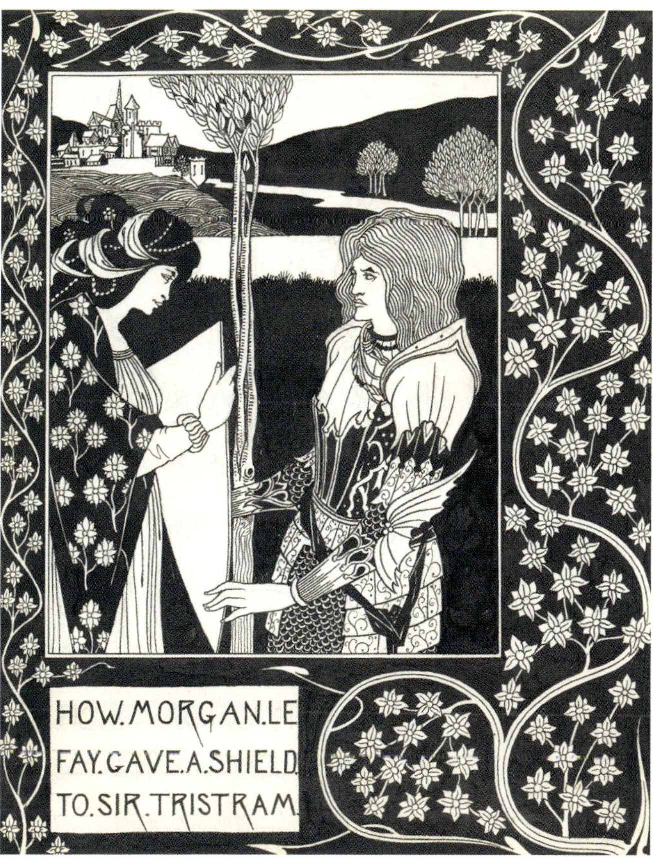

In 1893, Beardsley illustrated a lavish edition of Thomas Malory's *Le morte D'Arthur* (1485), published in parts by J. M. Dent from June 1893. The edition ran to 1500 copies, with a further 300 printed on Dutch hand-made paper. Beardsley designed hundreds of chapter headings, borders, initials and tail pieces, as well as this full-page illustration of an exchange between Tristram and Morgan le Fay. In doing so, he responded to a body of illustrative work celebrating the Arthurian legends, and sought to recover the literary and artistic traditions of Malory's medieval world (see no. 42).

85. Blast: Review of the great English vortex

London, John Lane
2 vols., 1914-15
Displayed: vol.1

Blast was the magazine-cum-manifesto of Vorticism, the self-consciously avant-garde literary and artistic movement which declared cultural war on Victorian Britain in 1914. Produced by Percy Wyndham Lewis, artist, writer and Vorticist leader, *Blast* jolted the typographical traditions of the private press movement into the twentieth century. Machine aesthetic replaced Arts-and-Crafts pastoral, as Lewis 'blasted' everything Morris and his disciples had held dear: aesthetes, France, 'the sacripant past'; and 'blessed' everything modern and popular, from industry to aviators and music-hall entertainers. 'Blast will be popular, essentially', it declared, contradicting the exclusive ethos of limited edition journals such as *The Dial*. Yet despite its revolutionary rhetoric and flamboyant design, it had much in common with the 1890s periodicals. Its expressive typography built on their assertion that text and page design must cohere; and like them, it was short-lived. After the second edition came out in 1915, Lewis went to war, and, like so many private press projects, *Blast* faded away.

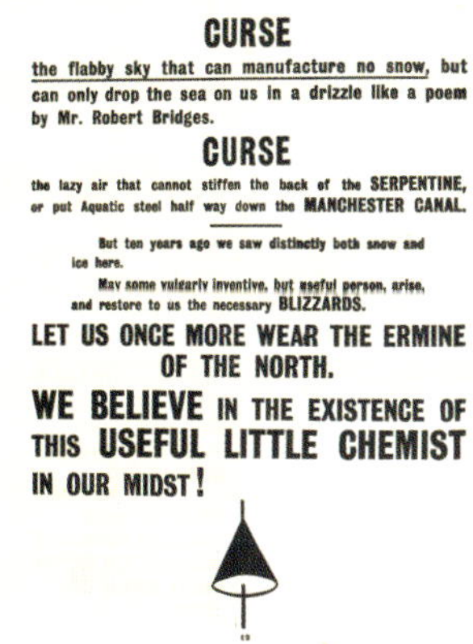

CURSE

the flabby sky that can manufacture no snow, but can only drop the sea on us in a drizzle like a poem by Mr. Robert Bridges.

CURSE

the lazy air that cannot stiffen the back of the SERPENTINE, or put Aquatic steel half way down the MANCHESTER CANAL.

But ten years ago we saw distinctly both snow and ice here.

May some vulgarly inventive, but useful person, arise, and restore to us the necessary BLIZZARDS.

LET US ONCE MORE WEAR THE ERMINE OF THE NORTH.

WE BELIEVE IN THE EXISTENCE OF THIS USEFUL LITTLE CHEMIST IN OUR MIDST!

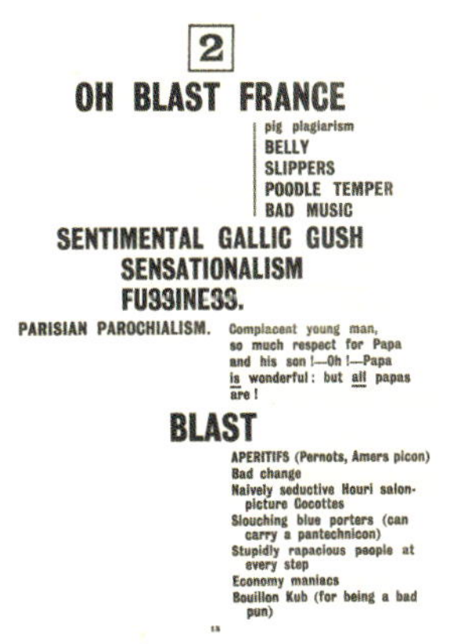

2

OH BLAST FRANCE

pig plagiarism
BELLY
SLIPPERS
POODLE TEMPER
BAD MUSIC

SENTIMENTAL GALLIC GUSH
SENSATIONALISM
FUSSINESS.

PARISIAN PAROCHIALISM.

Complacent young man, so much respect for Papa and his son!—Oh!—Papa is wonderful: but all papas are!

BLAST

APERITIFS (Pernots, Amers picon)
Bad change
Naively seductive Houri salon-picture Cocottes
Slouching blue porters (can carry a pantechnicon)
Stupidly rapacious people at every step
Economy maniacs
Bouillon Kub (for being a bad pun)

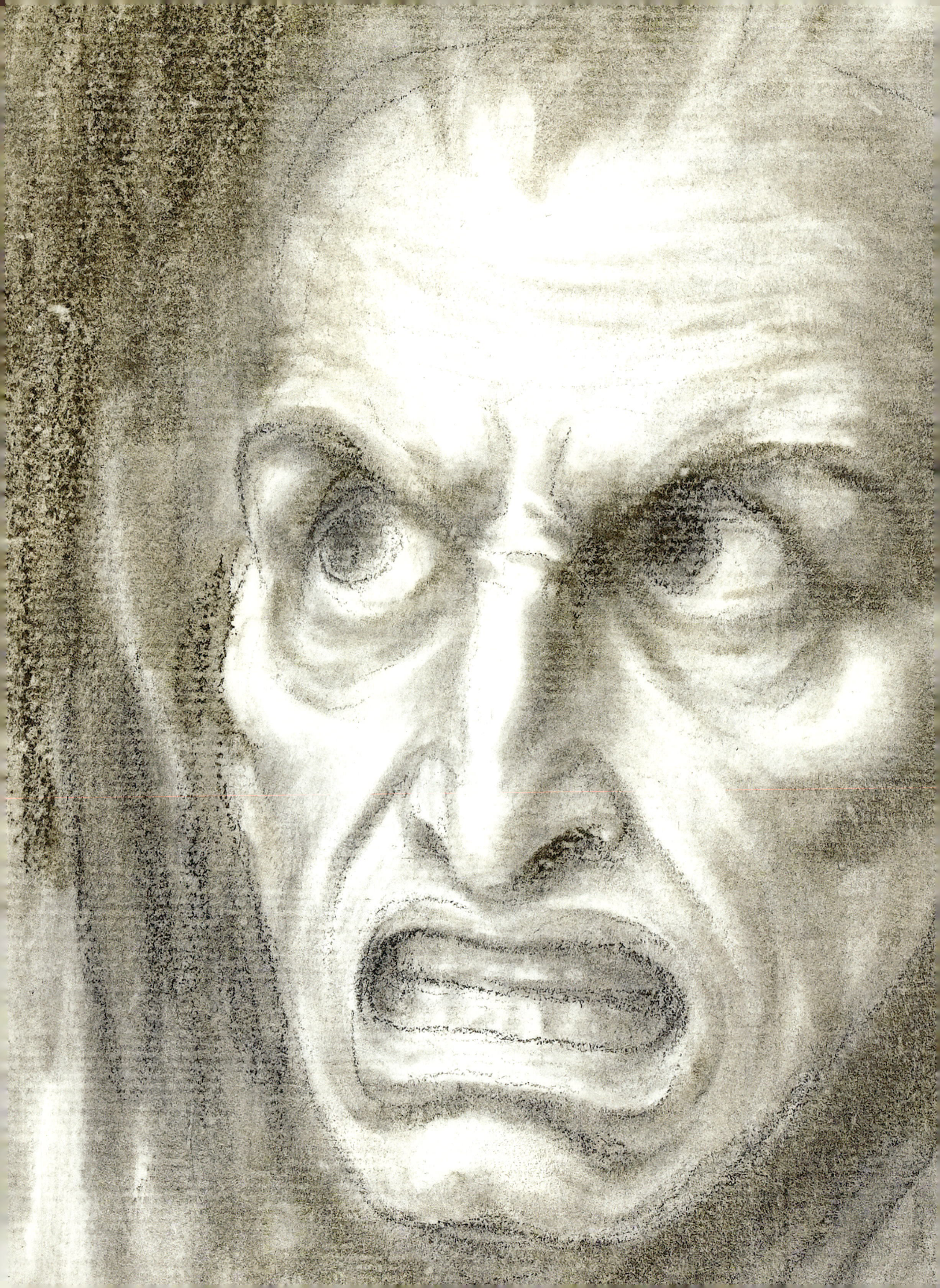

Imaging the Imaginary

Karolina Watras

Imaging the Imaginary

Karolina Watras

One response to Joshua Reynolds's call, in a series of lectures delivered at the Royal Academy between 1769 and 1790, for a 'Grand Style' of painting based on historical, allegorical and religious themes, was the creation of Alderman Boydell's Shakespeare Gallery in 1789. However, rather than promoting the morally elevated subject matter of the 'Historical Style,' Boydell's enterprise encouraged artists to explore their own creative flights of fancy. In this way, Shakespeare's literary legacy sanctioned such ventures into the imaginative and allowed them to enter the main stream of academic art. Henry Fuseli (1741-1825), a Royal Academician known for his visionary and disturbing interpretations of Shakespeare and Milton, serves as a good example of the integration of these extremes. When no literary precedent for the dream or the vision existed and fantasy scenes and characters were born of the artist's own imagination, a different set of standards was applied. Nowhere is this more apparent than in the work of William Blake, whose printed illustrations of Shakespeare found relatively wide public acceptance, but whose visionary and prophetic works, whether pictorial, poetic or combined works of 'double art', were generally dismissed as the product of a lunatic.

Significantly, Blake's and Romney's drawings of scenes from Shakespeare's plays (nos. 87, 89-92) do not strictly adhere to contemporary theatrical performances. Instead, they create an inventive visual commentary to parallel Shakespeare's plays, and in this succeed in capturing the fantastical element which was forcibly lost in performance. With their inherent theatricality and visionary nature, these drawings initiate their own dialogue with Shakespeare's literary inventions.

In mid-nineteenth-century England, with the first English translations of the the fables of the Brothers Grimm (1823) and Hans Christian Andersen (1847), and a growing interest in the

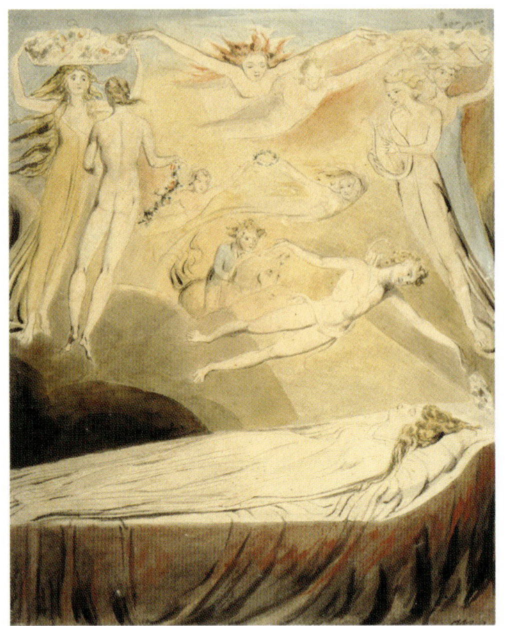

number of monkeys, baboons, & all of that species
chaind by the middle, grinning and snatching at
one another, but witheld by the shortness of their
chains; however I saw that they sometimes grew nu
merous, and then the weak were caught by the strong
and with a grinning aspect, first coupled with & then
devourd, by plucking off first one limb and then ano
ther till the body was left a helpless trunk, this after
grinning & kissing it with seeming fondness they devourd too; and here & there I saw one savourily pic-
king the flesh off of his own tail; as the stench ter
ribly annoyd us both we went into the mill, & I in
my hand brought the skeleton of a body, which in
the mill was Aristotles Analytics.

So the Angel said: thy phantasy has imposed
upon me & thou oughtest to be ashamed.

I answerd: we impose on one another, & it is
but lost time to converse with you whose works
are only Analytics.

TOP LEFT

92. William Blake

1757-1827

Queen Katherine's Dream

LEFT

97 William Blake

1757-1827

'...number of monkeys', The Marriage of Heaven and Hell, f.20

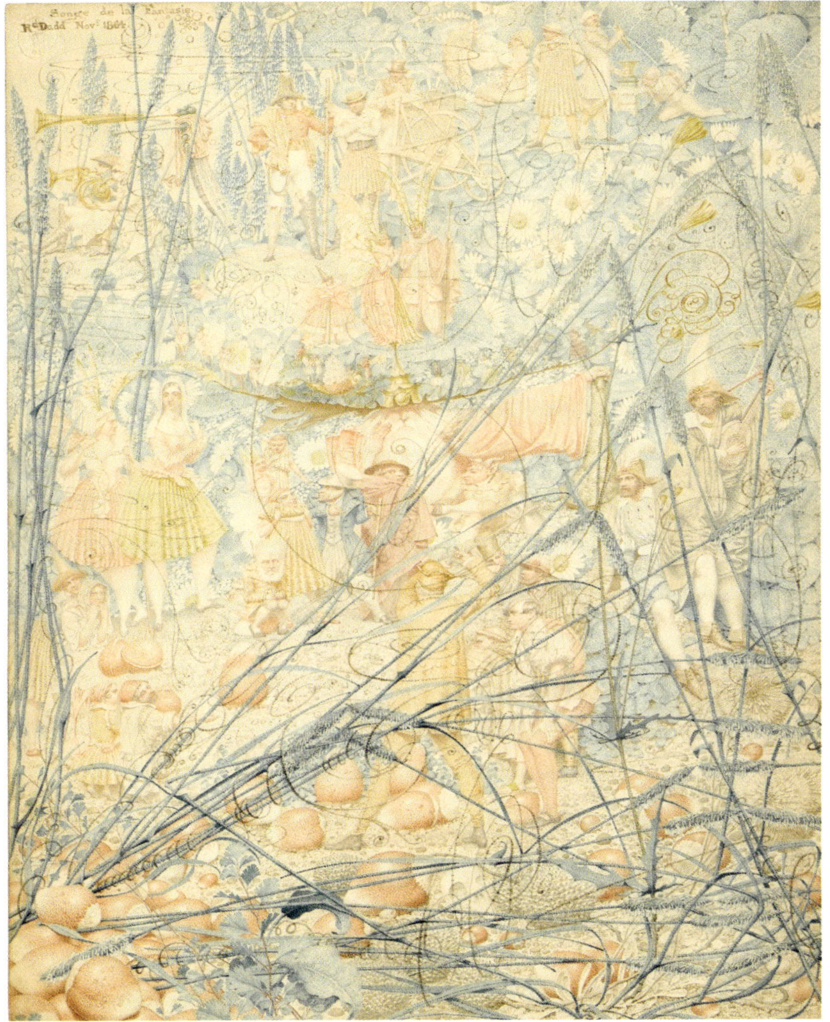

ABOVE
95. Richard Dadd
1819-1887
Songe de la Fantasie

subconscious, the potential for the fantastic and visionary in pictorial representation grew rapidly, and gave rise to a new, extremely popular genre of fairy painting. At the same time, the development of Romantic ballet with its reinvention of human movement, and technical advances in theatrical performance, offered an additional source of inspiration for more complex fantasy compositions. Whereas Blake's and Romney's purely imaginative 'stagings' had surpassed the dramatic practices of their contemporaries, it was now relatively difficult to match them. Consequently, fairy paintings became the vehicle for the most extreme pictorial fantasy, often reaching beyond established themes from literature or folklore.

Richard Dadd's progression from his acclaimed interpretations of Shakespeare to his independent fairyland creations (which coincided with his descent into mental illness) exemplifies this transition. Shakespearean characters such as Oberon and Titania from *A Midsummer Night's Dream* or Queen Mab from *Romeo and Juliet*, may still be found lurking in the intricate and essentially inexplicable narratives of *Songe de la Fantasie* (no. 101), and his earlier, almost identical oil painting on this theme, entitled *The Fairy Feller's Master-Stroke* (1855-64, Tate Gallery), but for the most part the inhabitants of this dreamscape are solely products of the artist's own imagination. The subject of these paintings preoccupied Dadd for at least a decade, and to the extent that he even composed a poem as a verbal commentary, notionally to elucidate their meaning. Dadd's various reprisals of the subject in word and image borders on the obsessive. It is as if, through constant repetition, he was evolving his own mythological vocabulary 'by rote.' In a not dissimilar sense, Swinburne, in copying Blake's prophetic poem, *The Marriage of Heaven and Hell* (no. 98), was applying an equally concentrated, mechanical mode to expand the trajectory of Blake's imaginative world, just as folk tales or legends gradually, through repetition, enter common cultural consciousness. The relationship between Dadd's poem and the two paintings is problematic, as the text bears little correspondence to the images and in itself fails to form any coherent narrative:

Turn to the Patriarch and behold
Long pendants from his crown are rolled,
In winding figures circle round
The grass and such upon the mound,
They represent vagary wild
And mental aberration styled.

This tension between the image and its meaning is already apparent in the poem's title: *Elimination of a Picture and Its Subject – Called the Feller's Master Stroke.* On the one hand, the poem can be seen as Dadd's frustrated attempt to clarify his two visualisations of the theme: it has been suggested, for example, that the use of the word 'elimination' was simply a pun on 'elucidation' or 'illumination.'[1] On the other, Dadd may have wished to convey a simpler message: that verbal description as we know it has no place in his fairyland. His final lines may well refer to the impossibility of translating visual fantasy into the rigid laws of logic and language:

For nought as nothing it explains
And nothing from nothing nothing gains.

Dadd's confused verses highlight the fact that, where words appear in relation to an image, most commonly in the form of inscriptions or the titles of paintings, we would expect them to play an instructive role in our reading. In fantasy paintings or drawings of the late nineteenth and early

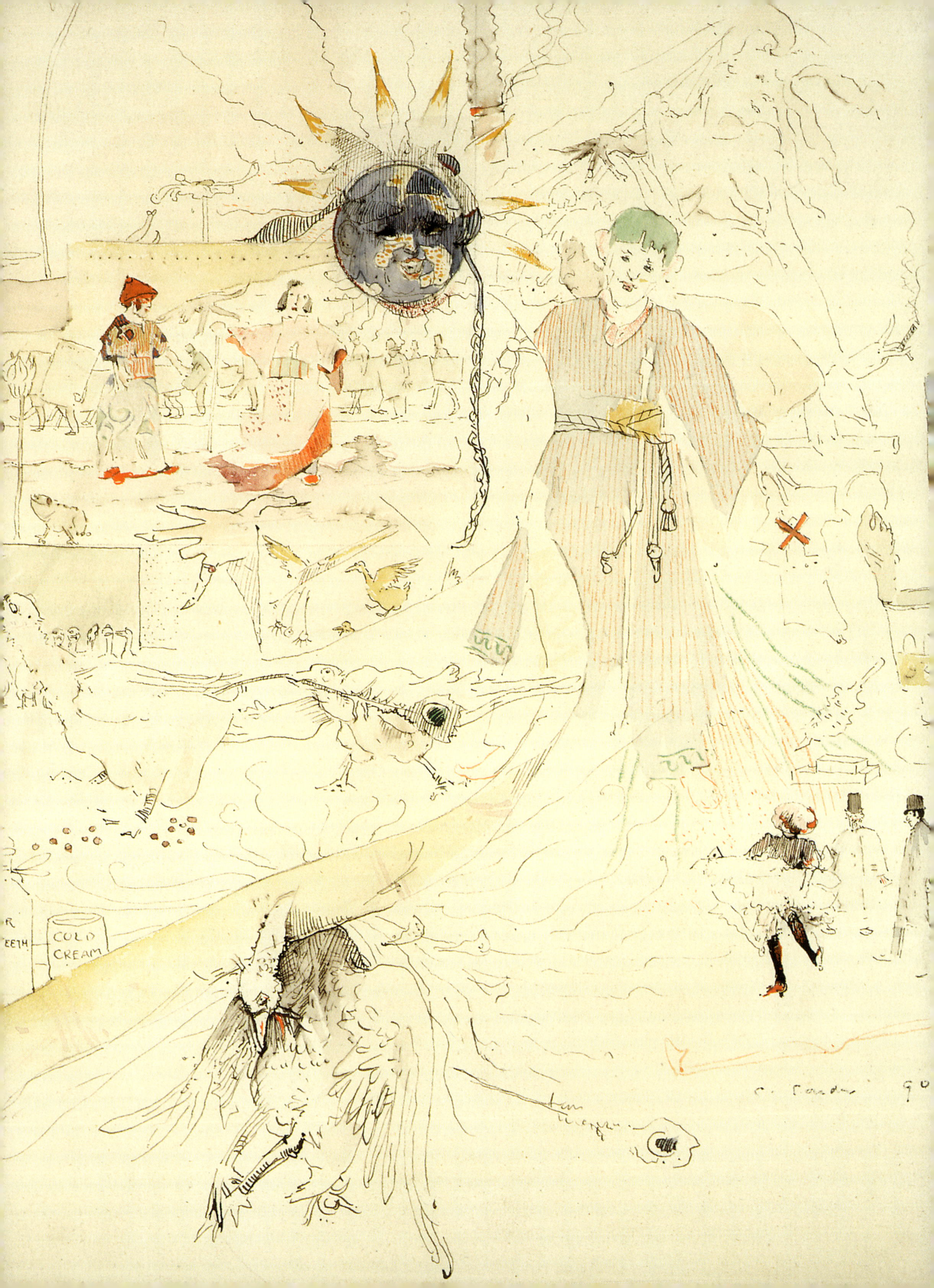
COLD
CREAM

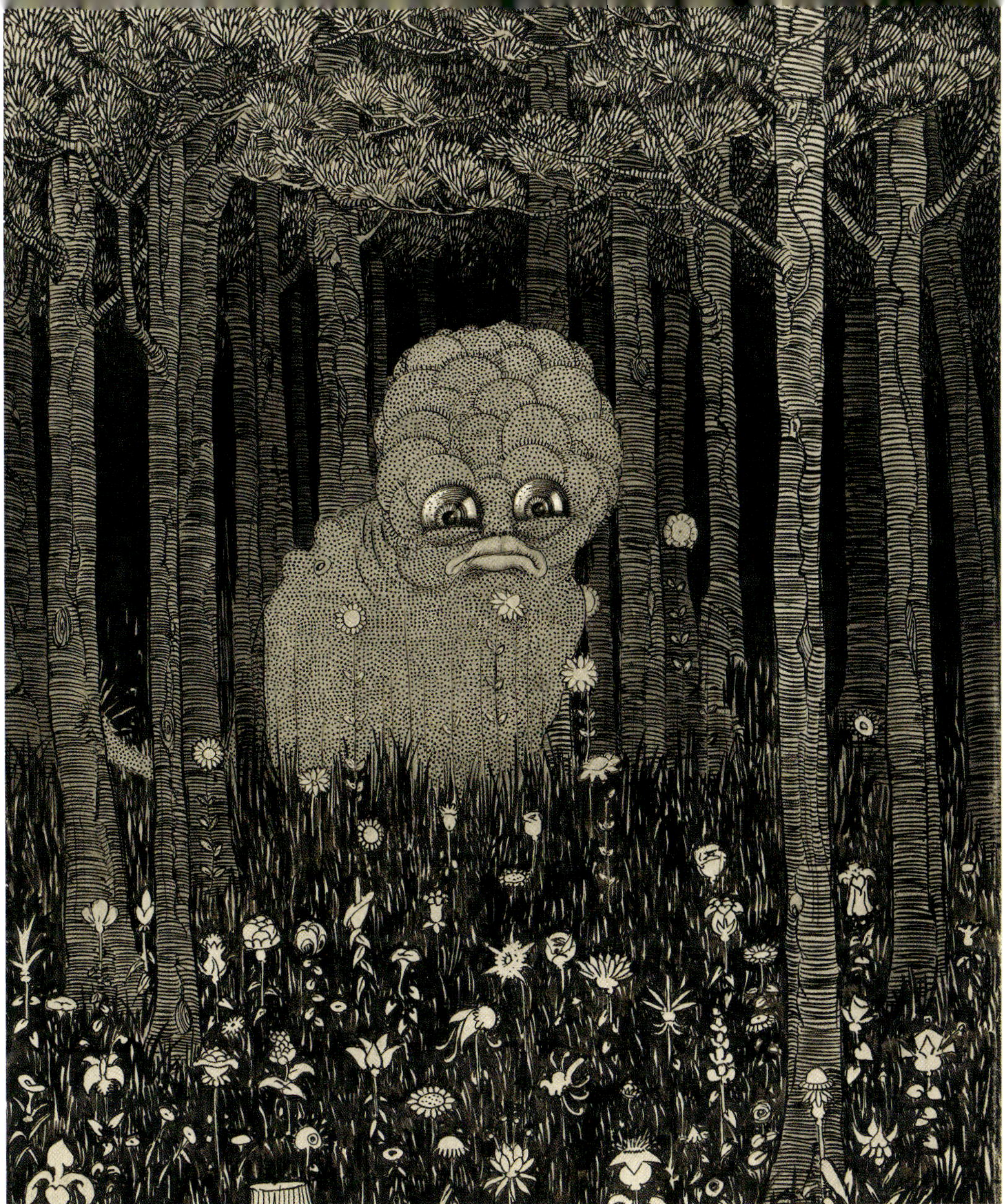

ABOVE
103. Sidney Sime
1867–1941
Bogey Beast, The Wily Grasser

LEFT
102. Charles Conder
1868–1909
A Dream in Absinthe

twentieth century, however, we look in vain to supporting text for any sort of clarification. The fantastic dominates and dismisses any logical discourse or categorisation. If anything, the verbal component raises the unreal to the level of reality. This can be seen in Sime's array of *Bogey Beasts*, or, in their earlier name, *Beasts that might have been*, as well as other invented characters with imaginary names. A fantasy 'bogey' creature is simply called Wily Grasser, as though it were a scientifically-classified species, and its real existence was taken for granted (no. 103). Sime took inspiration for his strange personages from passers-by in London streets, and their transubstantiation into his imaginative world only highlights the easy slippage between realistic observation, social caricature and fantasy.

For Blake, the 'reality' of a vision or fantasy translated itself into his powerfully expressed mystical prophecies. He, and subsequently Samuel Palmer (no. 99), blurred in their work the boundaries between the spiritual and the real, art and the material world. In Blake's famous series of visionary heads, such as that of Caractacus (no. 95), historical, legendary and purely imaginary characters assume equal physical substance and *raison d'être*. His prophetic books, such as *The Marriage of Heaven and Hell* (no. 97), unite text and image in defiance of the laws and language of reality, forming an alternative mystical paradigm in which the poet finds an appropriate means of expressing his beliefs and philosophies … and his dreams.

'Fancy', *songe* or dream: Blake's highly personal paintings and drawings set a powerful precedent for an art that was no longer bound by the imagination of the writer, but one where the only source for visual fantasy was the artist himself. Painters such as Dadd, Conder and Sime relied purely on their own dreams and visions to provide a title or commentary to their fantastical scenes. In Dadd's *Songe de la Fantasie*, the title denotes a sense of latency and recollection. When compared to

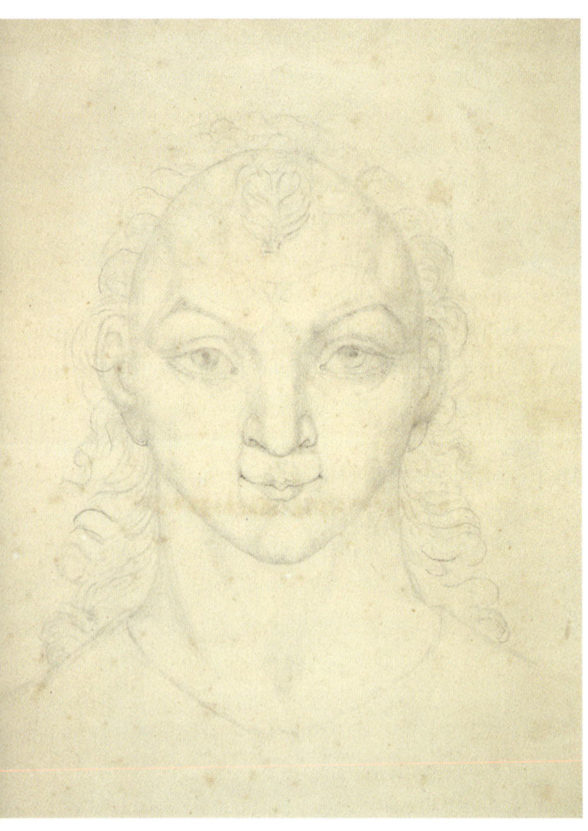

the earlier *Fairy Feller's Master-Stroke*, the watercolour's paler and more subdued tonalities introduce a sense of the passage of time, like a fading memory, or, indeed, an image displaced by a dream.[2] The change of title itself points towards this transition as it no longer focuses on the actual events within the picture, however elusive they may be, but rather repositions them in the author's own mental world. Conder's watercolour *A Dream in Absinthe* has a sounder base in the reality of the quotidian, in as much as it evokes the 'green goddess'-fuelled visions of the bohemian culture of Montmartre in which Conder so avidly immersed himself. However, if his representation is a reflection of reality, it is anything but realistic: instead it juxtaposes the scattered and distorted scenes of his Parisian experiences, recreating the immediacy and simultaneity produced by a reverie or hallucination.

Sidney Sime, when questioned about his drawings, often discussed them in terms of his own experiences and discoveries; as a critic of the *Strand Magazine* noted: '[Sime] has not sought after the grotesque; he has not, indeed, found it, the grotesque found him.'[3] Like Blake in his prophecies, Sime uses the first person singular in 'descriptions' of his pictures, as though he himself was a protagonist of the bizarre events he portrayed, and focuses on his own reactions and introspective observations.[4] They neither illuminate the picture's narrative, nor act as an additional commentary. Instead, the only relation they bear to the image is their mystifying and inconceivable mode of expression. In *Bogey Beasts*, Sime stretches the limits of his grotesque visions so that they can be shared – if not fully understood – by his public. Combined with his own jingles and Holbrooke's music, the artist stages a theatrical performance in which his fantastical creatures come to life in a way that Shakespeare's imaginary characters do on the stage.

Even within this brief outline of a transition from fantasy illustration to fantastic invention, we can perceive an evident breakdown in the reliance on literary narrative, and a growing emphasis on an introspective approach to the imaginary. In compositions drawn directly from the imagination, the fractured relationship between their various visual components is mirrored in the writings that arise from them. As fantastic pictorial inventions came to exist independently of their literary sources or prototypes, both language and vision rejected any remaining demands to adhere to literal transcription or traditional modes of pictorial expression. This process paved the way for the reliance on the subconscious as a key to artistic production in the twentieth century, the ultimate tribute to Blake's originality and uncompromised position as the outstanding champion of visionary art.

LEFT
95. William Blake
1757-1827
The man who taught Blake painting in his dreams

1 Patricia Allderidge, *The Late Richard Dadd*, London,1974, 125-126.

2 Sacheverell Sitwell has pointed out that some of the characters in the original oil wear dresses from the 1840s, two decades before the final date of the painting and the last opportunity Dadd would have had to observe society before being committed to Bethlam hospital, *Narrative Pictures: A survey of English genre and its painters*, London, 1937, 71.

3 E. S. Valentine, 'S. H. Sime and his Work', *Strand Magazine*, October 1908, 394.

4 See, for instance, Sime's description of his *Illustration to an Unknown Tale*: '… The sudden discovery of this infamous den – that renowned and impregnable stronghold, the fear and envy of universal wizardry – not only drowned my memory of the quest, it involved me in perilous side issues. The malevolence underlying the Pophoff's hospitable greeting unheeded by me, absorbed as I was – for how long I know not – in a profound and fatal curiosity…' *ibid*, 397.

George Romney
1734–1802

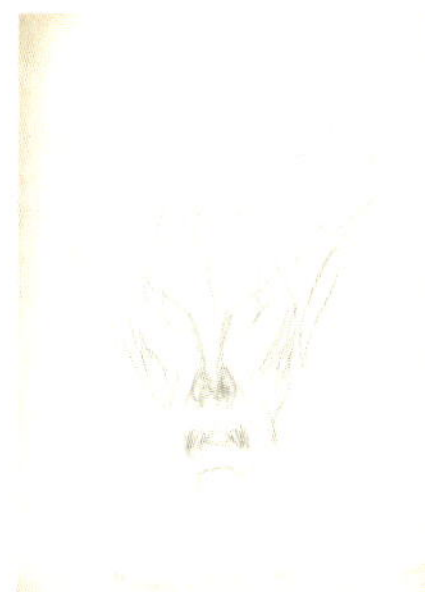

86. Study for a Fiend's Head

Graphite on paper | 538 x 390 mm
Bought, 1874 | LD.136

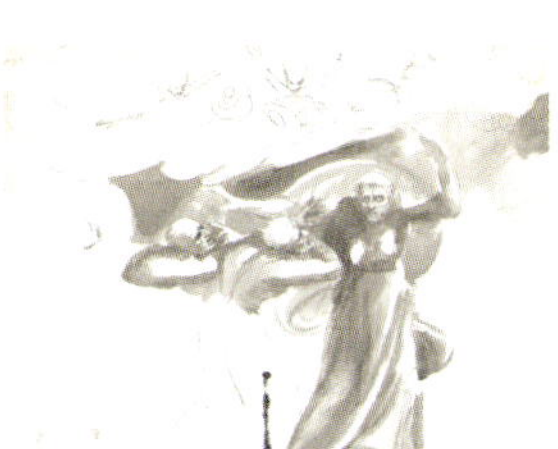

87. Meeting of the three Witches and Hecate

Pen with black ink and grey watercolour wash over graphite, on paper | 392 x 516 mm | Given by the artist's brother, John Romney, 1818 | BV. 141

88. Study for a Fiend's Head

Black chalk and brown chalk worked with stump on paper | 521 x 370 mm
Given by the artist's brother, John Romney, 1818 | BV.137

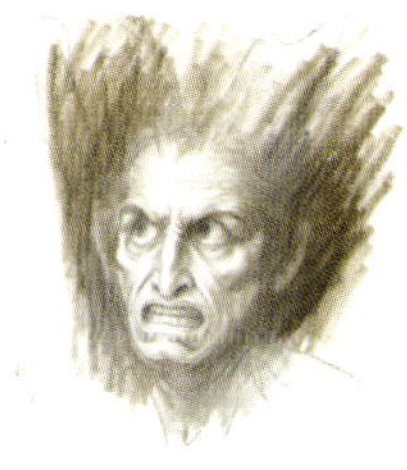

Trained as a portrait painter, Romney found the genre of large-scale historical painting difficult. In 1790 he completed a storm scene from *The Tempest*, his main contribution to Boydell's Shakespeare Gallery, which was often criticised for its overcrowded and clumsy composition. Instead, it is in his sketches for those works that he engaged most fully, and imaginatively, with the visual and dramatic challenges of Shakespeare's plays. While working on *The Tempest*, Romney began to prepare studies for two other paintings for Boydell: *Macbeth* and *Margery Jourdain and Bolingbroke conjuring up the Fiend* from *Henry VI Part II*. In both cases he was frustrated in his efforts, as both Reynolds and a young painter, John Opie, submitted their respective representations of these themes before him. Nonetheless, a great number of his preparatory sketches remain in the Fitzwilliam Museum and Folger Shakespeare Library, Washington.

The Meeting of the three witches and Hecate from *Macbeth*, Act III, scene v, can be traced to the early 1790s, when the artist executed a series of drawings related to the play, including a number of representations of witches (Jaffé, 1977, 55). The sketchy finish of this drawing and the summary description of the witches reflect the dramatic, infernal character of Shakespeare's scene.

Romney's expressive renditions of the fiend most likely derive from *Henry VI Part II*, Act I, scene iv, in which Bolingbroke, Southwell and Margery Jourdain, witnessed by the Duchess of Gloucester and an accompanying priest, question the spirit about the future of the King, the Duke of Suffolk and the Duke of Somerset. The political upheaval and uncertainty in Europe following the French revolution might underline Romney's choice of a scene that represents the anxieties provoked by the challenge to an accepted order. At the same time, he used the opportunity to expand his mastery of portraiture, possibly drawing on his early studies of physiognomy and expression after Charles Le Brun's hugely influential published treatise on *The Expression of the Passions* (1688). The unnerving appearance of the fiends powerfully evokes the fear and uneasiness in Shakespeare's text:

> *...wizards know their times*
> *Deep night, dark night, the silent of the night,*
> *The time of night when Troy was set on fire;*
> *The time when screech-owls cry, and ban-dogs howl,*
> *And spirits walk, and break up their graves.*

George Romney
1734–1802

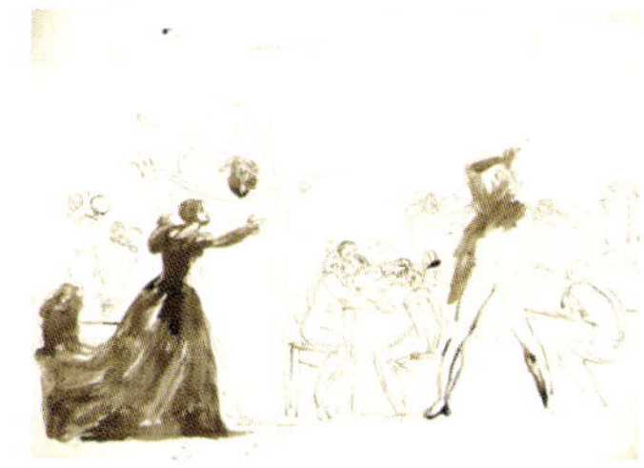

89. The Banquet scene, Macbeth

Pen, brown ink and brown wash over graphite on paper
371 x 527 mm
Bought, 1874 | LD.126

William Blake
1757–1827

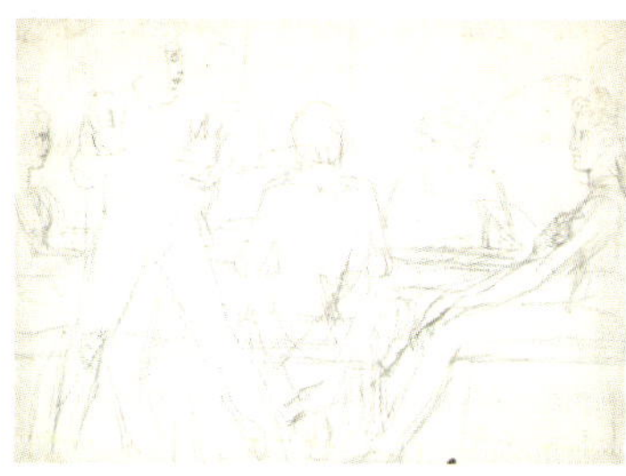

90. Macbeth and the Ghost of Banquo

Graphite on paper | 378 x 522 mm | Inscribed, lower right (not by Blake): *71*
Bequeathed by Geoffrey Keynes, 1985 | PD.170-1985

Between 1769 and 1790 the president of the Royal Academy of Art, Joshua Reynolds, delivered a series of lectures in which he called for an English School of History Painting that would draw strongly on literary tradition. In reaction, a wealthy publisher, Alderman Boydell, proposed an ambitious project in 1786 to commission leading painters to execute a series of paintings inspired by subjects from British plays. Both George Romney and William Blake, who already knew each other through the poet William Hayley and shared politically radical views, became involved. The Shakespeare Gallery opened in 1789 in Pall Mall and eventually comprised no less than 167 paintings, which were to be engraved for luxury Folio editions of Shakespeare's plays, with the final nine-volume folio published in 1802. Financially, the project turned out to be a failure; its founder was brought to near-bankruptcy, the entire collection was dispersed, and many artists (including Blake) were left without payment. Boydell's enterprise nevertheless gave rise to a new interest in literary subject matter and prompted similar short-lived ventures such as Fuseli's Milton Gallery (opened 1799) and James Woodmason's Irish Shakespeare Gallery (opened 1793). Moreover, many of the engravings produced under Boydell's patronage were subsequently used in later editions of Shakespeare's plays, thus establishing a set of fixed visual representations in the public's mind.

A number of artists used this opportunity to explore the fantastic and imaginative potential of Shakespeare's plays, giving visual form to 'invisible' visions and ghosts. In their interpretations of the banquet scene from Macbeth, both Romney and Blake, in his drawing of c. 1785, achieve highly theatrical effects. The dramatic contrasts of light created by the varying strengths of ink in Romney's drawing evoke a powerful sense of alarm, while Blake's sketchiness and rushed execution, together with Macbeth's highly expressive gesture, brilliantly convey a scene of paralysing fear and astonishment.

William Blake

1757-1827

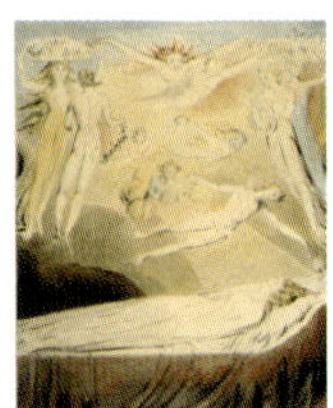

91. Queen Katherine's Dream

Pen and black ink, grey wash and watercolour over graphite on paper | 203 x 161 mm
Bought, 1935 | no. 1771

Blake treated this subject, from Shakespeare's *Henry VIII*, Act IV, scene ii, on four separate occasions, each time subtly reinterpreting the stage directions: *'Enter, solemnly tripping one after another, six personages, clad in white robes, wearing on their heads garlands of bays, and golden wizards on their faces; branches of bay palms in their hands. They first congee unto her, then dance; and, at certain changes, the first two hold a spare garland over her head, at which the other four make reverent curtsies: then the two that held the garland deliver the same to the other next two, who observe the same order in their changes, and holding the garland over her head: which done they deliver the same garland to the last two, who likewise observe the same order: at which – as it were by inspiration – she makes in her sleep signs of rejoicing, and holdeth up her hands to heaven: and so in their dancing they vanish, carrying the garland with them.'*

In 1880 Rossetti referred to the earlier watercolour (no.91) as 'The Dream,' thus emphasising as the principal subject the parade of 'invisible' angels soaring in an ascending spiral above the Queen's sleeping body. The later drawing from 1807 (no. 92) presents a more dynamic approach to the subject as the Queen, framed by the figures of Griffith and Patience asleep, is shown to participate actively in the events taking place around her. It may be that Blake's revised visual conceptualisation was the result of his interim collaboration with Fuseli on Rivington's 1805 edition of *The Plays of William Shakespeare* (Merchant, 1959, 30). Blake's renditions noticeably deviate from contemporary stagings of this scene, paralleling instead the visionary character of his own poetry and 'prophecies,' and thus assimilating Shakespeare's literary imagination into the artist's own visual language and mythology.

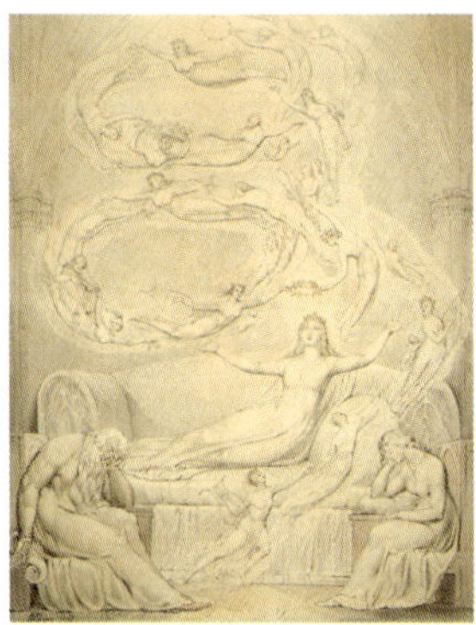

92. Queen Katherine's Dream

Pen, grey wash, with traces of graphite underdrawing, and watercolour on paper | 399 x 314 mm
Bought by the Friends of the Fitzwilliam Museum, 1911 | no. 712

John Linnell

1792 – 1882

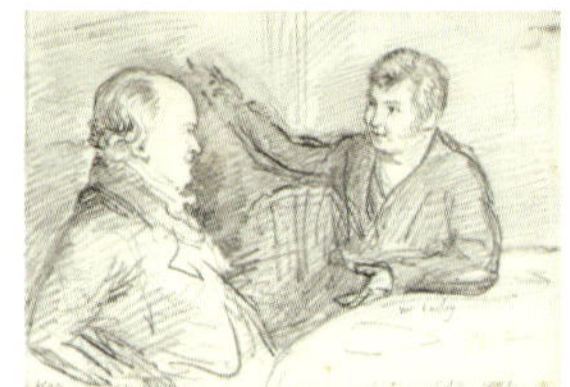

93. Blake in conversation with John Varley

Graphite on paper | 113 x 176 mm
Bequeathed by T. W. Riches, 1950
PD.59-1950

94. Head and shoulders of William Blake

Graphite on paper | 201 x 155 mm
Bequeathed by T. W. Riches, 1950 | PD.57-1950

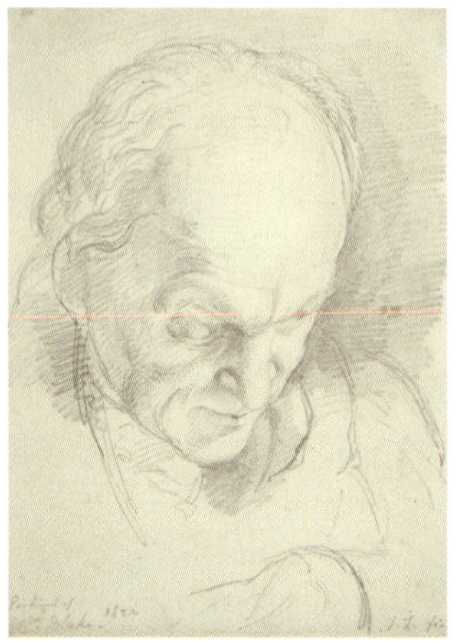

In 1818 Blake met John Linnell, a young landscape and portrait painter who soon became one of his closest friends and supporters. Linnell commissioned Blake to execute a series of watercolours on biblical and literary themes, most significantly for the *Book of Job*, Dante's *Divine Comedy*, and Milton. The following year Linnell introduced Blake to his former teacher John Varley (1778-1842), a watercolour painter of landscapes with a keen interest in astrology (see no. 96). Varley's fascination with what he saw as Blake's mystical character resulted in a number of late night conversations between the two men. According to Linnell's and Blake's own accounts, Varley would question Blake about the visionary personages and legendary figures that 'visited' the poet, providing him with his own sketchbooks so that he might see them for himself through Blake's drawings. In this way conversation, rather than any printed source, provided verbal inspiration for works by the two artists. In 1821, Linnell, who was an occasional witness, captured the energetic exchange between them in this rapidly-executed sketch (no. 93); later, he recalled, 'Varley believed in the reality of Blake's visions more than even Blake himself – that is in a more literal and positive sense that did not admit of the explanations by which Blake reconciled his assertions with known truth. I have a sketch of the two men as they were seen one night in my parlour near midnight, Blake sitting in the most attentive attitude listening to Varley who is holding forth vehemently with his hand raised – the two attitudes are highly characteristic of the two men, for Blake by the side of Varley appeared decidedly the most sane of the two…' Linnell's portrait of Blake from 1820 (no. 94) further confirms the contemplative nature of the poet. Ironically, Linnell himself was known to have disapproved of the excessive mysticism of Samuel Palmer, his son-in-law (no. 99).

William Blake

1757-1827

95. Caractacus

Graphite on paper | 195 x 152 mm | Inscribed, lower left: *Caractacus*

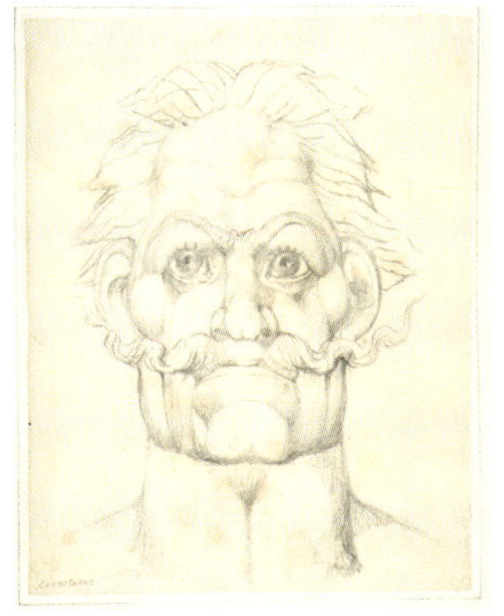

Bequeathed by Geoffrey Keynes, 1985 | P.D. 183-1985

This drawing belonged to the so-called Blake-Varley sketchbook of 1819, first used by Varley for his landscapes and subsequently by Blake for his 'visionary heads'. The sketchbook contained forty-six leaves, with some twenty-one, including the present sheet, cut out, and now all dispersed. Some of Blake's drawings in the sketchbook were subsequently engraved by Linnell and illustrated Varley's *Treatise on Zodiacal Physiognomy* of 1828.

The title, identifying this extraordinary head as that of Caractacus, King of the Catuvellauni, was most likely added by one of Blake's friends, John Linnell or John Varley. One of the leaders of British resistance against the Romans, Caractacus was captured with his family and taken to Rome in 50 A.D., where he delivered an impressive speech to the Emperor Claudius. It was traditionally believed that his children, upon their return to Britain, brought Christianity to England. Blake's choice of Caractacus as one of his visionary characters (if one can 'choose' a vision) reflects his strong religious beliefs as well as his conviction that the original spiritual and heroic values of the past had to be restored in order to prevent the moral decay of his own time, in the wake of years of the Absolutist rule of church and monarchy. The figure of Caractacus became a symbol of patriotism to British poets and composers throughout the period covered by this exhibition, as evoked by William Wordsworth in his *Ecclesiastical Sonnets* of 1821-1822,

The Spirit of Caractacus descends
Upon the Patriots, animates their task.

– and later, too by Edward Elgar in his cantata, *Caractacus*, with accompanying libretto by H.A. Acworth, written for the Leeds Music Festival in 1898 and dedicated to Queen Victoria.

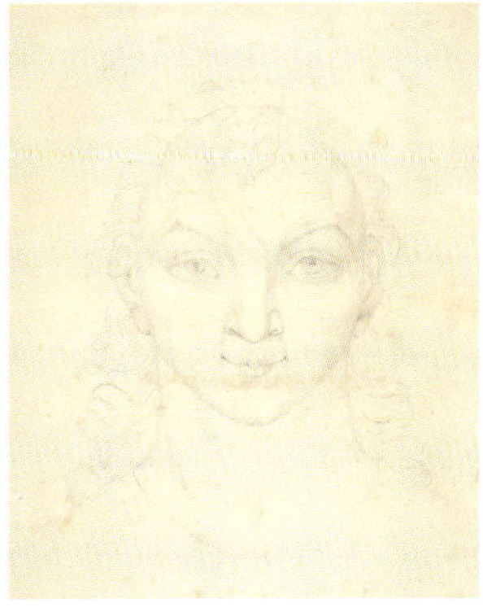

96. The Man who taught Blake painting in his dreams

Graphite on paper | 300 x 215 mm
Bequeathed by Geoffrey Keynes, 1985
P.D.166-1985

Between 1819 and 1825 Blake frequently visited the artist and amateur astrologer, John Varley, at his home in the evening, and the two men sat late into the night discussing Blake's dreams and visions. Executed some time during this period, *The Man who taught Blake painting in his dreams* was a direct result of these conversations and is one of numerous visionary drawings documenting this period of Blake's life. Its subject has been identified on the basis of similarities to two similar drawings of heads by Blake (Butlin 754 and 755), both of which bear inscriptions describing them as the figure that offered Blake instruction as he slept.

Blake believed that aesthetic judgement and artistic genius came from within, and strongly opposed the notion most forcefully represented by Sir Joshua Reynolds, as President of the Royal Academy, that art could be taught. This drawing has sometimes been thought to represent Blake himself, the visual manifestation of his perception of himself as artist and divine mystic, his visionary gaze and flames of inspiration rising from his forehead. The oddly shaped skull of Blake's 'teacher' have been related to J. Spurzheim's contemporary theories on phrenology, according to which two prominent bumps on the left and right of the head would suggest strong powers of imagination (Hamlyn and Phillips, 2001, 178).

Blake's insistence on vision as a fundamental source of inspiration had a profound impact on subsequent generations of artists. It resonated in particular with twentieth-century movements such as Surrealism, which explored the subconscious as the key catalyst of the creative process.

William Blake

1757-1827

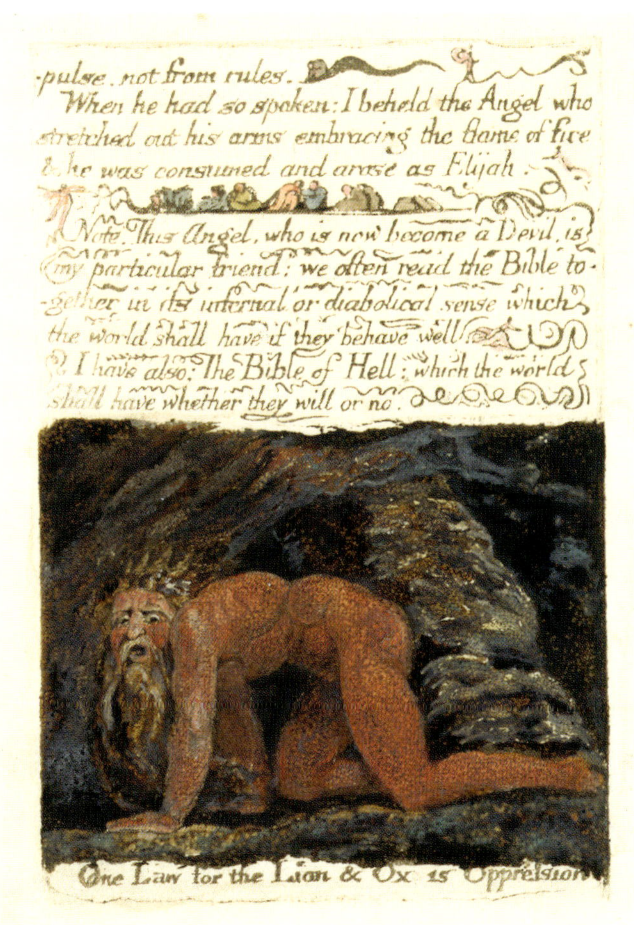

97. The Marriage of Heaven and Hell

Copy E, 1794, '...number of monkeys'; f.20 and 'Pulse, not from rules; f.24
Relief etchings | 153 x 104 mm
Bequeathed by Geoffrey Keynes, 1985 | P.669-1985

Blake's prose masterpiece, *The Marriage of Heaven and Hell* (1790-1793), of which the Fitzwilliam Museum owns three illuminated copies, combines his activities as writer, artist and visionary. His intensely personal prophetic vision celebrates art as a vehicle for the imagination, in which painting, poetry and philosophical thought carry equal weight. A satire on Swedenborg's *Treatise Concerning Heaven and Hell* and *New Jerusalem and its Heavenly Doctrine* (both 1757-1758), it expresses Blake's distrust of institutionalised religion and materialism. Blake's belief that the laws that rule the physical world restrain man's true spirituality and imagination can be seen in the penultimate image of the book, before the final 'Song of Liberty' (f.24), in which a crawling slave-like figure illustrates the poet's authoritative proverb: 'One Law for the Lion and the Ox is Oppression.' The tail-piece illustrating the end of one of the *Memorable Fancies* (f.20) culminates in an exchange of apocalyptic visions between Blake and the Angel as they show each other their 'eternal lots.' The image seems to relate to Blake's vision of Leviathan: '... we discovered two globes of crimson fire from which the sea fled away in clouds of smoke, and now we saw, it was a head of Leviathan.' In his *Critical Essay* of 1868 (see p. 14), the poet Algernon Swinburne celebrated the elusive significance of Blake's prophecy and allowed it a degree of mystical inexplicability, referring the reader to Blake's own symbol of the soul that is 'inseparable but yet incompletely expressible through the body.' This split between the tangible and intangible elements of the world might be considered analogous with Blake's own creative process, oscillating between mystical thought and its verbal and visual expression.

Algernon Charles Swinburne

1837-1909

98. The Marriage of Heaven and Hell

Autograph manuscript, c. 1864
Given by Charles Fairfax Murray, 1916

With Dante Gabriel Rossetti, the poet and critic Algernon Charles Swinburne was one of the greatest champions of Blake's artistic genius in mid-nineteenth century Britain (see p. 14). Blake perfectly embodied Swinburne's ideal of the poet as an assimilator of past traditions and a torchbearer for his civilisation. In *William Blake, A Critical Essay* (1868), Swinburne vehemently defended the artist against the charges of insanity which had been published during his lifetime. Swinburne was deeply moved by the lack of recognition that Blake had suffered and the profound contrast between his modest life and the spiritual richness that underlined his poetry. He saw Blake as a visionary giant, outgrowing his own age, 'for there is no record of a man's being so far in advance of his time, in everything that belongs to the imaginative side of art, as Blake was from the first in advance of his.' Of all Blakes's prophecies, *The Marriage of Heaven and Hell* stood out for Swinburne as representing 'the high-water mark of his Intellect.' He demonstrated his admiration for Blake's text by transcribing it in full, from a copy lent to him by his friend Rossetti around 1864. Although appreciative of the original visual 'decorations', Swinburne scarcely commented on Blake's extraordinary illustrations and was most taken by the vivacity and eloquence of his language and thought, 'how much of lofty love and of noble faith animates these rapid and fervent words; what greatness of spirit and of speech there was in the man who, living as Blake lived, would write as Blake has written' (1868, 225).

Samuel Palmer

1805 – 1881

99. The Magic Apple Tree

Pen and Indian ink, and watercolour, in some areas mixed with a gum-like medium on paper | 349 x 273 mm | Given by A. E. Anderson, 1928 | no. 1490

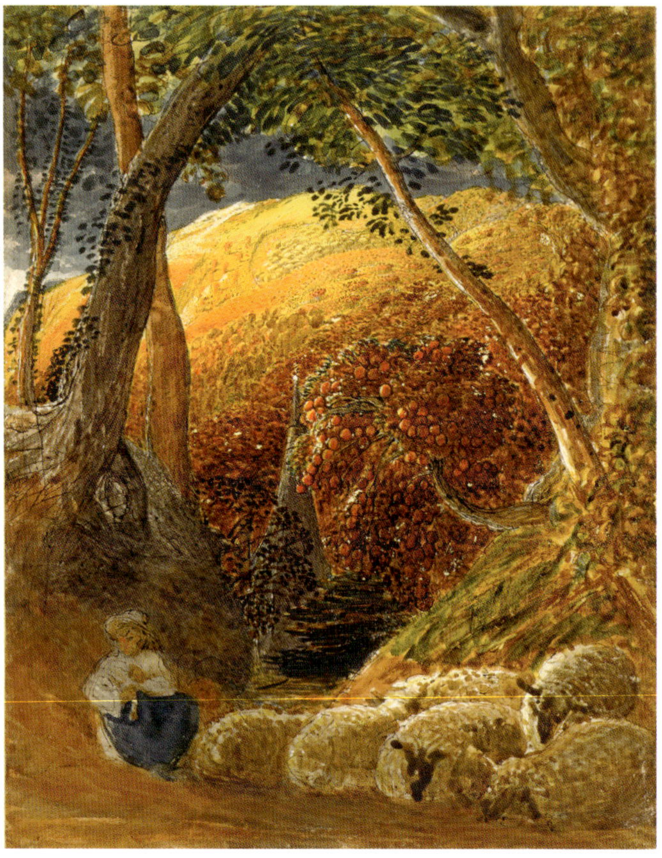

In 1824, at the age of nineteen, Palmer met a seventy-year-old Blake, three years before the master's death, and, with a small group of other young disciples, formed a literary and artistic circle called the 'Ancients'. About two years later Palmer moved to the village of Shoreham, in Kent, where he lived for five to six years in relative seclusion, visited occasionally by members of Blake's circle. With a keen interest in mysticism and asceticism, he spent most of his time reading poetry and taking long walks into the countryside. In his own work, despite John Linnell's advice to concentrate on more realistic, and financially lucrative, landscape painting, this resulted in a number of poetic representations of nature, of which *The Magic Apple Tree*, painted around 1830, is one of the most intense and visionary. The scene of a shepherd and his flock, set against a rich harvest, has both pastoral and religious resonances, its luminescent colours evoking the radiance of Gothic illuminated manuscripts. The work clearly represents Palmer's profound belief in a mystical relationship between art and nature and is best summed up by the painter's own words: 'The visions of the soul, being perfect, are the only true standard by which nature must be tried.'

100. Samuel Palmer (1805-1881) to John Linnell Autograph manuscript, Shoreham Kent, 21 December 1828

From the John Linnell Archive.
Bought with a grant from the Heritage Lottery Fund, together with contributions from the Friends of National Libraries, the Pilgrim Trust and the Charlotte Bonham-Carter Charitable Trust, 2000
MS. 148-2000

In this letter to John Linnell, his mentor and future father-in-law, Palmer argues for the supremacy of imaginative art over realistic representation. He passes from an apparently prosaic comment about the unavailability of a very particular type of apple that Linnell had asked him to find, to a description of a landscape, 'sprinkled and showered with a thousand pretty eyes and bud and spires and blossoms, gemm'd with dew, and … clad in living green', which stands in remarkable poetic correspondence with the most visionary of his Shoreham period drawings and watercolours.

Richard Dadd

1819-1887

101. Songe de la Fantasie

Pen, ink, point of the brush and watercolour on card
383 x 314 mm | Signed, dated and inscribed by the artist in ink, upper left: *Songe de la Fantasie / Rd. Dadd. Novr. 1864* | Provenance unknown
no. 3713

Dadd first ventured into the fantastic and imaginary by illustrating subjects from Shakespeare, including *Titania Sleeping* (c. 1841) and *Puck* (1841), both from *A Midsummer Night's Dream.* These established his reputation as a fairy painter, but his career took a dramatic turn around 1843 when he killed his father and was subsequently committed to Bethlam Hospital. This watercolour is a later version of a painting, *The Fairy Feller's Master-Stroke* (1855-1864, Tate Britain), which he executed during his stay at the institution, for its director G. H. Haydon. The unfinished oil remained at Bethlam after the artist was transferred to Broadmoor prison in 1864, where he spent the remaining years of his life. Within the first four months at Broadmoor, Dadd returned to the subject again and produced this watercolour, which, although not a direct copy of the earlier painting, closely corresponds to the original. Since the artist was most likely working from memory, the title of the work could be read literally as a recollection or indeed a 'dream' of a past fantasy that had haunted him. Most noticeably, Dadd introduced a complex network of swirling calligraphic lines across the surface, giving the work an even more abstract character and further distracting from its hermetic and barely-penetrable narrative. A year after its execution in 1865, Dadd wrote a long-winded and incomprehensible explanation of his *Fantasy* entitled, somewhat perversely, the *Elimination of a Picture and Its Subject- Called the Feller's Master Stroke.*

The Great-War poet Siegfried Sassoon (no. 28), who fought in the trenches with the painter's great nephew, Julian Dadd, once owned the oil version of this subject; he donated it to the Tate Gallery in 1963.

Charles Conder

1868-1909

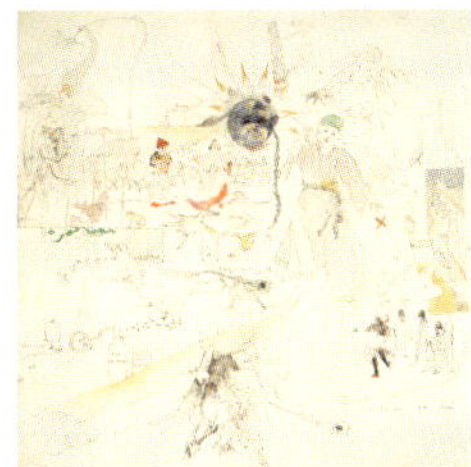

102. A Dream in Absinthe

Pen and ink with watercolour on paper
240 x 253 mm
Signed and dated, lower right: *C. Conder 90 Paris*; inscribed, in ink, upper right: *A DREAM IN ABSINTHE*
Given by Harold Wright, 1947 | PD.21-1947

Conder was one of the main exponents of a peculiarly Anglo-Saxon form of Impressionism in Australia and England. Born in London, he lived in India, Australia, Paris and finally, England, where he settled in 1897. He painted this semi-autobiographical watercolour soon after his arrival in Paris in August 1890. Its fragmentary composition conveys an idea of his multiple and disjointed first impressions of the city, as well as its bustling, lively street life. As the inscription shows, the title is evidently Conder's own, and reflects his energetic immersion in the bohemian life of Paris bars and cabarets. Conder rapidly became known as an English eccentric with a phenomenal capacity for drink, not least the hallucinogenic delights of the 'green goddess', absinthe. As the Symbolist writer and critic Arthur Symons recalled, Conder 'lived a wild life in Paris… He was sensual, casual in his *leves amores*, drawn incessantly into the thralls of Liliths' (Beckson, 1977, 184); some of these 'ferocious and over-nervous creatures' lurk in the corners of this dreamscape – somewhat sinister, for all its cartoon-like appearance. Next to Dadd's poetic *Songe de la Fantasie*, it stands as an intoxicating (or intoxicated) mockery of fairyland dreams.

Sidney Sime

1867-1941

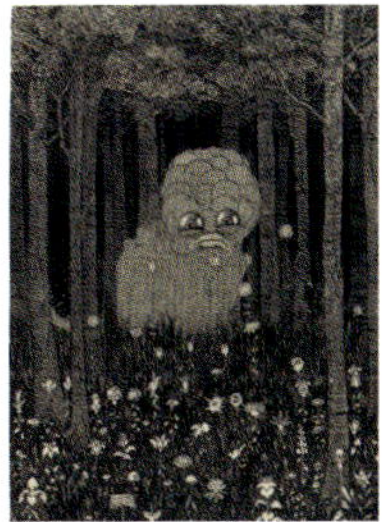

103. Bogey Beast, The Wily Grasser

Pen and ink with grey wash on paper
227 x 168 mm
Given by C.D. Rotch, 1942 | no. 2489

A cartoonist, caricaturist and illustrator, Sime enchanted his audiences with a characteristic combination of the mysterious and the humorous. His drawings appeared on the pages of papers and magazines such as *The Sketch*, *Punch*, *Pick-Me-Up* and *The Idler*. Despite the pervasive grotesqueness of his work, its visionary nature drew comparisons with Blake. Like him, Sime was drawn to the fantastic potential of religious and mystical subjects, and spent a considerable amount of time working in seclusion, away from London, on a series of paintings illustrating 'The Revelations of St. John the Devine'.

The Wily Grasser was executed as part of a 1905 series called 'The Sime Zoology: Beasts that might have been' and first appeared in *The Sketch* on 18 January. The was later enhanced and published in 1923 as *Bogey Beasts*, with highly obscure doggerel written by the artist, and musical accompaniment by the composer Joseph Holbrooke, who, like Sime, was generously patronised by Lord Howard de Walden. In association with Herbert Trench, De Walden, one of the leading patrons of the Theatre Royal, Haymarket, staged Maeterlinck's *The Blue Bird* in 1909 and Ibsen's *The Pretenders* in 1913, both of which had sets and costumes designed by Sime. In fact, the artist showed a strong interest in theatre from the beginning of his career, executing a series of caricatures of famous London actors and music-hall singers.

Sime cited Edgar Allen Poe, Heinrich Heine, Thomas De Quincey and George Meredith as key influences. He cultivated his relationship with the literary world by illustrating fantasy books by Lord Dunsany between 1905 and 1916 and designing covers for de Walden's (under the pseudonym of T.E. Ellis) and Holbrooke's collaborative trilogy: *Dylan*, *The Children of Don* and *Bronwen*, published in parts between 1910 and 1922. However, Sime's own inventions were praised by his contemporaries for their independence from written sources and avoidance of verbal explanation or narrative. The occasional commentaries on his drawings that he provided are so mystifying and convulsive that they only create an even greater state of bewilderment. One such example is the nonsensical jingle accompanying the *Wily Grasser* in the *Bogey Beasts*, which was added to the image at a later stage, and supplements it with a separate set of imaginative evocations:

Once I saw
The Grasser
Sit,
Where
The Wuffle Wood
Leaves a lot
And barks
A bit,
Like a grown wood should…

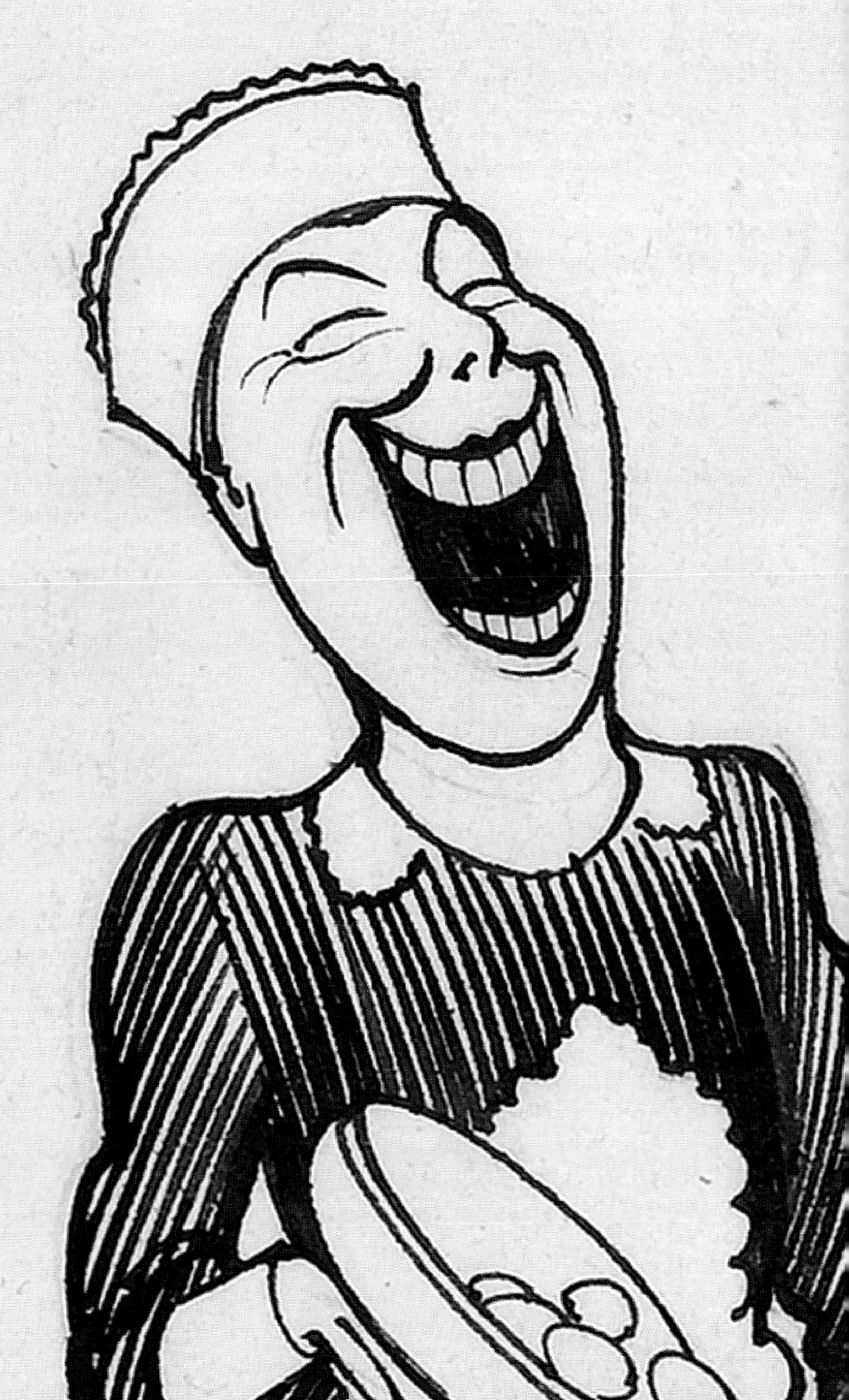

Where's the Joke?

Rosie Ibbotson

Where's the Joke?

Rosie Ibbotson

The distinctive images which fall under the term 'caricature' are unique in the word/image relationship in having a single purpose: to make us laugh.

While caricature has often been labeled 'low-art', this very status allows it to enjoy infinite scope, in both the subject-matter it addresses, and the ways in which it communicates meaning, through text, image, or a combination of the two. However, for the joke to emerge, more is required. Both text and image demand that the viewer engage with the broad base of their existing knowledge. This, the 'beholder's share', is an interpretive response to a work of art, and will vary according to the spectator's memory, knowledge and cultural background.[1] Understanding the humour in a caricature therefore depends on the extent and relevance of the viewer's knowledge, and whether this sufficiently overlaps with the caricaturist's intentions. When both are attuned, a complicity between creator and beholder ensues: 'getting the joke' is the reward.

The role of the 'beholder's share' in understanding a caricature is twofold. Firstly, it requires the ability to 'read' highly abbreviated images, drawn with a rigorous economy of line. Although this by no means applies to caricature alone, the spare draughtsmanship of artists such as Phil May (no. 109) serves to illustrate how problems can arise with the legibility of this particular pictorial shorthand: *Punch* readership's initially lukewarm reception of May's caricatures prompted one editor to ask, 'Couldn't you finish up your drawings a bit more?'[2]

Secondly, to respond to the humour of the caricature, the viewer must often engage with its topicality, and match the lifespan of the joke. For, while as drawings caricatures are arguably timeless, as they can be admired for their draughtsmanship and composition long after their humour has expired, their subject clearly affects the durability of the joke, and one concerning a universal truth or an ageless observation about humanity is less likely to date than one drawing on the etiquette, events or social mores of a particular era. If the caricatures included in this section of the exhibition continue to amuse, they do so to varying degrees. For example, both George du Maurier's *Putting his foot in it* (no.107) and May's *Bad business or Wasted Efforts* (no.109) are set in situations which are less familiar to the modern viewer than they would have been to their original audience. Despite this, May's joke emerges completely unscathed, since its parody of penny-pinching businesses strikes a chord with viewers of any era. In contrast, du Maurier's joke suffers slightly. The Victorian obsession with daintiness having long since ended, a joke about a man accidentally insulting a woman by drawing attention to her large feet loses much of its impact before a more 'liberated' modern audience. Both of these cartoons appeared in the satirical weekly *Punch*, whose concern with the topical, and status as a periodic publication, is likely to have encouraged the treatment of subjects of a more transient nature.[3] The extent to which the jokes represented in these particular examples *have* endured, speaks much for the wit of du Maurier and May, who, unlike certain of their contemporaries on *Punch*, including Charles Keene, devised their own jokes for the majority of their caricatures.

Caricature proper – as first practiced in the sixteenth century by the Bolognese painter Annibale Carracci – originally referred to drawings in which people's physiognomies and proportions had been distorted. More recently, however, caricature has become associated with the cartoon, a term first used to denote satirical drawings in *Punch* in 1843, so that now, even drawings devoid of human figures can be counted as caricatures. Even when the 'still' (non-animated) cartoon lacks an amusing caption, it is immediately recognisable as comic, largely by virtue of what Gombrich and Kris describe as a 'peculiarly humorous style of draughtsmanship.'[4]

RIGHT
108. Charles Samuel Keene
1823-1891
Most Assuring

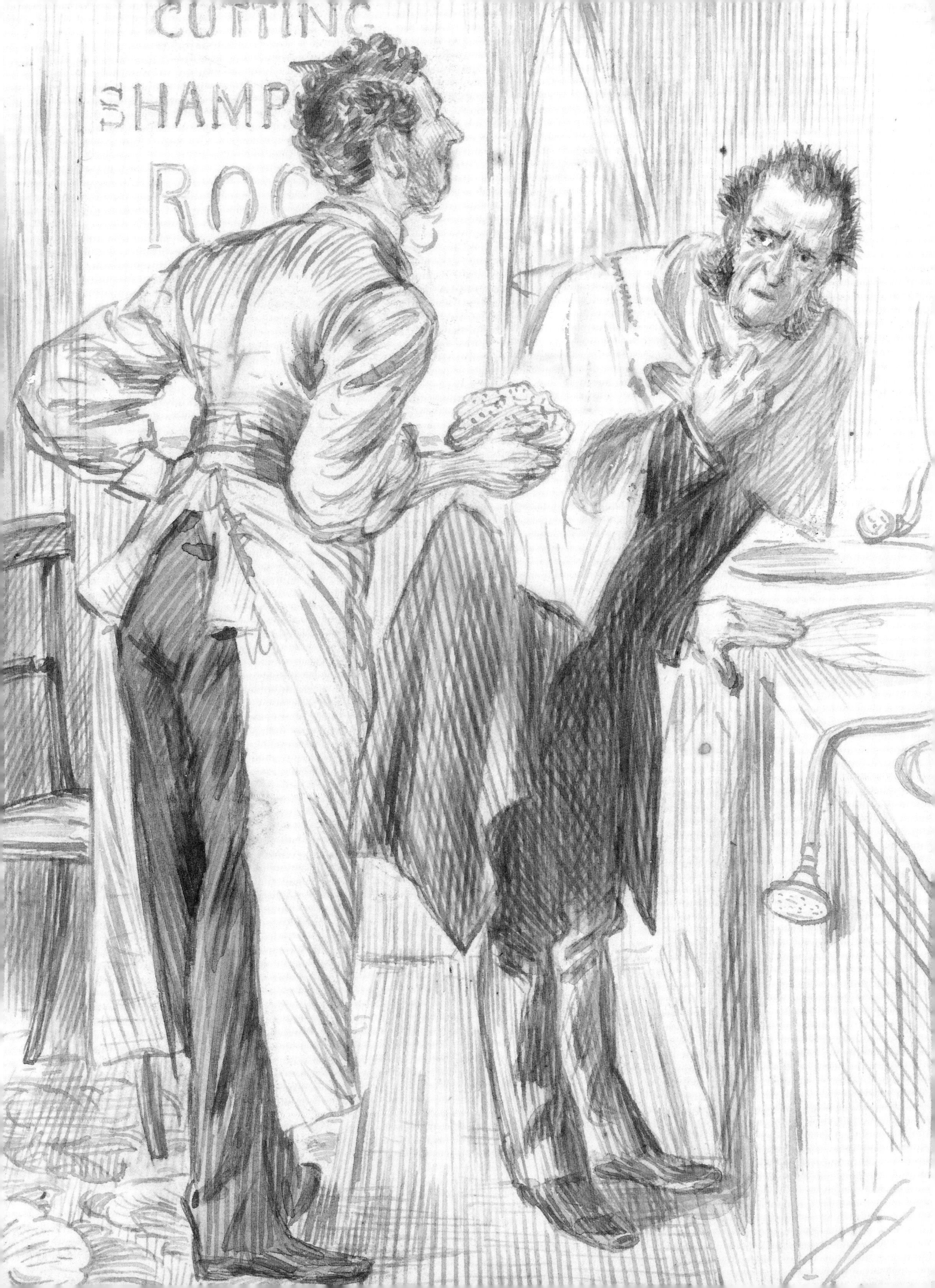
CUTTING
SHAMP
ROC

This style is best represented by Henry Mayo Bateman's *The maid who was but human* (no.116). As with mime, or in silent movies, the joke here is wholly in the image – a sort of visual slapstick – and relies in no significant way on text. This is true, too, of Edmund Dulac's *Caricature of Ricketts and Shannon* (no. 104), although each artist uses different methods to communicate the joke, exemplifying the two principal means by which an image can convey humour. The first, and the earliest in terms of the history of caricature, is the most predominantly visual. It involves either distortion, or the metamorphosis of one thing into another, and relies on the spectator's existing knowledge of appearances. In this scenario the beholder's share is to match (or rather enjoy the mis-match of) the image with an existing expectation of the subject's appearance. This is clearly the case with Dulac's portrait-parody: the fusion of famous faces with the fantastical but well-known forms of the Hindu god makes us laugh by its very absurdity. The second type relies less on the humour inherent in pictorial form than on a joke that is conveyed through the construction of a narrative. In Bateman's cartoon, this narrative is communicated using a strip-cartoon that shows a chronological sequence of events in a series of frames. Indeed, the only text relating to it is the title, and this simply as an adjunct to the image. More often than not, however, the comic narrative element is conveyed by texts of varying lengths, as other exhibits in this section demonstrate. Whether this text takes the form of a lengthy dialogue accompanying a single frame, as in certain examples by Keene, du Maurier and May, or a few deftly-placed words within the image – such as 'Beware of falling masonry' on a sign in the cartoon by William Augustus Sillince (no.112) – it plays a critical role in communicating the joke.

Dulac's gently mocking portrait of Ricketts and Shannon stands out in this group as the only caricature where no narrative, textual or pictorial, plays a significant role. Although Arthur Boyd Houghton's *Barber's Saloon, New York* (no.110), engraved for *Graphic America* in 1870, has no immediately visible text associated with it, the scene – from real life, we are assured – is elucidated in an accompanying article in the same journal, which unlocks the comedy merely suggested by the amusing anecdotes and characters. As such, Boyd Houghton's drawing also demonstrates how the presence of texts can affect the style of caricatural draughtsmanship, that is as the amount of text increases, the humoristic qualities of the drawing *per se* often correspondingly decrease. A comparison between George du Maurier's *De gustibus non disputandum* (no.106) and the Bateman highlights this point: in the former, it is the text that single-handedly carries the joke, relieving the drawing from the need to be funny. As a result, the image becomes something more akin to an illustration, and, considered in isolation, the style in which the figures are represented could be seen as sentimental rather than comic. In the Bateman, however, there is no explanatory text, so that the joke announces itself through the image, relying on the quick-paced legibility of the strip-cartoon format. These, of course, are extremes: on the whole a more equitable balance exists between text and image, as in Phil May's *Bad business or Wasted Efforts* (no.109), with its lengthy caption and amusing pictorial style.

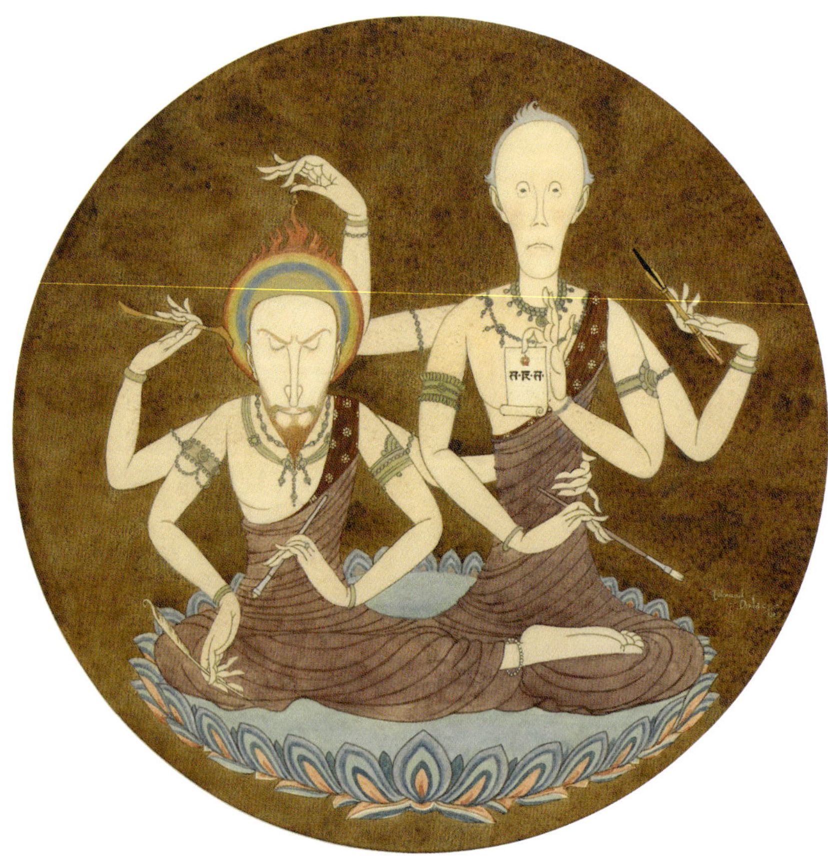

The cross-section of caricatures in this exhibition follows a more-or-less chronological trend in which the joke becomes increasingly grounded within the image. Whereas the joke in the du Maurier cartoon would remain more or less intact without the picture, detaching Max Beerbohm's images from his series *The Future, as beheld...* (nos. 113-115) would only leave three nonsensical sentences; yet remove these from the drawings, and they, too, would 'misfire'. In this case – appropriately for an artist who practiced

ABOVE
104. Edmund Dulac
1882-1953
Ricketts and Shannon as Hindu gods (Ri-Ké-Tsan-Dcha-Nhon)

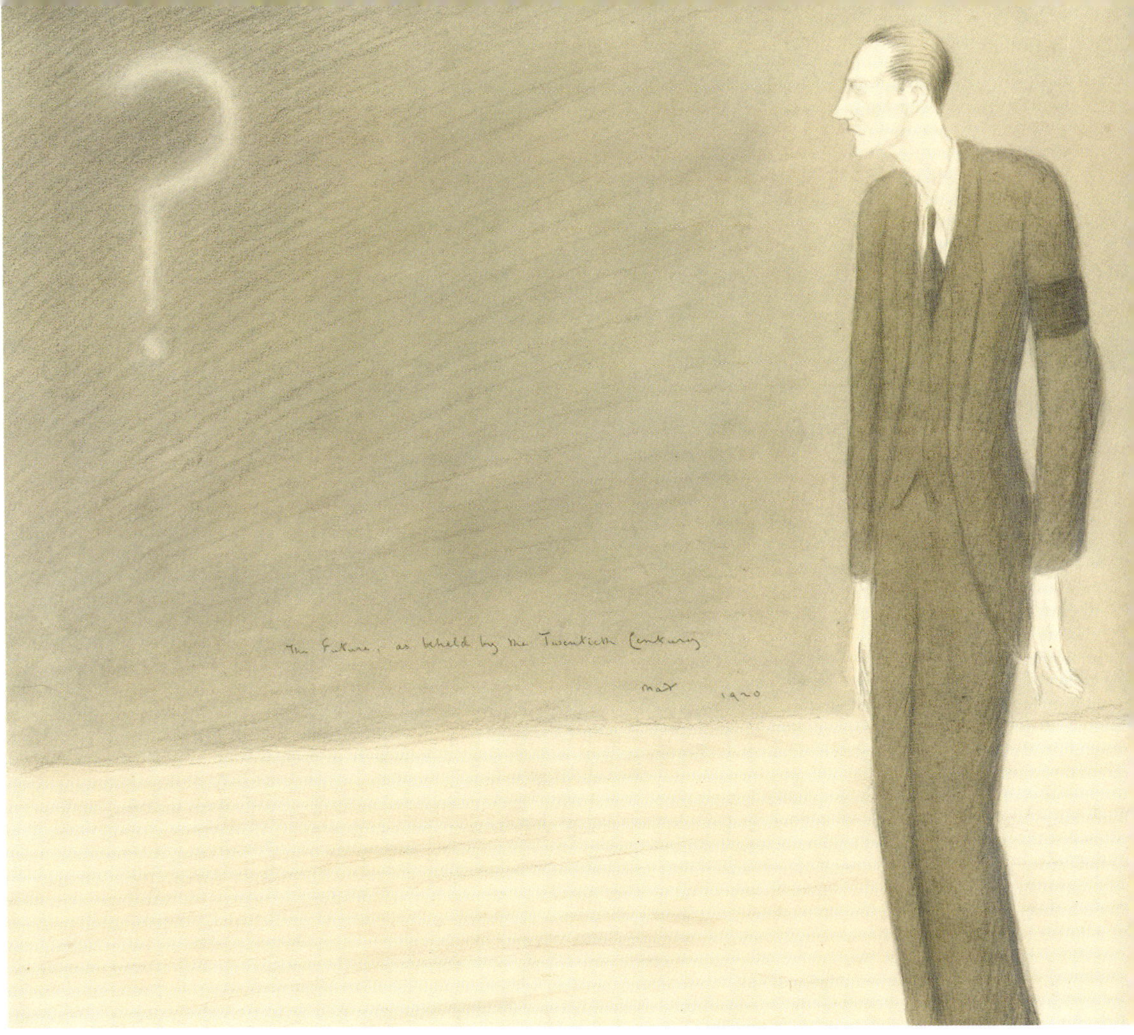

ABOVE
115. Max Beerbohm
1872–1956
The Future, as beheld by the twentieth century

both the literary and visual arts – the relationship between text and image is perfectly cyclical.

While the 'black and white' artists represented found common ground in the society and customs they parodied – albeit often different sectors of that society, from dandies to street urchins – many were also linked by their own circles, through their work, friendships and spheres of influence. At least five of the eight worked for *Punch*, three were members of the London Sketch Club, and three are linked seemingly arbitrarily by their enthusiasm for poking fun at the institution of the barber's shop.

Certainly, whether dealing with contemporary events, or the foibles of the human race, the caricaturist cannot afford to be a hermit or social pariah. Du Maurier and, to a greater extent, Beerbohm, for example, had many friends and connections in all walks of life, and several different countries; a role-call of Beerbohm's connections, in particular, would yield the names of many of those who feature elsewhere in this exhibition. In both of these cases, the caricaturist, defying his status as a practitioner of a 'lowly' art form, was located at the epicentre of the literary and artistic circles of his day.

1 The term 'beholder's share' is used by Ernst Gombrich in *Art and Illusion* (London, 1977) to describe the process whereby the formal components of a picture are converted into an intelligible image in the spectator's mind.

2 May responded, 'When I can leave out half the lines I now use, I shall want six times the money,' quoted in R.G.G.Price, *A History of 'Punch'*, London, 1957, 172.

3 However, the 'Even now' section in the late editions of *Punch* – where an old caricature was reprinted due to its striking relevance to much later events – draws attention to how many of *Punch*'s cartoons have stood the test of time. See introduction by David Thomas in Amanda-Jane Doran, ed., *The 'Punch' Book of Utterly British Humour*, London, 1989, 9.

4 According to Gombrich and Kris, the evolution of this style coincided with the development of pictorial humour in *Punch*, Ernst Gombrich and Ernst Kris, *Caricature*, Harmondsworth, 1940, 24.

Edmund Dulac

1882–1953

104. Ricketts and Shannon as Hindu gods (Ri-Ké-Tsan-Dcha-Nhon)

Watercolour on paper | Diameter: 290mm
Signed and dated, lower right: *Edmund Dulac / 1914*
Given by the Nicholson Gallery, 1972 | no. 2483

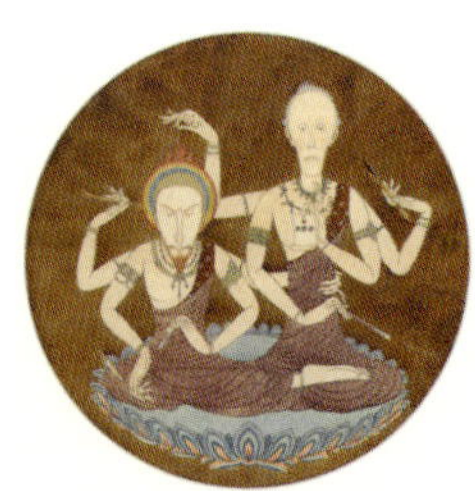

Falling somewhere between the fantastic and the comical, this watercolour portrait plays not so much on text as on the viewer's existing knowledge of the sitters' taste and appearances. Apart from the title, the only words associated with the image are the three letters 'A.R.A.' on the scroll held by Shannon, which celebrates his election as an associate member of the Royal Academy in 1911.

As well the scroll, Ricketts and Shannon – each seated cross-legged and Vishnu-like, their four arms signifying their presence in both the physical and the spiritual world – hold brushes and pens, the tools of their trade. In addition to being painters, the two men were among the most distinguished collectors of the day, amassing not only a large collection of antiquities, paintings and graphic art of the European schools (most of which they bequeathed to the Fitzwilliam), but also many fine examples of Japanese woodblock prints, Indian and Persian miniatures, oriental bronzes and ceramics, and it is this latter passion that is evidently the butt of Dulac's joke.

French by birth, and trained at art academies in Paris, Dulac moved to England in 1904 to work as an illustrator. It was through joining the London Sketch Club in 1905 that he developed his ability as a caricaturist, but he worked mostly as a book illustrator, and greatly admired the work of Morris and Beardsley. As the gentle mockery of this portrait suggests, Dulac was a close friend of Ricketts and Shannon, and one who shared their taste for all forms of oriental art and culture. His own dining room was adorned with 'dusky Chinese silk paintings' and his guests required to eat with chopsticks, seated on the floor, Japanese-style, while listening to Dulac's recordings of chants from Japanese *nō* plays; to his contemporary, the writer, Clifford Bax, his mind 'always seemed to be derived in equal parts from Toulon and from Tokyo' (1936, 180).

George-Louis-Palmella-Busson du Maurier

1834–1896

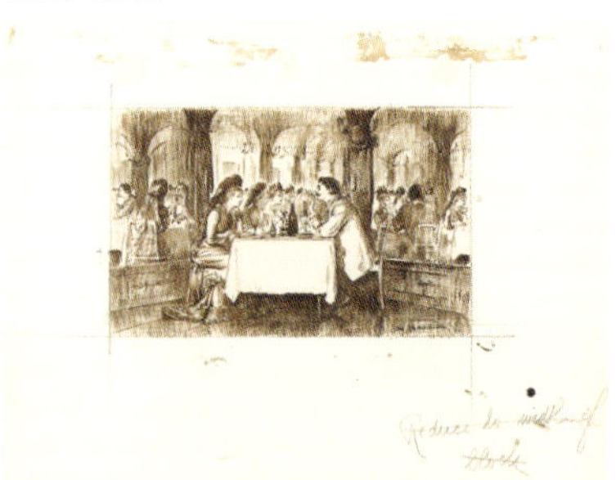

105. Edwin and Angelina in Paris

Pen and brown ink on paper
122 x 198 mm
Bequeathed by Dr J. W. L. Glaisher, 1928 | no. 1505e

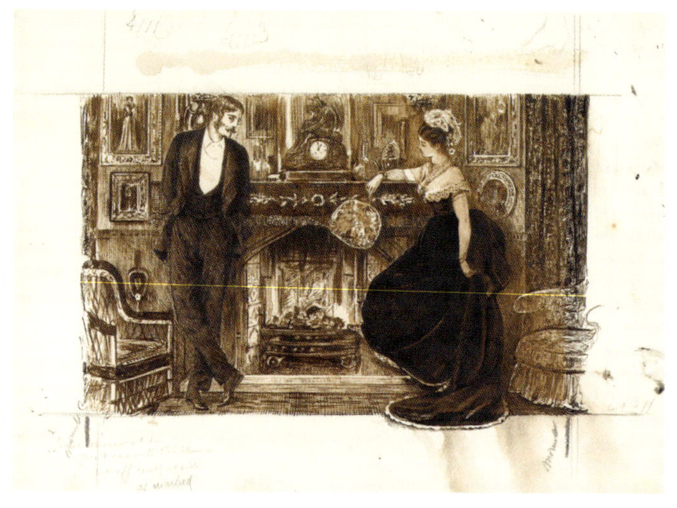

106. De gustibus non disputandum

Pen and brown ink on paper | 252 x 337 mm
Bequeathed by Dr J. W. L. Glaisher, 1928 | no. 1505d

107. Putting his foot in it

Pen, brown ink and brown wash on paper 254 x 177 mm
Given by the Trustees of the Estate of George du Maurier, 1934 | no. 1727c

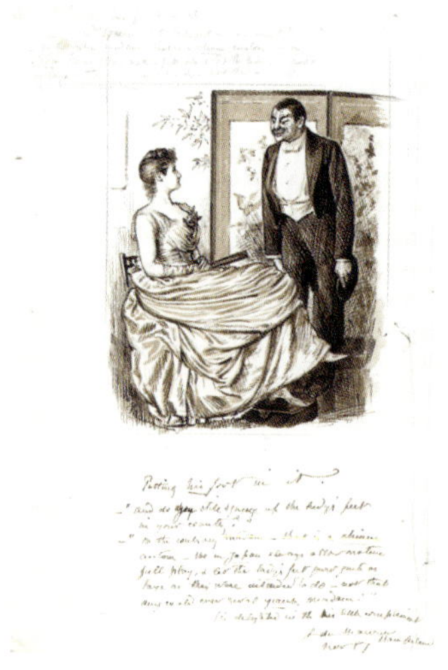

French-born, du Maurier moved to England as a teenager in 1851, but returned to Paris five years later to study art. In 1857, after travelling to Antwerp to continue his training, he suddenly lost his sight in one eye, which ended his ambitions of a serious painting career. While convalescing, he saw the *Punch Almanack*, and soon after began to contemplate a career in illustration. In 1860 he returned permanently to London, where he became a figure in Hampstead's bohemian artistic and literary circles.

These three drawings were executed by du Maurier for the satirical magazine *Punch* during his thirty-two years as a staff artist. This role naturally prompted comparison of his work with that of another of *Punch*'s major artists, Charles Keene, although du Maurier was quick to assert an independent terrain: 'I have generally stuck to the "classes" because C K seems to have monopolised the "masses". As his characters' attire, preoccupations and interior settings confirm, du Maurier made the English middle-classes his prime target for satire, and specifically those with artistic pretensions. In this he conformed fully to *Punch*'s editorial resolve in 1882 to 'persistently attack to the bitter end' (Savory and Marks, 1985, 150) the fashionable absurdities of the Aesthetic Movement.

Each of the caricatures demonstrates du Maurier's tendency to accompany his drawings with long captions, generally in dialogue, on which he relies heavily to transmit the humour of the scene. If these sometimes long-winded exchanges can appear like 'tiresome one-act-plays' to twenty- and twenty-first century audiences (Hillier, 1970, 106), du Maurier was by no means alone in using this mechanism, and Keene's drawings in particular often depend on extended textual commentaries. However, whereas most of Keene's captions were written by other people then sent to him to illustrate, du Maurier's jokes were for the most part of his own invention.

Edwin and Angelina in Paris combines two stock characters in du Maurier's satirical vocabulary, a vacuous-looking woman, struggling with *ennui*, and her companion, a narcissistic dandy. Characteristically, du Maurier does not resort to exaggeration of physiognomy or gesture to convey his joke, but instead uses a combination of the broader pictorial composition and text. At first glance, the couple appears to be sitting in a crowded restaurant, but closer inspection shows that they are surrounded by mirrors, enjoying only the reflection of themselves. Their vanity, already evident from their elegant dress, is highlighted by the dialogue which accompanied the drawing in an 1878 edition of *Punch* :

> *Angelina: "Do you like this style of mural decoration, Edwin?"*
> *Edwin: "Yes, love! It enables me to see on every wall the face and form I love best in the world."*
> *Angelina: "Oh, Edwin! DARLING! – you make me blush!"*
> *Edwin: "I didn't mean yours, love! I meant mine!"*

The characters Edwin and Angelina appeared on a number of occasions in du Maurier's *Punch* cartoons, and ultimately derive from Oliver Goldsmith's poem *The Hermit.* However, a much more likely, and more immediate, inspiration for the series was Violet Fane's delightfully mocking and hugely popular *Edwin and Angelina Papers*, which appeared in monthly instalments in *The World*, between January 1877 and May the following year, and was published in book form by the end of 1878. The serialised novel concerns the courtship, marriage and subsequent adventures of Edwin and his wife Angelina, 'a young married lady of literary aspiration,' too often led astray by the 'strange and evanescent vagiaries of Fashion' and by indulging in reading voguish romantic literature such as 'Swinburne-and-water,' a 'rather huggy and kissy and *warm*' account of an (over-) amorous young poet.

Du Maurier's other caricatures exhibited here function in identical ways. *Putting his foot in it*, which appeared in *Punch* in 1887, trades both on a compliment that has backfired, turning into an insult, and on the cult for Oriental – and particularly Japanese – art among 'aesthetic' households. *De gustibus non disputandum* of 1876 (no. 106), subtitled *at least not by beautiful people of either sex*, also parodies vain, patently self-obsessed individuals. As this couple's petty and point-scoring argument shows, matters of taste are indeed not to be disputed:

> *Adonis (after his guests have departed): 'By Jove, Maria, what a handsome woman Mrs Jones is! She looks better than ever!'*
> *His wife: 'Ahem! Well it may be bad taste, but I own I have hitherto failed to detect the beauty of Mrs Jones. Now Mr Jones is good-looking, if you like.'*
> *Adonis: 'Jones, good-looking! Come, hang it, Maria, Jones is a very good fellow, and all that; but I must say I never perceived his good looks!'*
> *&C., &C.*

The careful observance of speech patterns evident in du Maurier's texts is perhaps unsurprising considering that he worked as both an author and an artist, writing and illustrating three novels towards the end of his life.

Charles Samuel Keene

1823-1891

108. Most Assuring

Pen and black ink on paper | 199 x 135 mm
Signed in brown ink, lower right: *cK*; Inscribed: *'Bere(?) from his friend Charles S. Keene'*
Given by Sir Ivor and Lady Batchelor, 1996 | PD.3-1996

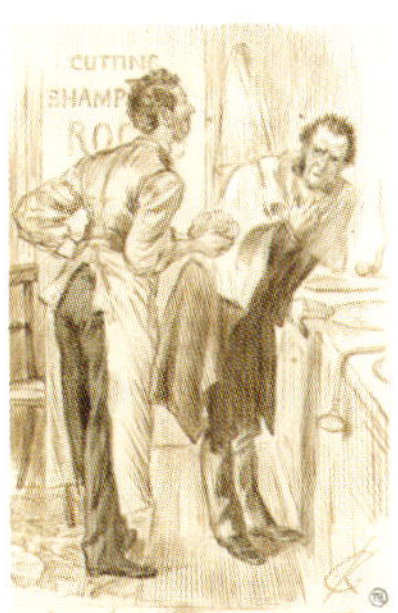

BROWN *[who is nervous about sanitary matters and detects something]* 'Hum (sniffs) Surely – this system of yours – these pipes now – do they communicate with your main drain?'
HAIR DRESSER *(with cheery grin)* – '*Di*-rect, Sir!!'

The illustrations for *Punch* brought about a revolution in the meaning of the word 'cartoon'. Until 1843, it was used to refer to any rough, preparatory drawing, but thereafter became associated with comic or humorous ones. In part, this change was caused by the need to define new satirical forms. The term 'caricature', originally used to refer to a grotesquely exaggerated physiognomy or portrait – a form of satire that all but disappeared by the end of the eighteenth century – came to encompass any separately issued copper-plate print sold or displayed in print shops. At the same time, it signalled a change in cultural climate: although the work of Hogarth and great caricaturists such as Gillray was still greatly admired, the Victorians felt uncomfortable with the more disreputable, or caustic, elements of their prints. The 'political sketches' or 'cuts' that replaced them were satirical and often denunciatory, but they never challenged the proprieties of the day, and the appearance of a new word to describe any humorous drawing was therefore no coincidence. Text became increasingly important, not only because the cartoon was no longer issued separately on a single sheet and was instead included in a text-based journal, but also because the cartoon itself was accompanied by a written joke. Keene's cartoon reverts back to the classic comedic contrast of extremes used constantly throughout the previous century, most skilfully by Thomas Rowlandson, but achieves the same result through the dialogue, rather than through the illustration alone, by contrasting the hesitant, broken speech of the uneasy customer with the cheery gusto of the proud barber.

EL

Philip William May

1864-1903

109. Bad Business or Wasted Efforts

Pen and black ink on card | 202 x 286 mm
Signed and dated in ink, lower right: *PHIL MAY / 95*
Given by Sir Ivor and Lady Batchelor, 1994 | PD.140-1994

New Assistant *(after Hair Cutting, to Jones who has been out of town for a few weeks)*: 'Your hair is very thin behind sir, try singeing?'
Jones: 'Yes, I think I will'
Assistant (*after a pause*): 'Shampoo Sir? Good for the 'air.'
Jones: 'Thank you, yes.'
Assistant: 'Your moustache curled, Sir?'
Jones: 'Please.'
Assistant: 'May I give you a friction, Sir?'
Jones: 'Thank you!'

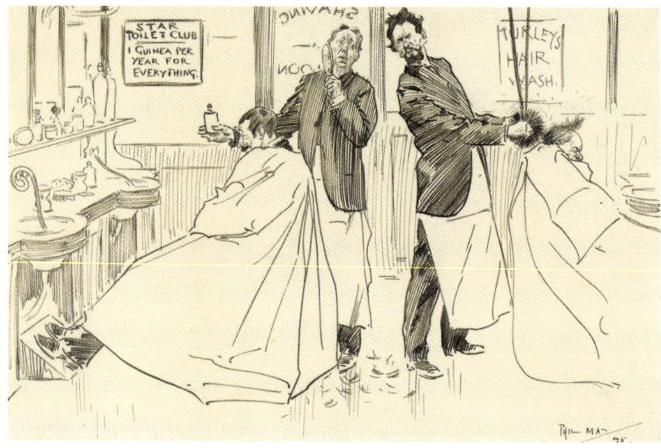

The Proprietor (*sotto voce*): 'Shut up, you fool, 'e 's a Member of the Toilet Club!!' Unlike the majority of eighteenth-century caricatures, in which a distinction between 'political' and 'social' satire was often difficult to draw, those of the late nineteenth century fell into much more distinct categories. Typically, an edition of *Punch* would be composed of several pages of text interspersed with cartoons, or 'cuts', and one full-page 'big cut' which was usually political in emphasis. Of the many comic journals in existence, *Punch* was most indebted to the French journal *Le Charivari*, founded in 1832, in which barbed political satire went hand-in-hand with a much gentler mocking of social foibles. For M. H. Spielmann, while *Punch's* power might have derived from its political cuts, its popularity came from its 'socials', whose sole aim was to produce 'the evanescent smile of a harmless satire'. May's cartoon, published in *Punch*, 25 May 1895, is a good example of the attempt to raise such a smile. The joke lies in the give and take of a conversation, not least in the use of a phonetic shorthand to convey the sound of the dialogue : the barbers dropping their 'h's contrasted with the eloquently monosyllabic answers of the gentleman customer. Within the drawing itself there are also touches of humour outside the joke's parameters, most especially the seated customer on the right undergoing rough treatment (Turley's hair wash, perhaps?).

EL

Arthur Boyd Houghton
1836-1875

110. The Barber's Saloon, New York

Wood engraving | 312 x 418mm | Letterpress on *verso*
Bequeathed by J.R. Holliday, 1927 | P.1196-R

In February 1870 the *Graphic* set amongst the other advertisements a short notice announcing the launch of Houghton's special assignment series entitled 'Graphic America'. The notice began by lamenting British artists' neglect of the manners and customs of the New World, and admitted that the real American was almost certainly as unlike his stereotype 'as the modern Englishman is unlike the gross fat man in a low-crowned hat, top boots, and with a bludgeon in his hand, whom our humorists typify as John Bull.' Houghton was offered the chance to record in illustrations and accompanying articles the new sights and experiences from his trip. This caricature was published as part of the 'Graphic America' series on 16 April 1870.

However, as both image and text show, Houghton in every case reverted back to familiar stereotypes. In the related article he recounts how, as a guest at the Fifth Avenue Hotel on Madison Square in New York, he finds himself transformed into a bewildered John Bull, baffled by the larger-than-life New Yorkers, complaining of the lack of privacy and the quality of the food, and dreaming instead of the cosiness of English inns. The barbers' saloons, attached to every hotel, are one 'convenience' that escape complaint. In this illustration Houghton conveys the sheer luxury of the establishment, with its glass doors and cushioned chairs, but even here relies on visual precedent: the comic distortions of the characters – most notably the upturned nose and affected pose of the central barber – and the contrast of extremes between the stocky attendant and his gaunt customer, are comic ploys that were frequently exploited in eighteenth-century caricature.

EL

Charles Samuel Keene
1823-1891

111. The Barber's Shop

Pen and black ink heightened with white ink on paper | 145 x 185 mm
Private collection

Male grooming fell victim to the wit of the satirist from the eighteenth century onwards. Along with the pole, the bowl, the apron and other implements of the barber's trade that identified his business to the viewer, another common feature of the barber's shop was the newspaper, signalling that it, like the coffee shop, was an exclusively male environment, a place for men to discuss politics and public affairs. However, if the types are recognisable, the figures themselves are highly individual, a quality that George du Maurier attributed to Keene's exceptional powers of observation. He was, moreover – as this drawing shows – an exceptionally gifted draughtsman, admired by artists of the stature of Edgar Degas. Here, he brilliantly exploits the cramped compositional space to enhance the comic close encounters of the protagonists.

EL

William Augustus Sillince
1906-1974

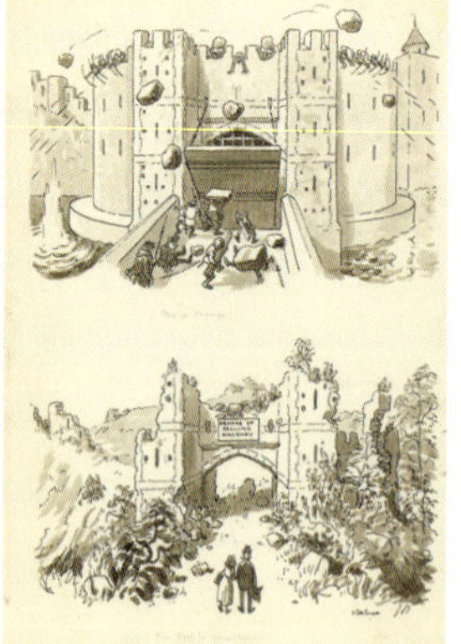

112. *Plus ça change… plus c'est la même chose*

Pen, ink and grey wash on board
(Windsor and Newton, Fashion Plate)
381 x 269 mm
Signed in ink, lower right: *Sillince*
Bought, 1973 | PD.44-1973

Sillince was yet another cartoonist of the *Punch* stable, and worked on the magazine's staff from 1936 until his death in 1974.

In this cartoon he employs a favourite format: the juxtaposition of comparable images as a means to highlight an absurdity, in this case, that of a constructional and cultural 'before and after', with the laconic inscription, 'The more things change, the more they stay the same.'

Max Beerbohm

1872–1956

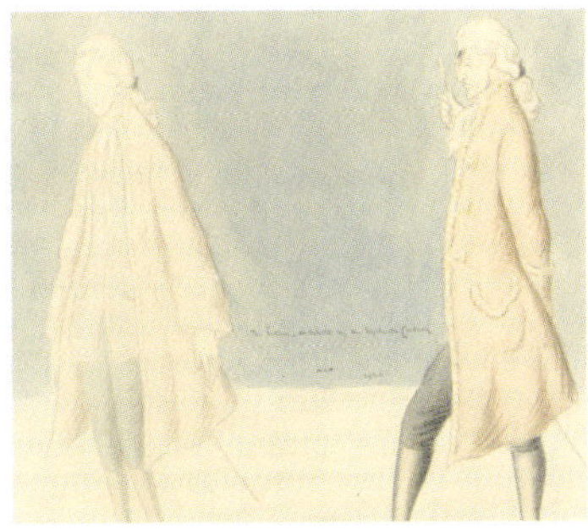

113. The Future, as beheld by the eighteenth century

Graphite and watercolour on paper, laid down | 261 x 295 mm
Signed and dated in graphite, centre: *Max 1920*; Inscribed: *The Future, as beheld by the Eighteenth Century*
Given by the Friends of the Fitzwilliam Museum, 1923
no. 1089a

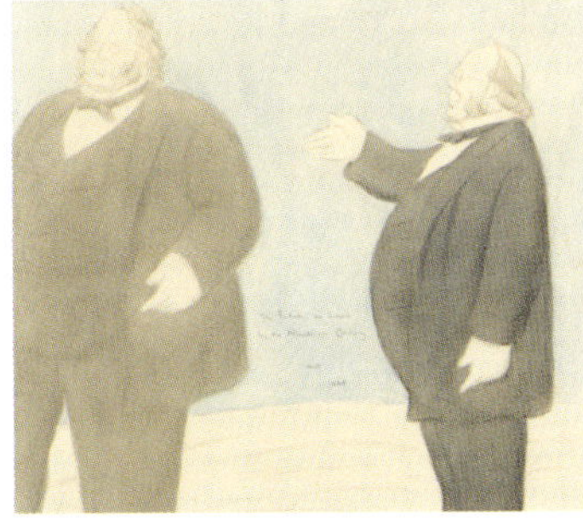

114. The Future, as beheld by the nineteenth century

Graphite and watercolour on paper, laid down | 259 x 296 mm
Signed and dated in graphite, centre: *Max 1920*; Inscribed: *The Future, as beheld by the Nineteenth Century*
Given by the Friends of the Fitzwilliam Museum, 1923
no. 1089b

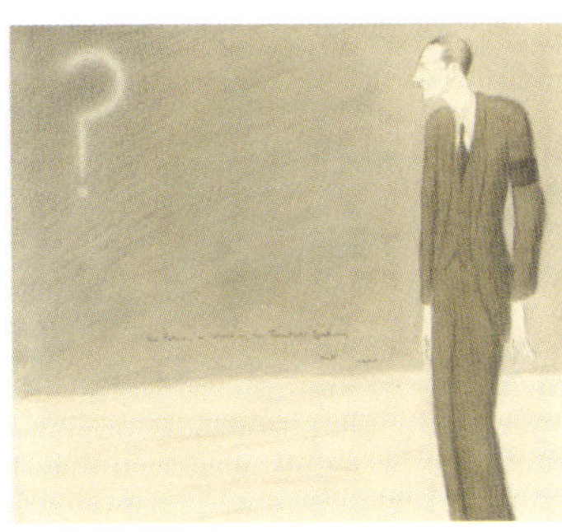

115. The Future, as beheld by the twentieth century

Graphite and watercolour on paper, laid down | 253 x 296 mm
Signed and dated in graphite, centre: *Max 1920*; Inscribed: *The future, as beheld by the Twentieth Century*
Given by the Friends of the Fitzwilliam Museum, 1923 | no. 1089c

These drawings occupy an ambiguous place in caricature. Not only is their 'joke' not strictly comical but they also could stand alone in a way that an individual frame in a strip-cartoon could not. Like the two separate images in Sillince's cartoon (no. 112), each frame summarises an epoch rather than a series of moments. Using the caricaturists' technique of exaggeration, Beerbohm has shown three men, on the right-hand side of each image, contemplating – in every case bleakly – future versions of themselves.

The thin apparition of 'the future as beheld by the eighteenth century' suggests difficult times ahead, whereas the overweight and prosperous-looking Victorian premonition appears to symbolise capitalist gain. The question mark in the final frame needs no explanation; nor does it give one. These three visions recall the ghosts of Christmas Past, Present, and Yet to Come in Charles Dickens's *A Christmas Carol*, in which the third forecast is the similarly the most ominous. Not only is the vision of the twentieth century uncertain, but the use of monochrome, which only appears in the third of the trilogy, suggests that the twentieth century's prospects appeared especially gloomy when the series was executed. The gaunt man in the final frame wears a black armband, perhaps evoking the War which had ended two years earlier and shaken the morale of the nation, and more broadly, mourning the end of an epoch.

In order for the 'joke' to be understood, both image and the text, for all its brevity, are necessary. This is unusual in Beerbohm's caricatures, which on the whole take the form of physical distortions of recognisable political and society figures, many of whom were his personal friends. All three drawings were bought for the museum by its director, Sydney Cockerell, in 1923. In a letter to Cockerell in June that year Beerbohm proclaimed himself delighted with his 'enshrinement among the augustusnesses of the Fitzwilliam' (Meynell, 1956, 30).

Henry Mayo Bateman

1887–1970

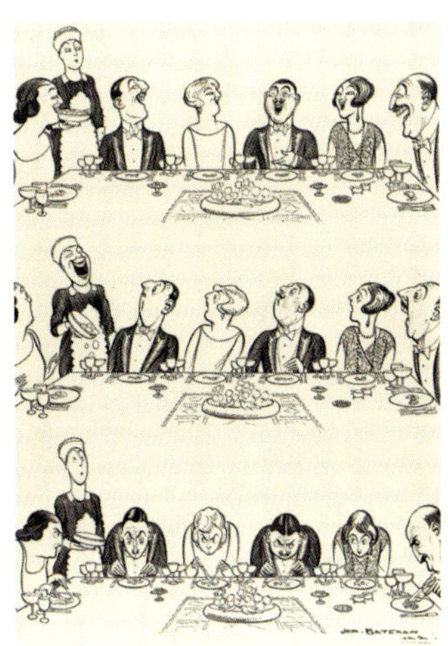

116. The maid who was but human

Pen and black ink on paper, laid down | 450 x 330 mm
Signed and dated lower right: *H. M. Bateman / 1922*
Bequeathed by J. R. Holliday, 1927 | no. 1207

Australian by birth, Bateman enjoyed a long and successful career as a book illustrator and caricaturist, working extensively for *Punch*, but also for other journals such as *The Sketch*, *The Tatler* and – at the peak of his popularity – *The Radio Times*. He also worked in advertising, producing posters for film and theatre.

Bateman's early work was influenced by both Henry Osporvat and Sidney Sime (see no. 103), and like them he drew many of his subjects from the world of the theatre, but around 1911 he evolved his own, instantly recognisable, style of visual farce. Drawn in 1922, this cartoon is a classic example of his most famous series, *The man who …* Typically, these include a character whose 'social incompetence, ineptitude, ignorance or folly' (Jensen, 1983, 43) incite snobbish shock and ridicule from those around them, but the viewer's sympathy is invariably directed towards the humiliated *naïf*. Bateman mocks the social codes being breached, but in doing so is gentle, and his style lacks the malice on which the humour of caricature is so often founded.

A casual glance through *Punch* of 13 December 1922, in which this cartoon was published, highlights the modernity of Bateman's lively, minimalist draughtsmanship. Unlike the majority of the single-frame images that fill its pages, heavily dependent on often lengthy associated texts in the Victorian tradition, Bateman's fast-paced visual narrative unfolds itself in a punchy, easily legible sequence. In fact, Bateman has been recognised as the British pioneer of the wordless strip-cartoon. Filling a whole page in *Punch*, and unconnected to the text on the facing page, the joke is communicated through the image alone. The title, printed below the image in the journal, is the only text that accompanies it, and serves only to comment on, not to explain, the visual narrative.

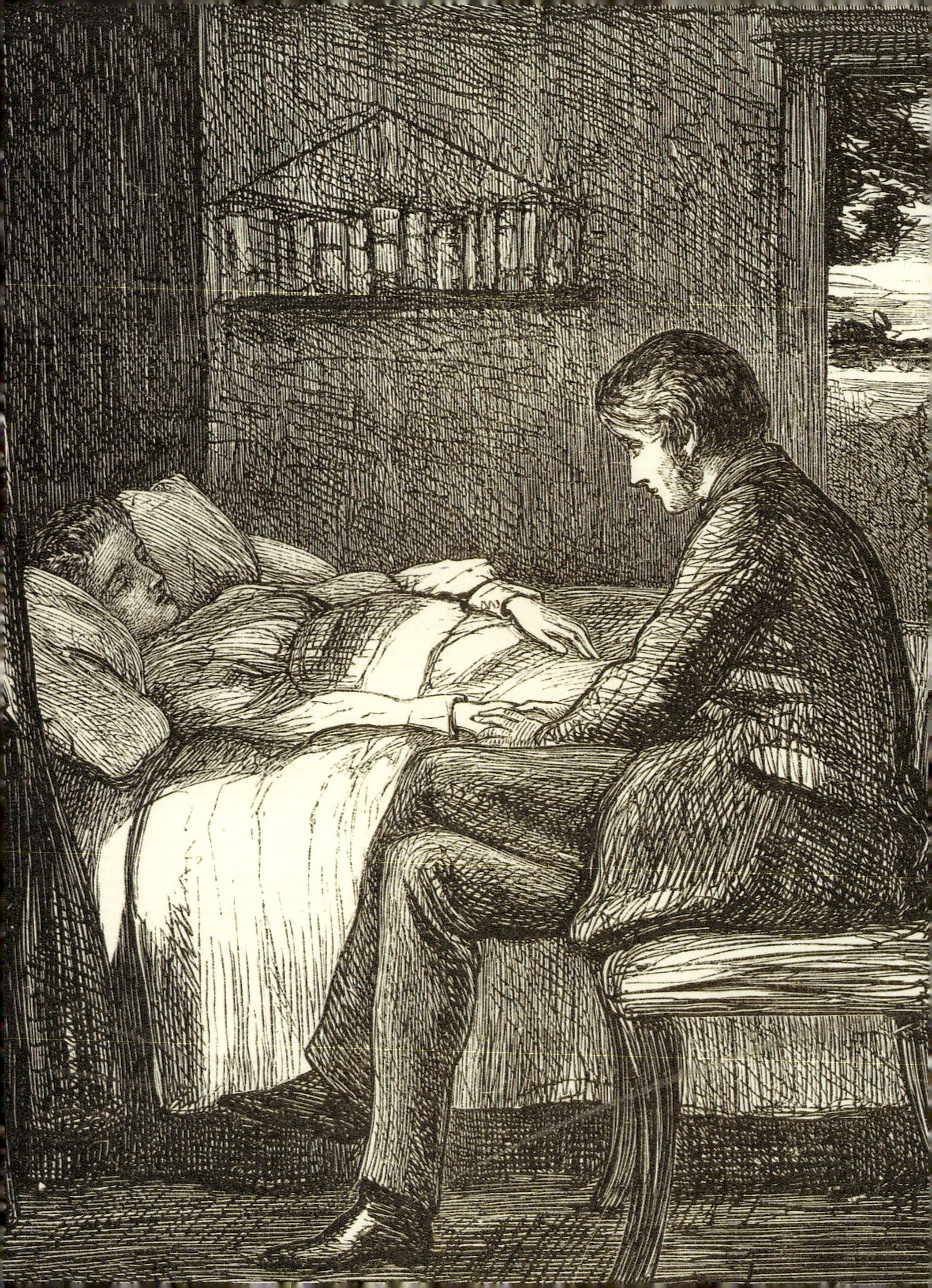

Select Bibliography

Mark Abley, ed., *The Parting Light: Selected writings of Samuel Palmer*, Manchester, 1985

Patricia Allderidge, *The Late Richard Dadd*, exh. cat., London, Tate Gallery, 1974

Richard Daniel Altick, *'Punch': The lively youth of a British institution, 1841-1851*, Columbus, 1997

Anthony Anderson, *The Man Who Was H. M. Bateman*, Exeter, 1982

Helen Rossetti Angeli, *Dante Gabriel Rossetti: His friends and enemies*, London, 1949

Henry Mayo Bateman, ed. John Jensen, *The Man Who ... and Other Drawings*, London, 1975 (1983 ed.)

Clifford Bax, *Ideas and People*, London, 1936

Karl Beckson, ed., *The Memoirs of Arthur Symons: Life and art in the 1890s*, University Park, 1977

David Bindman, *William Blake: Catalogue of the collection in the Fitzwilliam Museum*, Cambridge 1970

David Bindman, *The Complete Graphic Works of William Blake*, London, 1978

Shiela Birkenhead, *Illustrious Friends: The story of Joseph Severn and his son Arthur*, London, 1965

William Blake and his Contemporaries, exh. cat., Cambridge, Fitzwilliam Museum, 1986

The William Blake Archive, eds. Morris Eaves, Robert N. Essick and Joseph Viscomi: http://www.blakearchive.org/blake/

Wilfred Blunt, *Sydney Carlyle Cockerell, Friend of Ruskin and William Morris and Director of the Fitzwilliam Museum, Cambridge*, London, 1964

Robert Browning, *Critical Comments on Algernon Charles Swinburne and D. G. Rossetti*, London, 1919

Georgiana Burne-Jones, *Memorials of Edward Burne-Jones*, 2 vols., London, 1904

Martin Butlin, *The Blake-Varley Sketchbook of 1819*, London, 1969

Martin Butlin, *The Paintings and Drawings of William Blake*, 2 vols., New Haven and London, 1981

Susan P. Casteras, *Pocket Cathedrals: Pre-Raphaelite book illustration*, exh. cat., New Haven, Yale Centre for British Art, 1991

Gilbert Keith Chesterton, *Autobiography*, London, 1939 (1969 ed.)

Sidney Colvin, *John Keats, his Life and Poetry, his Friends, Critics and After-Fame*, London, 1917

Sidney Colvin, *Memories and Notes of Persons and Places 1852-1912*, London, 1921

Walter Crane, *An Artist's Reminiscences*, London, 1907

Joseph Darracott, ed., *All for Art: The Ricketts and Shannon Collection*, exh. cat., Cambridge, Fitzwilliam Museum,1979

Amanda-Jane Doran, ed., *Punch Lines: 150 years of humorous writing in 'Punch'*, London, 1991

Oswald Doughty and John Robert Wahl, eds., *Letters of Dante Gabriel Rossetti*, Oxford, 1965, I, 1835-1860; II, 1861-1870

Rodney Engen, *Richard Doyle*, Stroud, 1983

Kate Flint, *The Victorians and the Visual Imagination*, London, 2000

Peter Forbes, 'The Implosive Animation of the Still Cartoon', *Modern Painters*, 9:1, Spring 1996, 65-67

John Geipel, *The Cartoon: A short history of graphic comedy and satire*, Newton Abbot, 1972

Marcella D. Genz, *A History of the Eragny Press 1894-1914*, London, 2004

Robert Gibbings, *John Keats*, London, 1968

Robin Gibson, *Glyn Philpot, 1884-1937: Edwardian aesthete to thirties modernist*, exh. cat., London, National Portrait Gallery, 1984

Alexander Gilchrist, *Life of William Blake*, London, 1880

Gail Lynn Goldberg, 'Rossetti's Revising Hand: His illustrations for Christina Rossetti's poems', *Victorian Poetry*, 20: 3-4, Autumn-Winter 1982, 145-159

Paul Goldman, *Victorian Illustrated Books 1850-1870: The heyday of wood-engraving*, London, 1994

Paul Goldman, *Victorian Illustration: The Pre-Raphaelites, the Idyllic school and the High Victorians*, Aldershot, 1996

Ernst Hans Gombrich and Ernst Kris, *Caricature*, Harmondsworth, 1940

Ernst Hans Gombrich, *Art and Illusion: A study in the psychology of pictorial representation* (5th edition), London, 1977

Edmund Gosse, *The Life of Algernon Charles Swinburne*, London, 1917

June Steffensen Hagen, *Tennyson and his Pre-Raphaelite Illustrators*, London, 1979

John Hall, *Trollope and his Illustrators*, London, 1980

Robin Hamlyn and Michael Phillips, *William Blake*, exh. cat., London, Tate Gallery, 2001

Martin Hardie, *English Coloured Books*, London, 1906

Rupert Hart-Davis, *A Catalogue of the Caricatures of Max Beerbohm*, London, 1972

Rupert Hart-Davis, ed. and intro., *Siegfried Sassoon Diaries*, London, *1915-1918*, 1983; *1920-1922*, 1981; *1923-1925*, 1985

Antony H. Harrison, *The Letters of Christina Rossetti*, 4 vols., Charlottesville, 1997-2000

Martin Harrison and Bill Waters, *Burne-Jones*, London, 1973 (1989 ed.)

Bevis Hillier, *Cartoons and Caricatures*, London, 1970

Paul Hogarth, *Arthur Boyd Houghton*, London, 1981

William Holman Hunt, *Pre-Raphaelitism and the Pre-Raphaelite Brotherhood*, 2 vols., London, 1905

Michael Holroyd, *Augustus John*, 2 vols., London, 1972

Simon Houfe, *Phil May: His Life And Work, 1864-1903*, Aldershot, 2002

Simon Houfe *The Work of Charles Samuel Keene*, Aldershot, 1995

Laurence Housman, *A. B. Houghton: A selection from his work in black and white*, London, 1896

Patricia Ingham, 'The Evolution of *Jude the Obscure*', *Review of English Studies*, nos. 27, 1976, 27-37, 159-169

Patricia Jaffé, *Drawings by George Romney from the Fitzwilliam Museum*, exh. cat., Cambridge, Fitzwilliam Museum, 1977

Lorraine Janzen Kooistra, *Christina Rossetti and Illustration: A publishing history*, Athens, 2002

Dan H. Laurence, ed., *Bernard Shaw: Collected letters*, London, 1898-1910, 1972; 1911-1925, 1985

George Somes Layard, *Tennyson and his Illustrators: A book about a book*, London, 1894

Eileen Leach, *Walter Crane and After: A century of changing fashions in the illustration of children's books, 1865-1965*, London, 1966

Cecil Lewis, ed., *Self-Portrait taken from the Letters and Journals of Charles Ricketts, R.A.*, London, 1939

Lionel Lindsay, *Charles Keene: The artists' artist*, London, 1934

Boyd Litzinger and Donald Smalley, eds., *Robert Browning: The critical heritage*, London and New York, 1968 (1995 ed.)

George Locke, *The Land of Dreams: A review of the work of Sidney H. Sime, 1905 to 1916*, London, 1975

Edward Verrall Lucas, *The Colvins and their Friends*, London, 1928

Jeremy Maas, *Victorian Fairy Painting*, London, 1997

Jan Marsh, 'Hoping you will not think me too fastidious: Pre-Raphaelite artists and the Moxon Tennsyon', *Journal of Pre-Raphaelite and Aesthetic Studies*, 2:1, 1989, 11-18

Jane Martineau *et. al.*, eds., *Shakespeare in Art*, London, 2003

Frank McLynn, *Robert Louis Stevenson: A Biography*, London, 1993

William Moelwyn Merchant, *Shakespeare and the Artist*, Oxford, 1959

Viola Meynell, ed., *The Best of Friends: Further letters to Sydney Carlyle Cockerell* London, 1956

Michael Millgate, *Thomas Hardy: His career as a novelist* , London, 1994

Jane Munro, *Shakespeare and the Eighteenth Century*, exh. cat., Cambridge, Fitzwilliam Museum, 1997

Jane Munro, *Tennyson and Trollope: Book illustrations by John Everett Millais (1829-96)*, exh. cat., Cambridge, Fitzwilliam Museum, 1996

Jane Munro and Paul Stirton, *Burne-Jones and William Morris: Designs for the Aeneid and the Kelmscott Chaucer*, exh. cat., Cambridge, Fitzwilliam Museum, 1996

Norman Page, ed., *Oxford Reader's Companion to Thomas Hardy*, Oxford, 2000

Leslie Parris, ed., *The Pre-Raphaelites*, exh. cat., London, Tate Gallery, 1984

William S. Petersen, *The Kelmscott Press: A history of William Morris's typographical adventure*, Oxford, 1991

Richard Geoffrey George Price, *A History of 'Punch'*, London, 1957

Richard Little Purdy and Michael Millgate, eds., *The Collected Letters of Thomas Hardy*, Oxford, 1984, II, 1893-1901; IV, 1909-1913; 1985 V, 1914-1919

Forrest Reid, *Illustrators of the Sixties*, London, 1928

Jan Reynolds, *Myles Birket Foster*, London, 1984

Jacobus Gerhardus Riewald, *Sir Max Beerbohm, Man and Writer: A critical analysis with a brief life and a bibliography*, The Hague, 1953

Duncan Robinson, *A Companion Volume to the Kelmscott Chaucer*, London, 1975

William Michael Rossetti and Algernon C. Swinburne, *Notes on the Royal Academy Exhibition, 1868*, London, 1868

William Michael Rossetti, *Ruskin, Rossetti and Pre-Raphaelitism*, London, 1899

William Michael Rossetti, *Some Reminiscences of William Michael Rossetti*, 2 vols., London, 1906

Rossetti Hypermedia archive: http://www.rossettiarchive.org/

John Rothenstein, *The Life and Death of Conder*, London, 1938

William Rothenstein, *Men and Memories, Recollections, 1872-1938, of William Rothenstein*, London, 1978

Jerold Savory and Patricia Marks, *The Smiling Muse: Victoriana in the comic press*, London, 1985

Grant F. Scott, *Joseph Severn: Letters and memoirs*, Aldershot, 2005

William Bell Scott, *Autobiographical Notes of the Life of William Bell Scott*, 2 vols., London, 1892

Shakespeare in Art: A visual approach to the plays, exh. cat., Nottingham University Art Gallery, 1961

Sacheverell Sitwell, *Narrative Pictures: A survey of English genre and its painters*, London, 1969

Marion Harry Spielmann, *The History of 'Punch'*, London, 1895

Richard Stein, 'The Pre-Raphaelite Tennyson', *Victorian Studies*, 24:3, Spring 1981, 279-301

Lionel Stevenson, *The Pre-Raphaelite Poets*, Chapel Hill, 1973

Virginia Surtees, *The Paintings and Drawings of Dante Gabriel Rosetti (1828-1882): A catalogue raisonné*, 2 vols., Oxford, 1971

Virginia Surtees, ed., *The Diary of Ford Madox Brown*, New Haven and London, 1981

Virginia Surtees, *Rossetti's Portraits of Elizabeth Siddal*, Oxford, 1991

J. Don Vann and Rosemary T. Van Arsdel, *Victorian Periodicals and Victorian Society*, Toronto, 1994

Colin White, *Edmund Dulac*, London, 1976

The End.

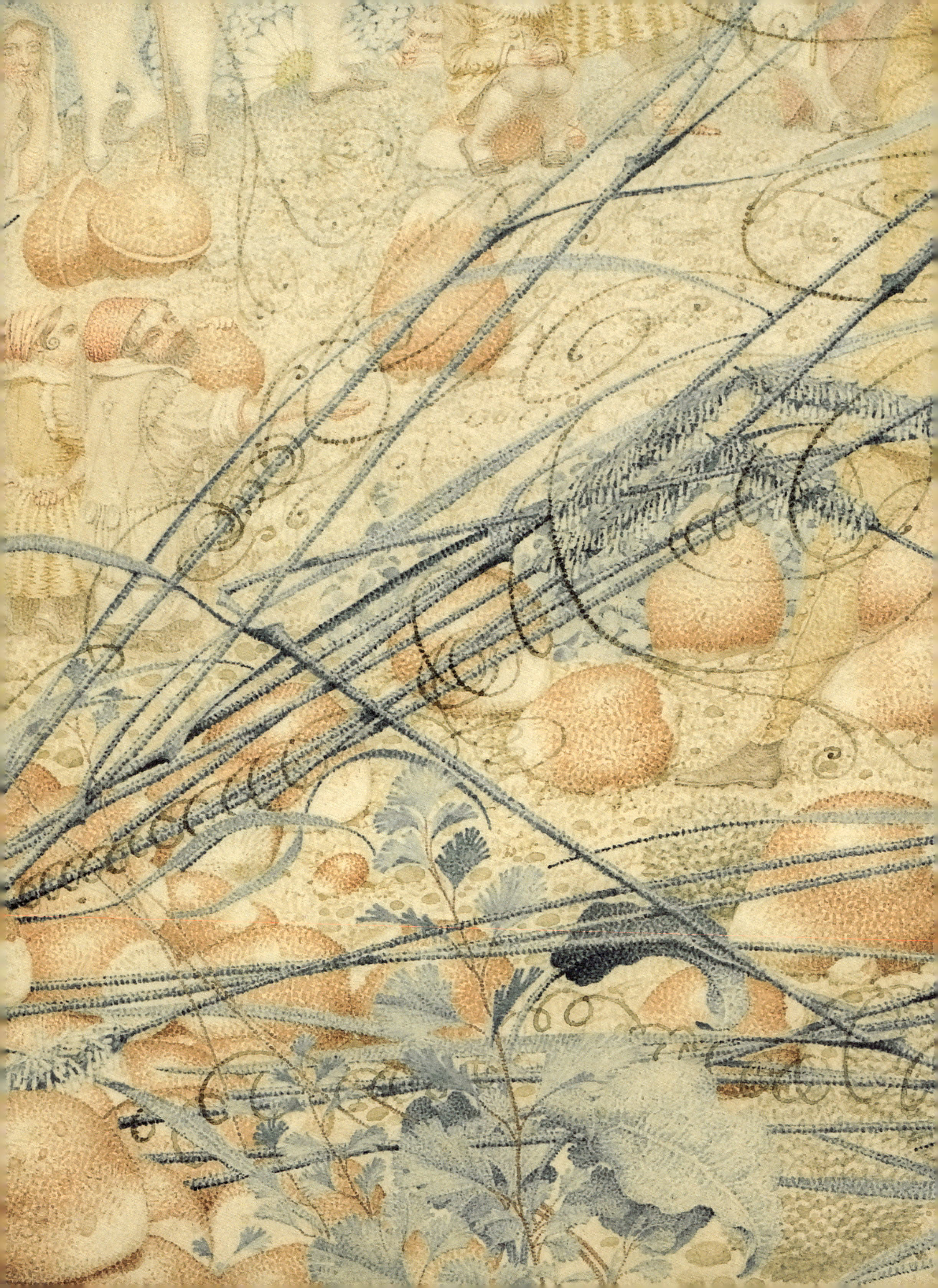